SHADOWSIDE

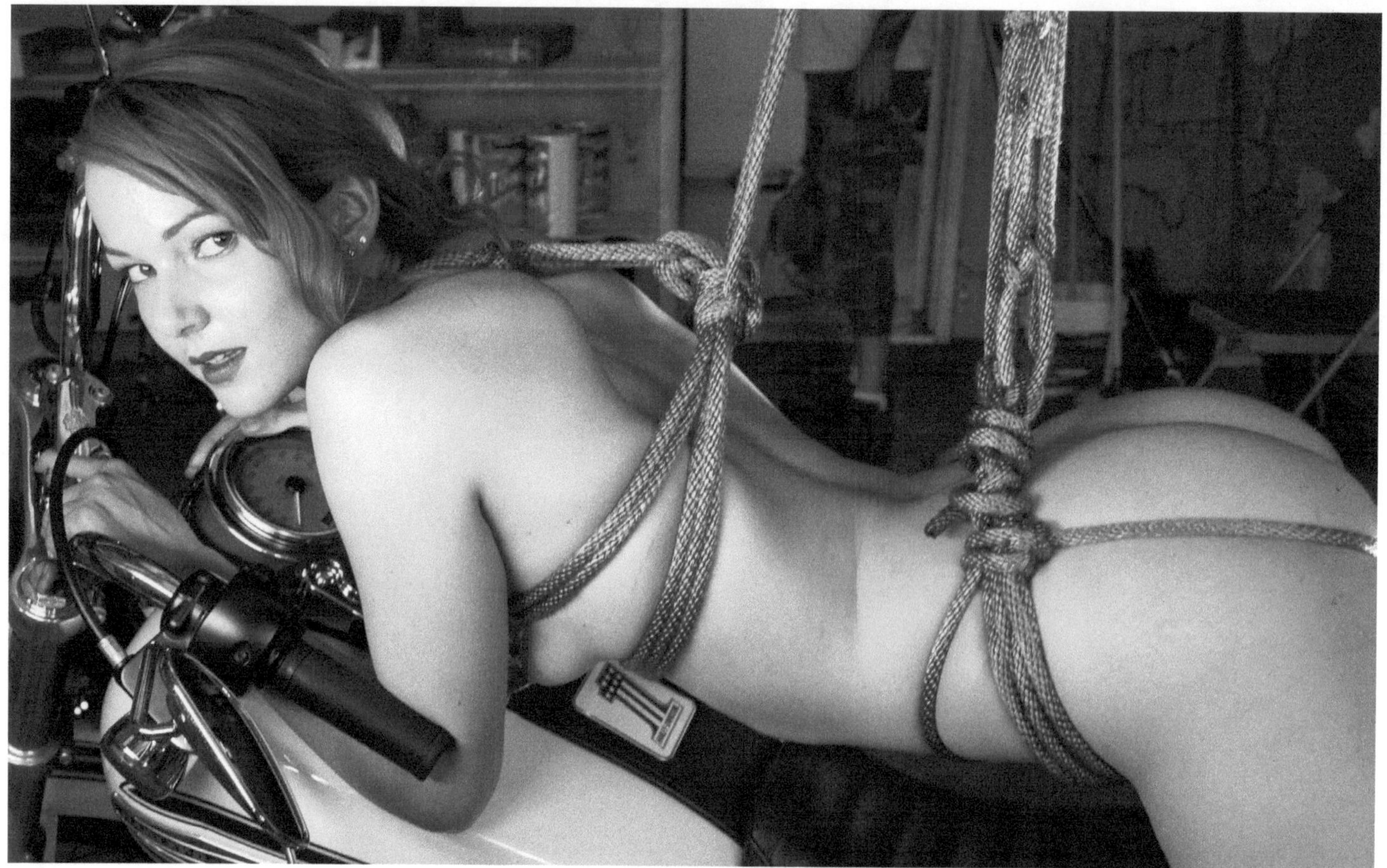

Shadowside

ISBN 978-0-9858999-4-3

Dedicated to Sheila, Mary and Jacquelyn Higgins.

Published by
Nakedcomix.com
793 South Tracy Blvd #210
Tracy CA., 95376

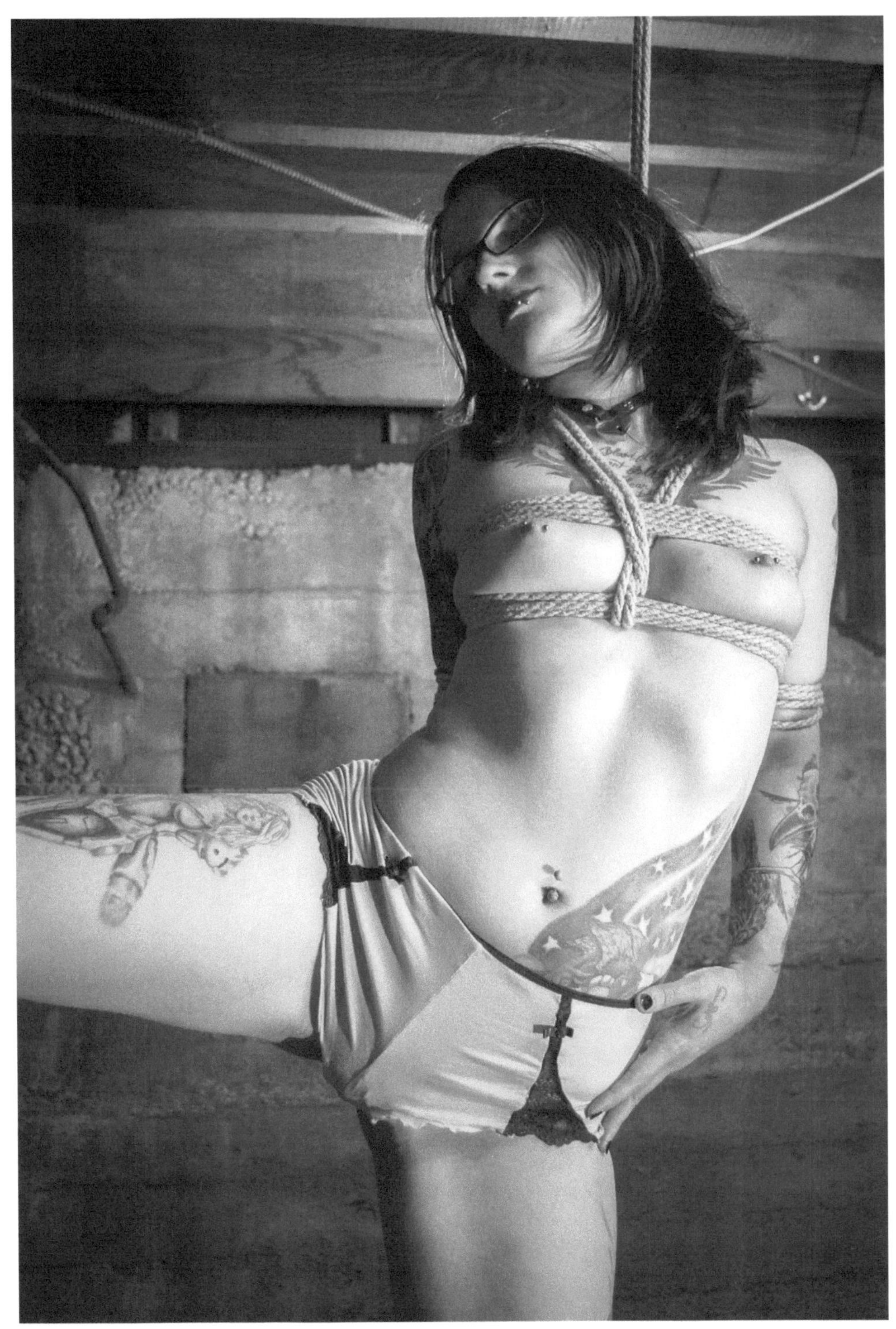

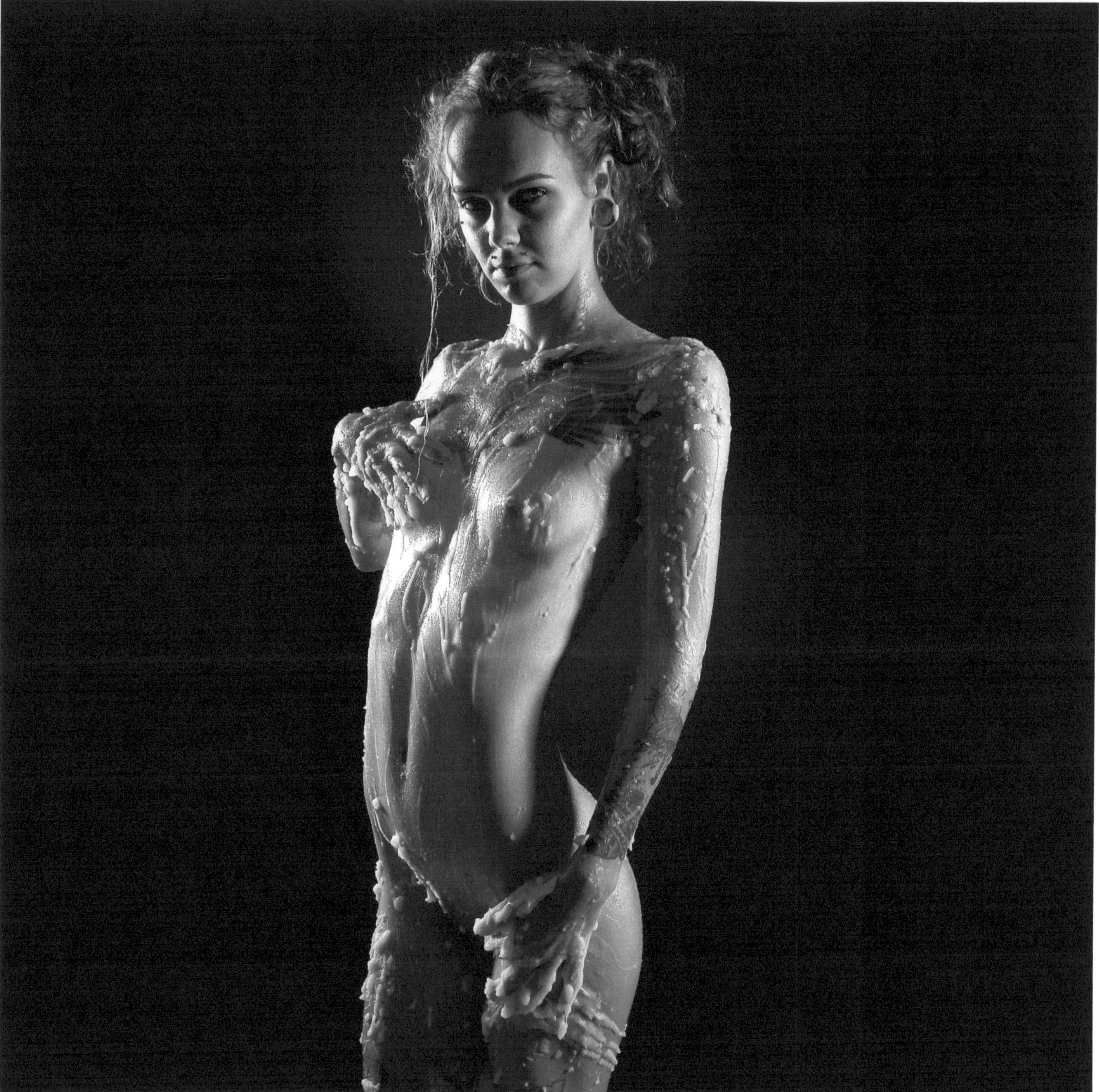

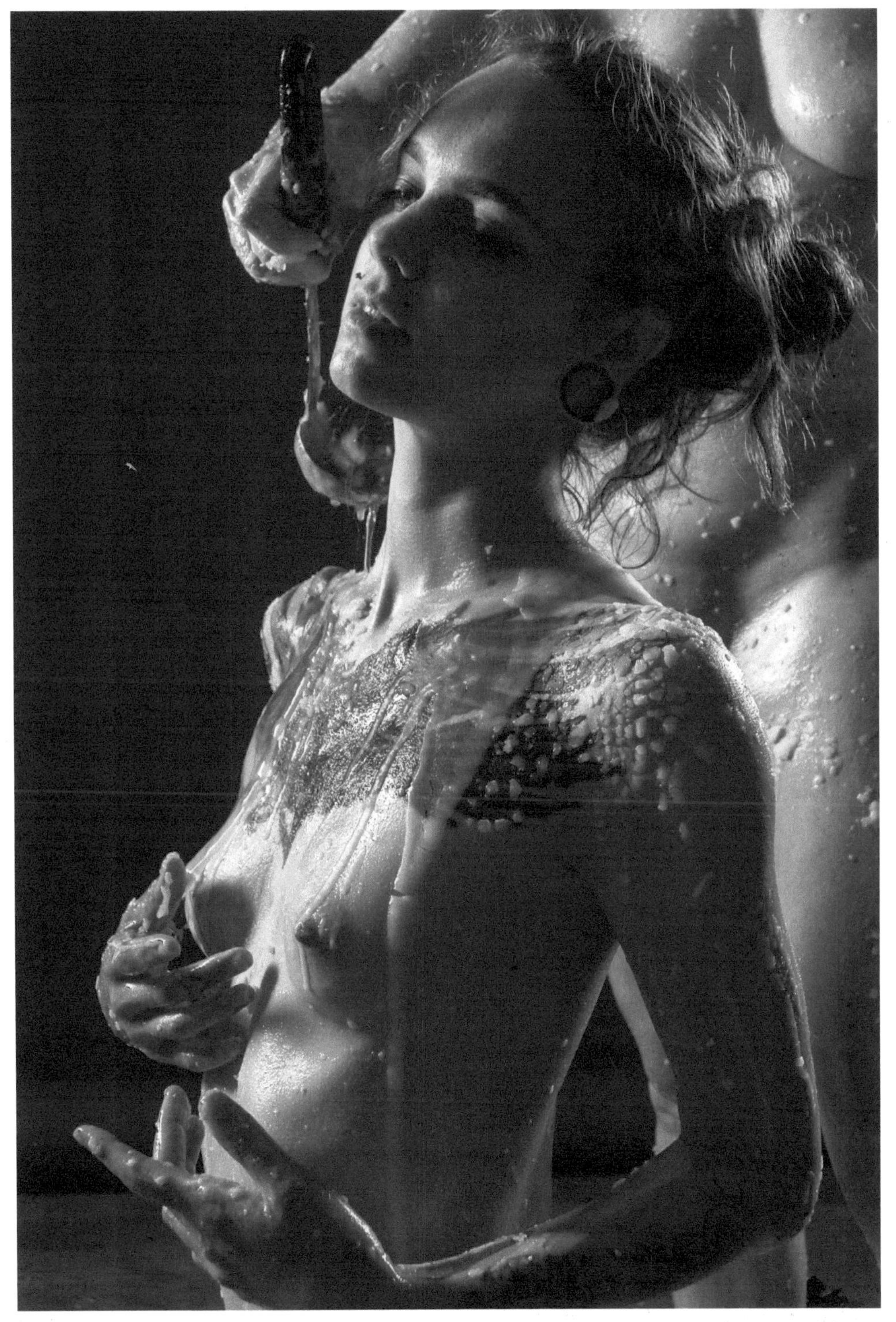

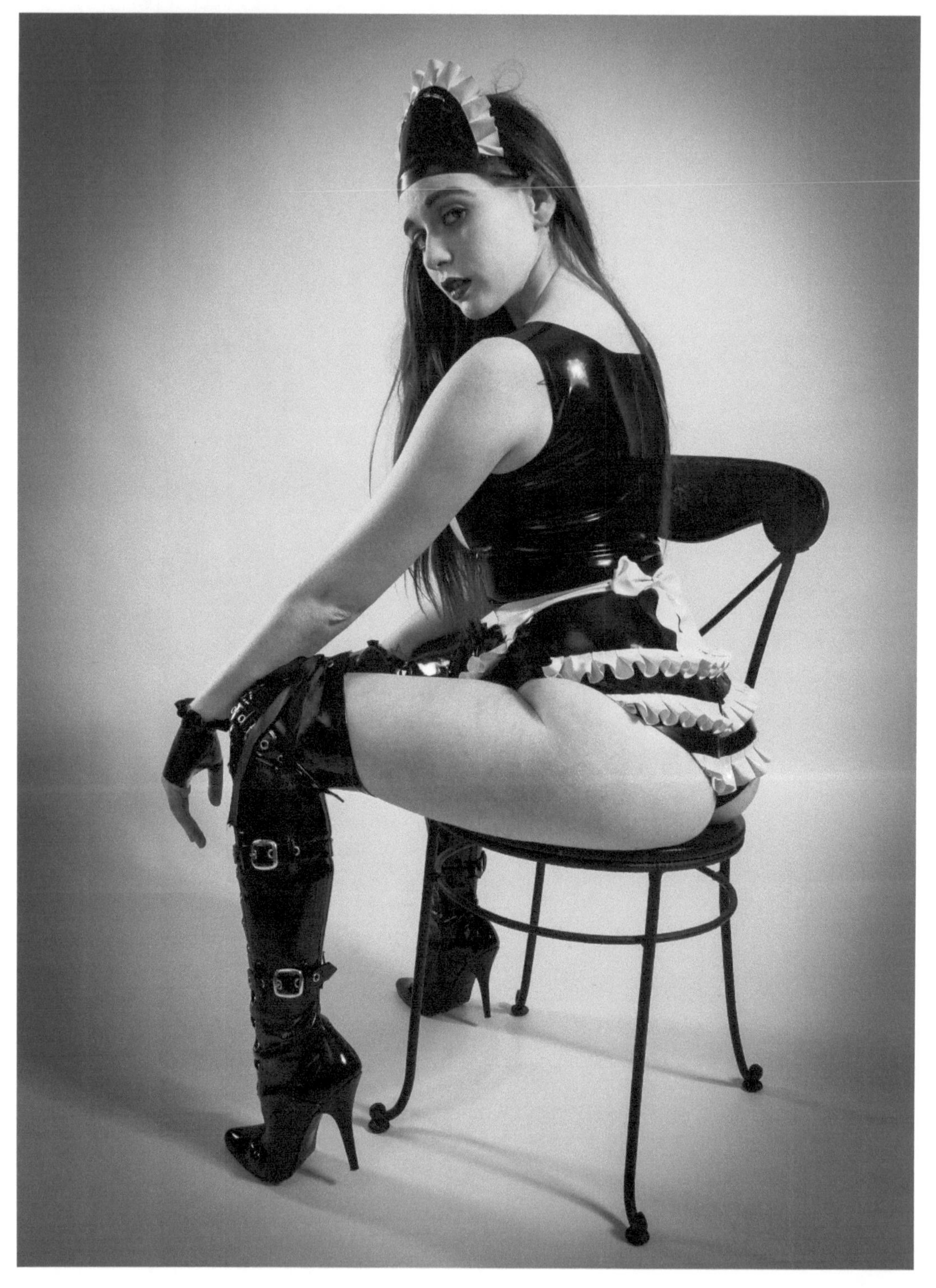

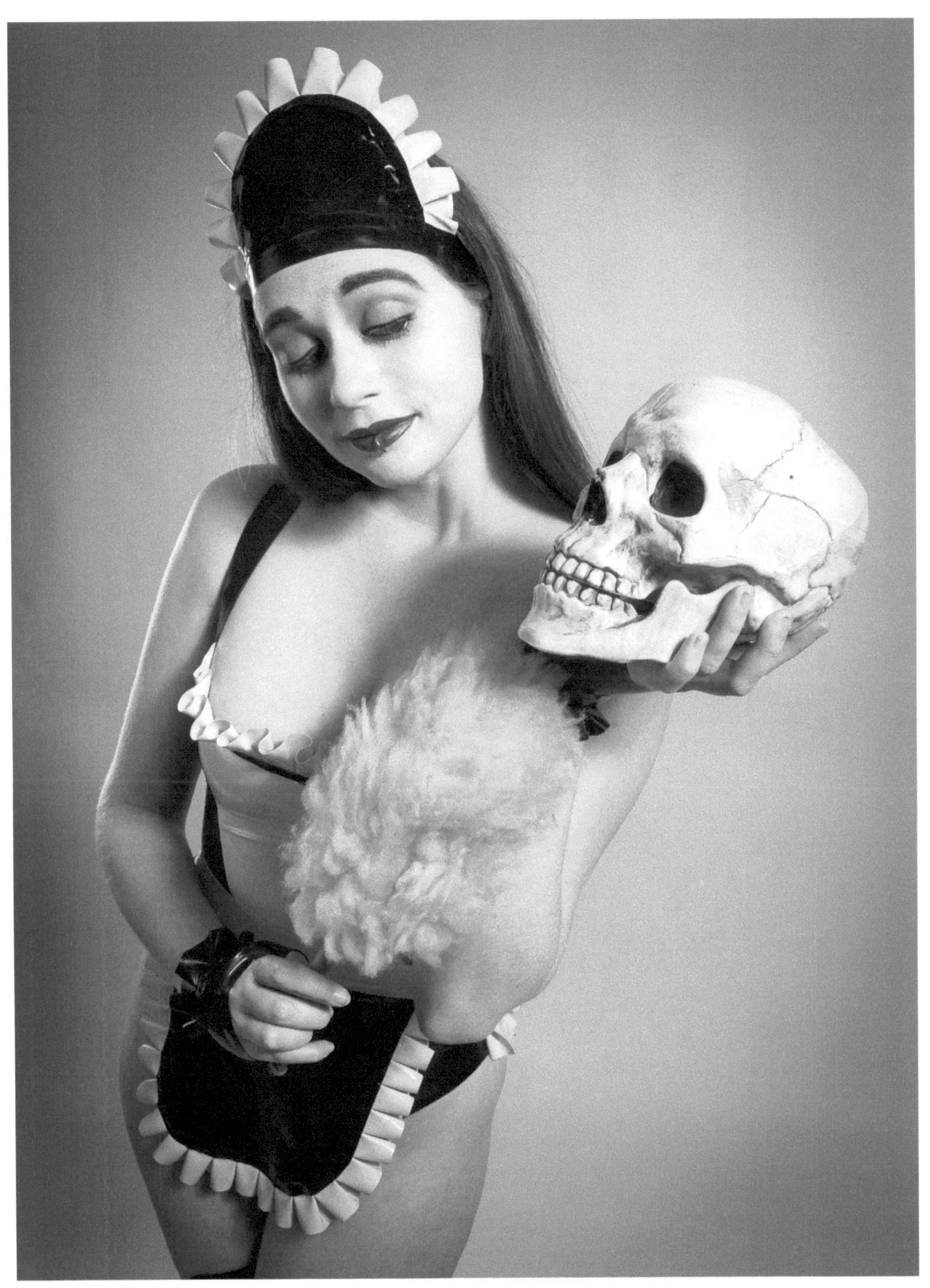

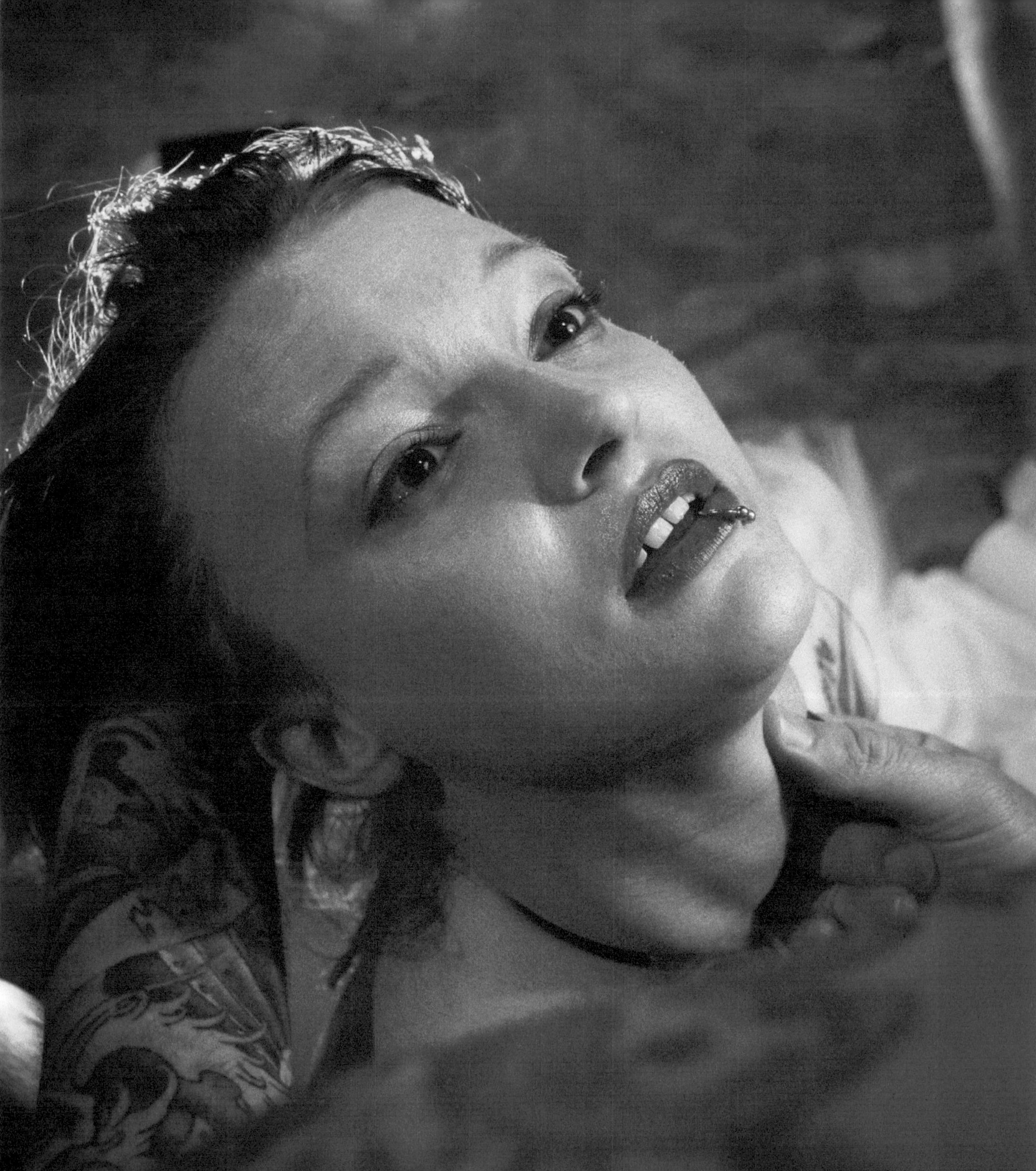

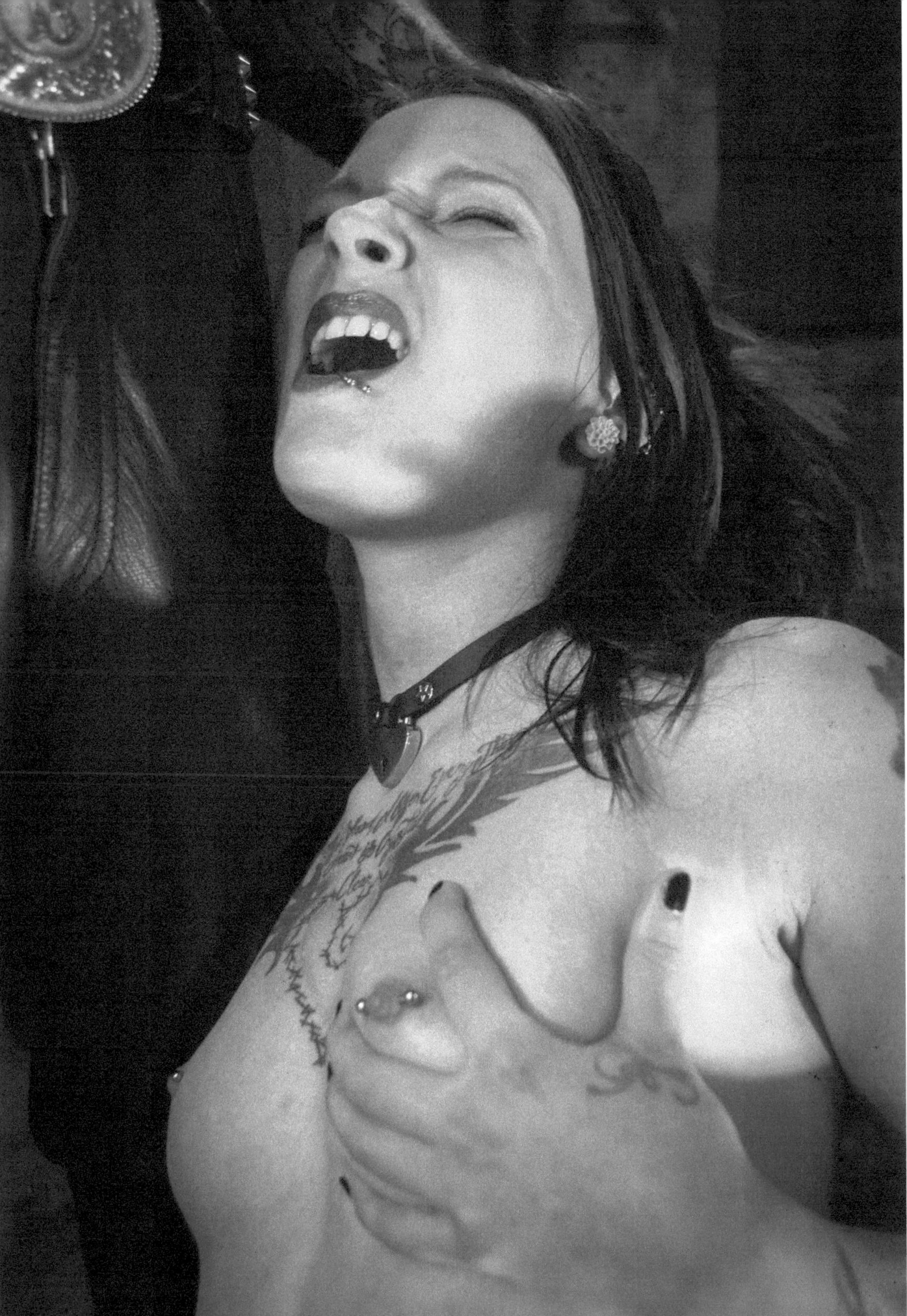

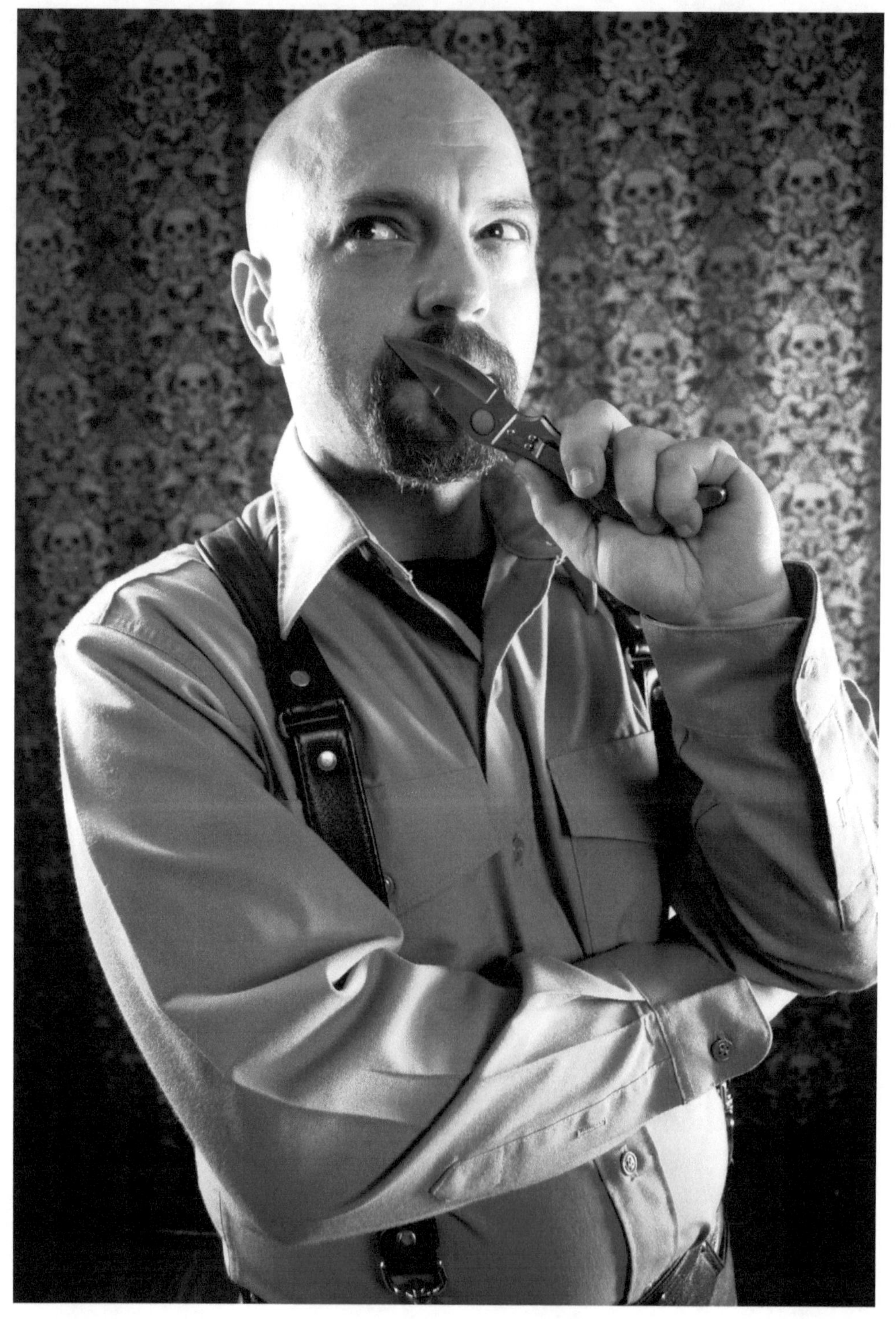

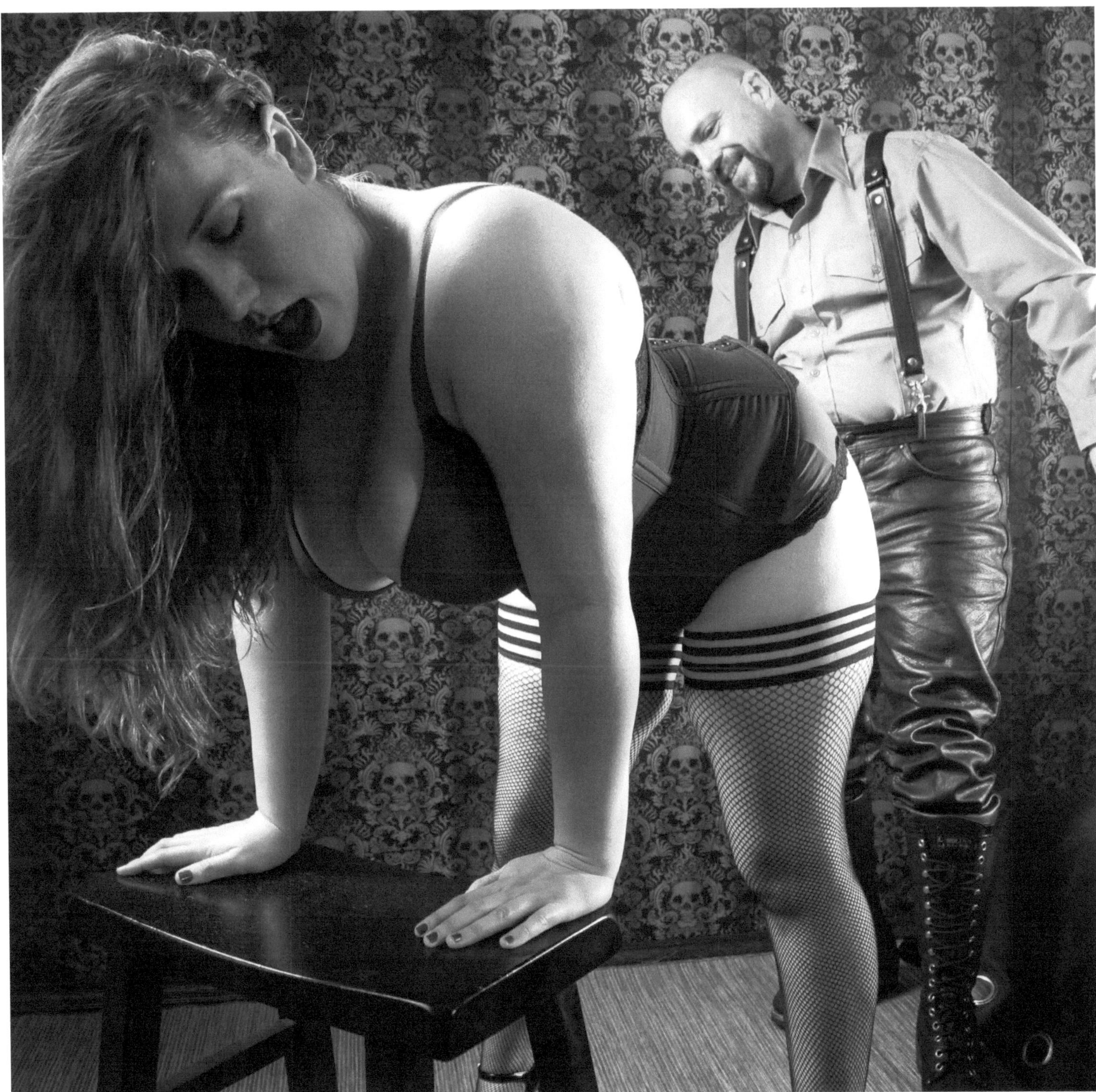

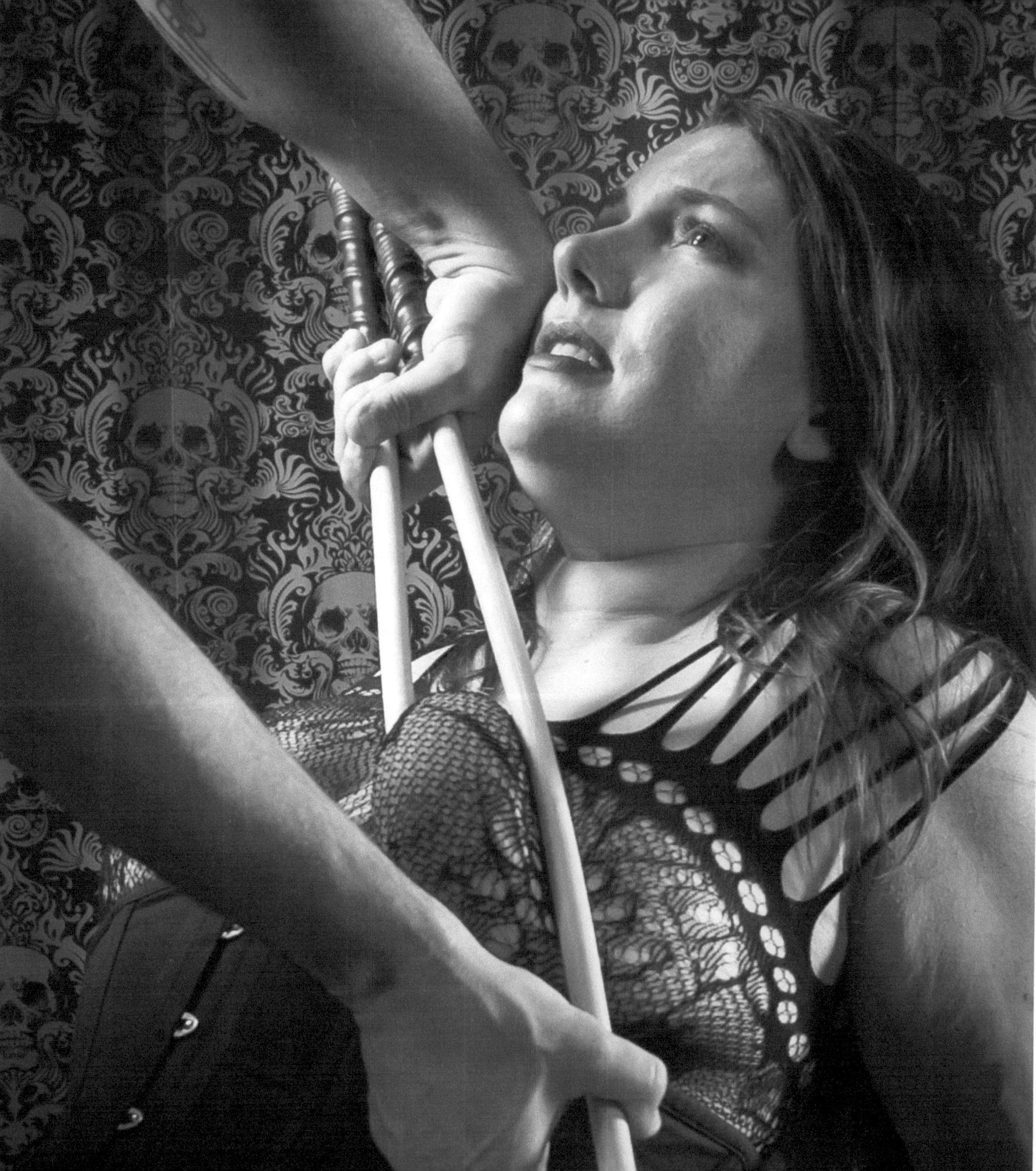

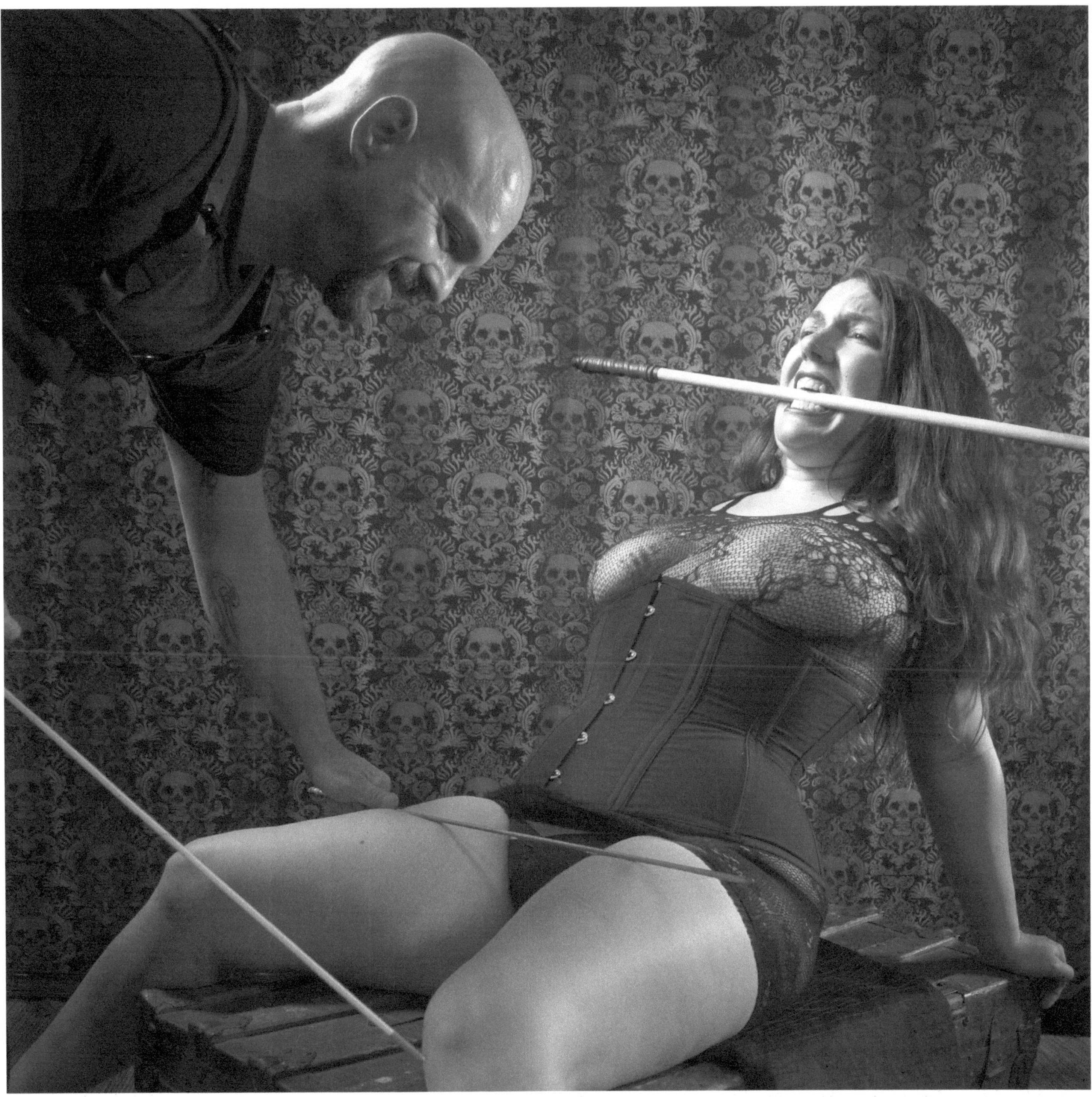

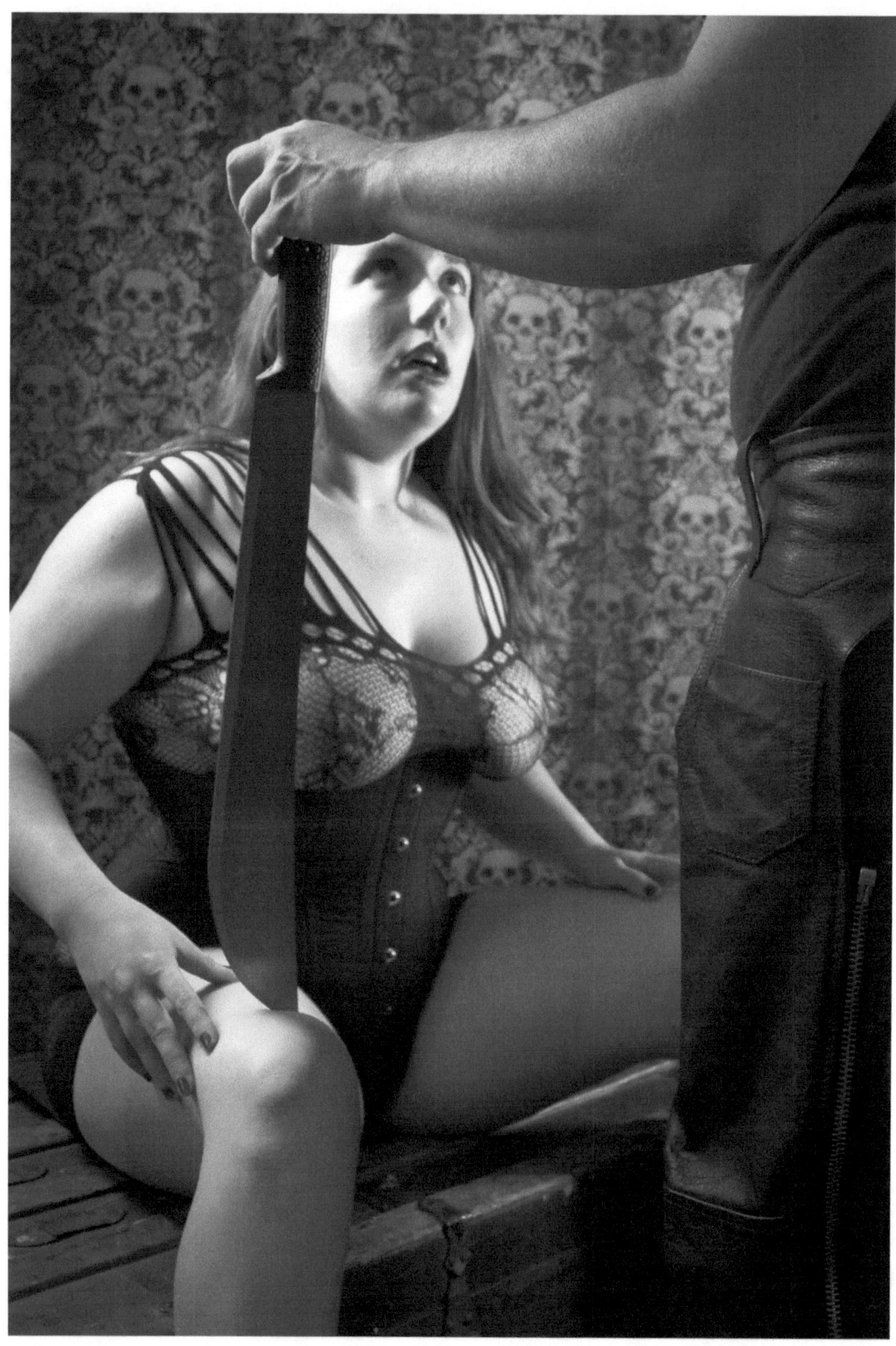

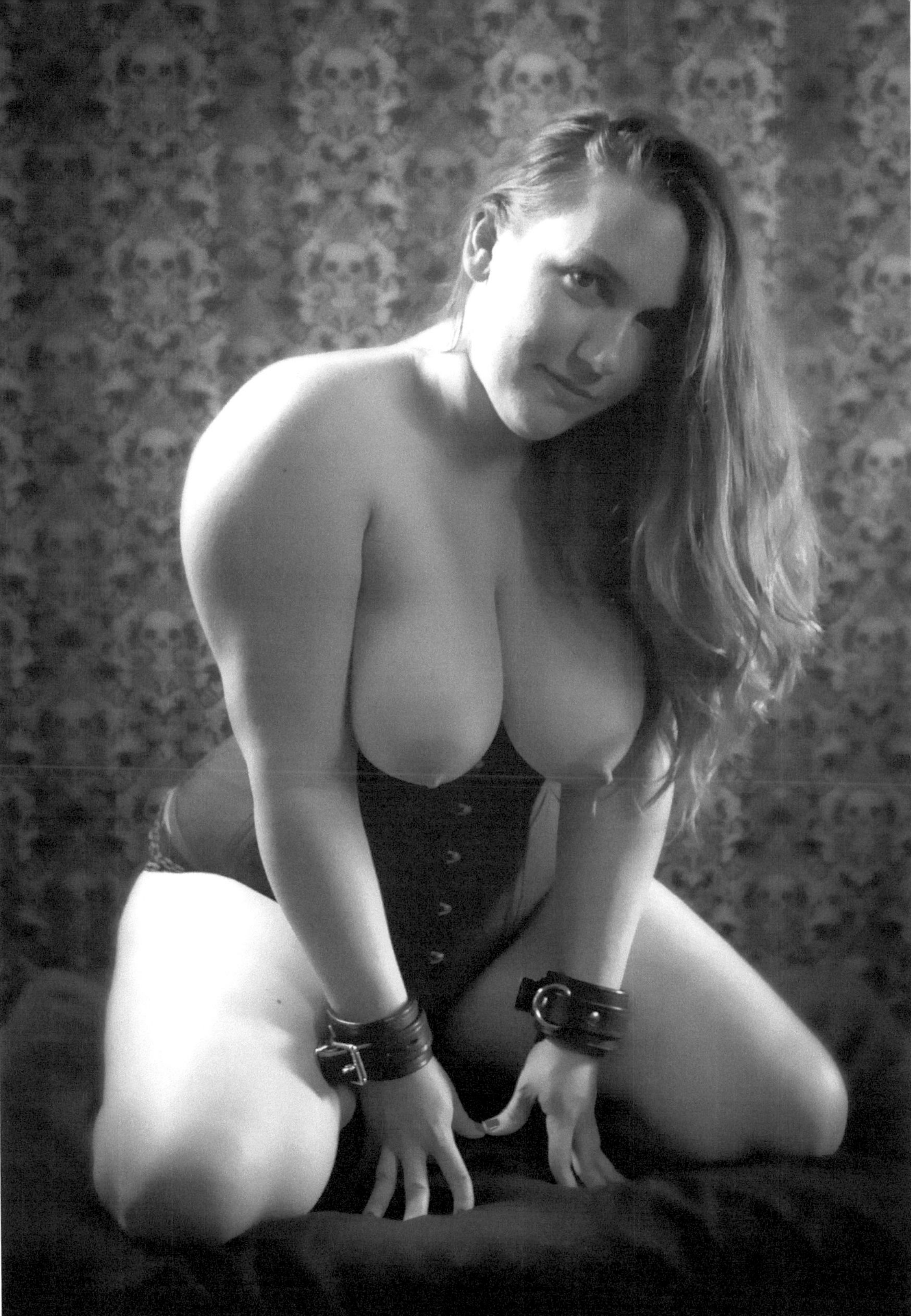

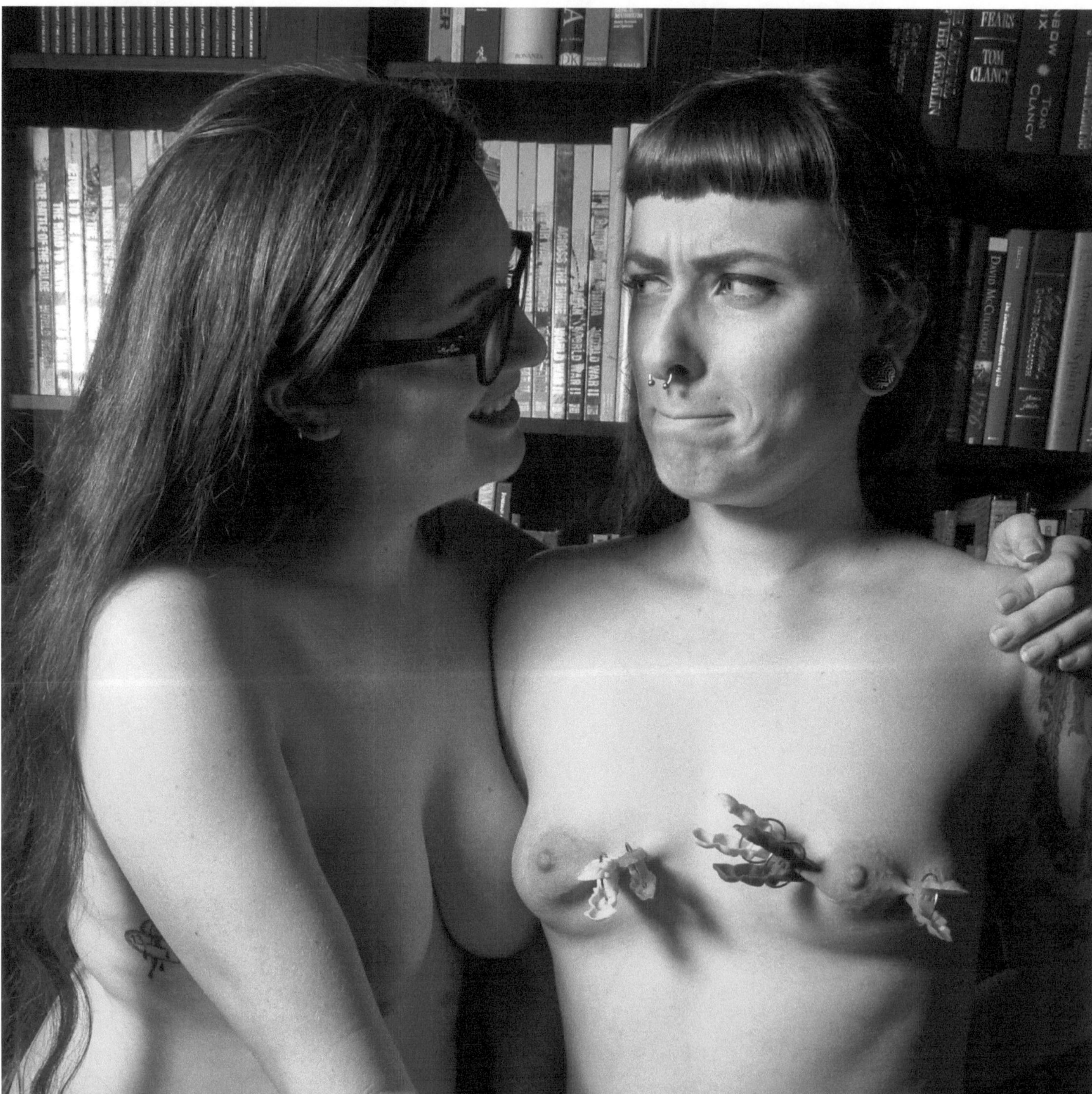
FEARS
TOM CLANCY
TOM CLANCY
THE KREMLIN
DAVID McCULLOUGH
1776
WORLD WAR II
WORLD WAR II
ACROSS THE RHINE
THE BATTLE OF THE BULGE
THE ROAD TO

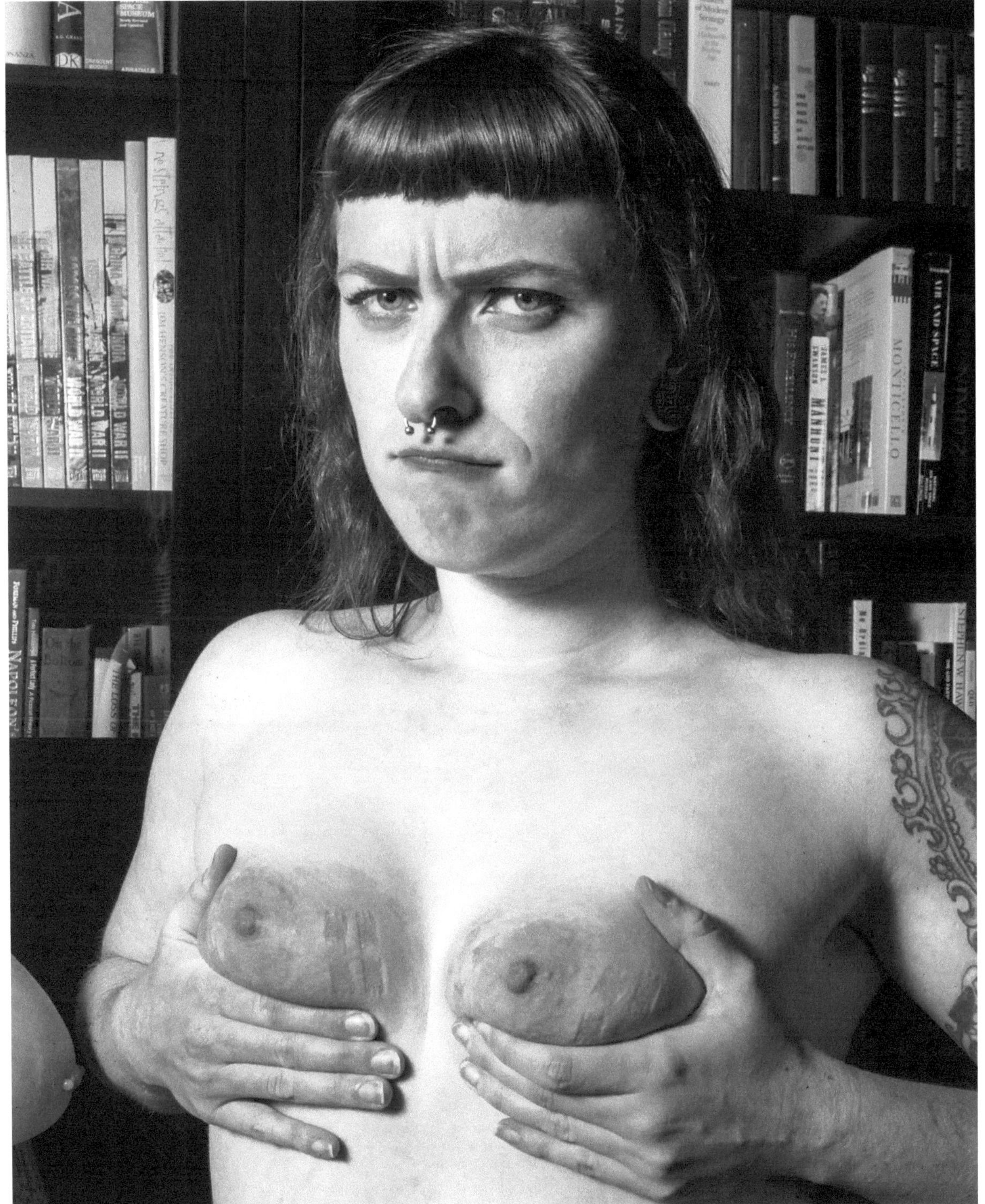
SPACE MUSEUM
WORLD WAR II
AIR AND SPACE
MONTICELLO
MANHUNT

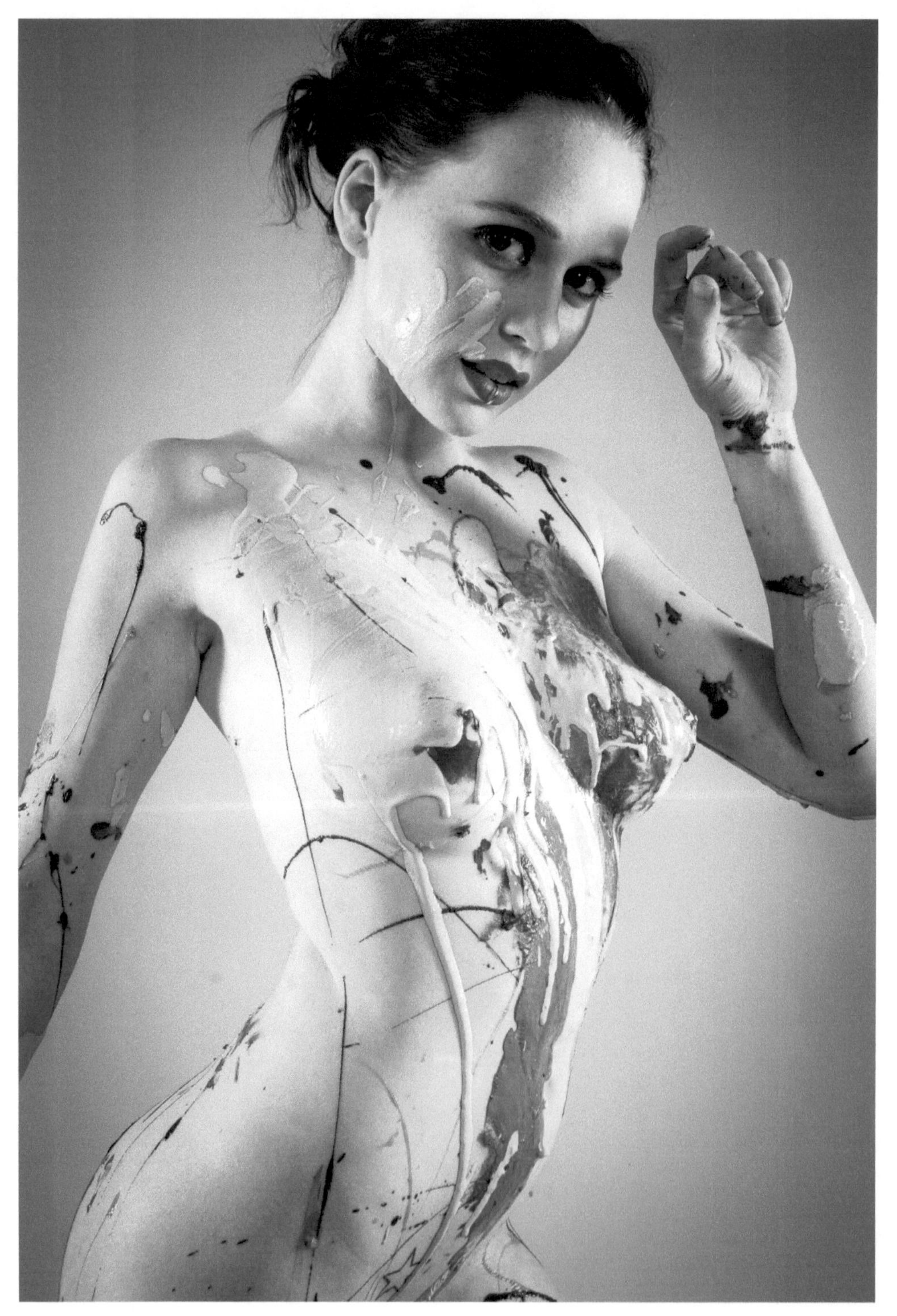

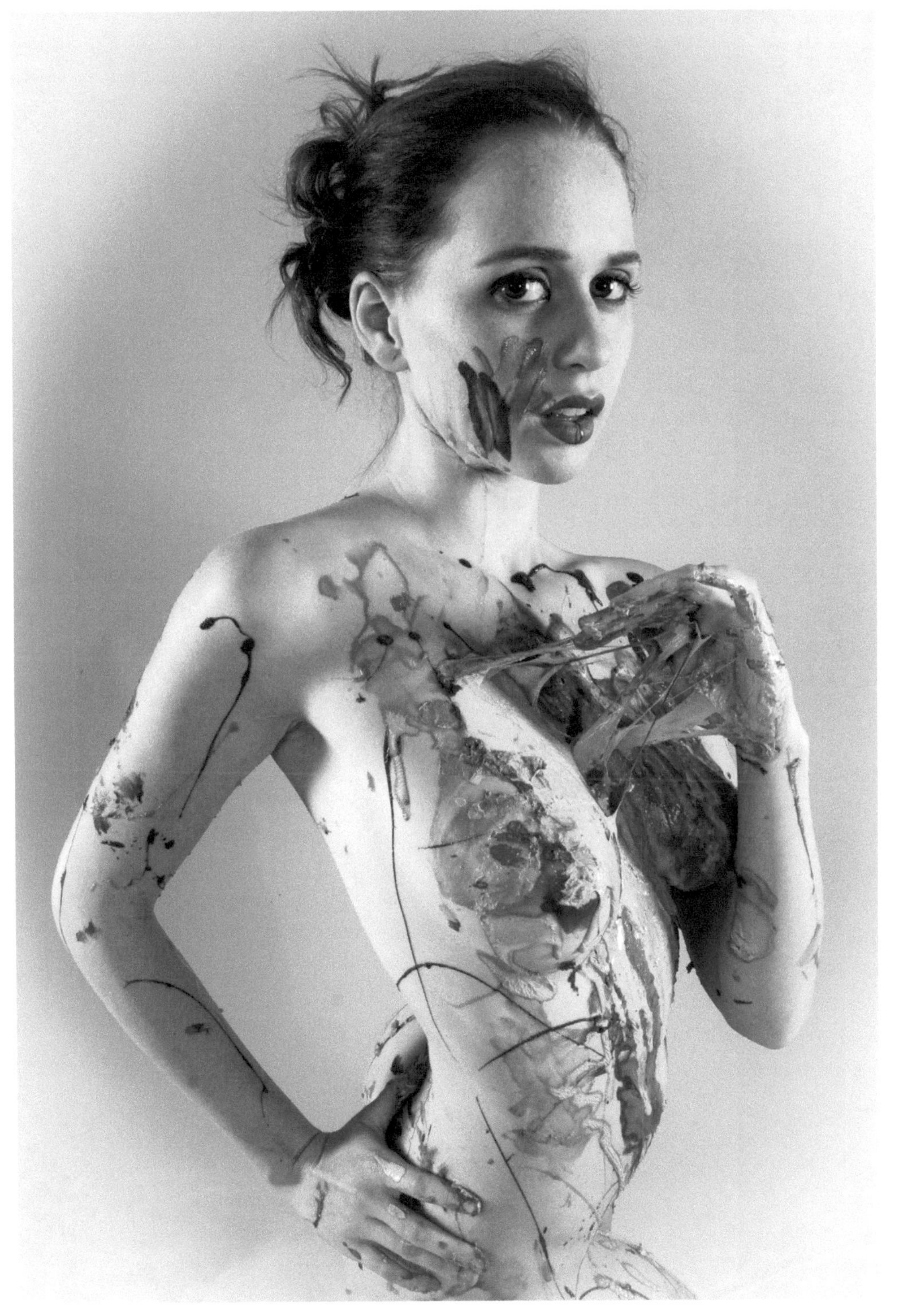

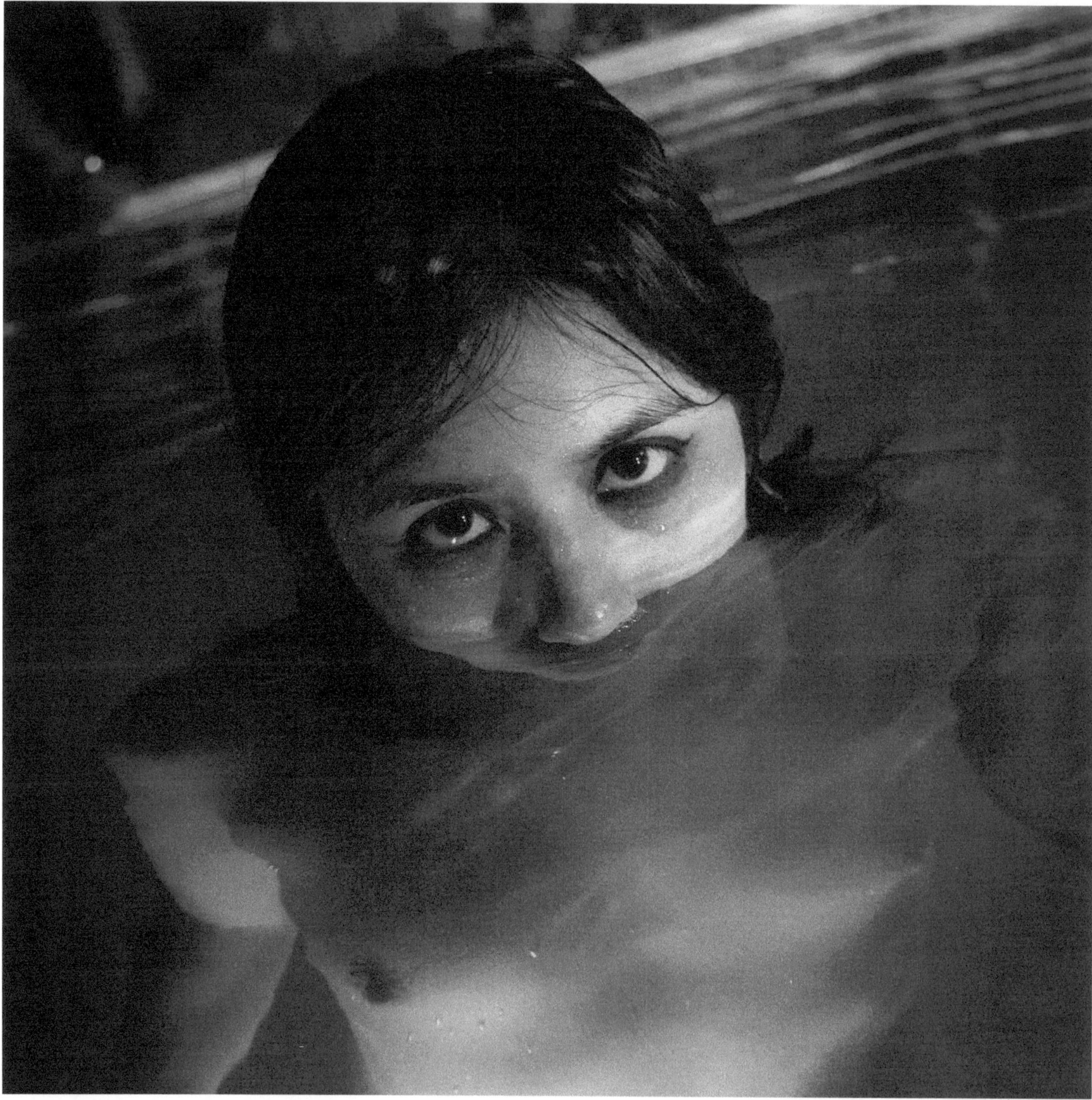

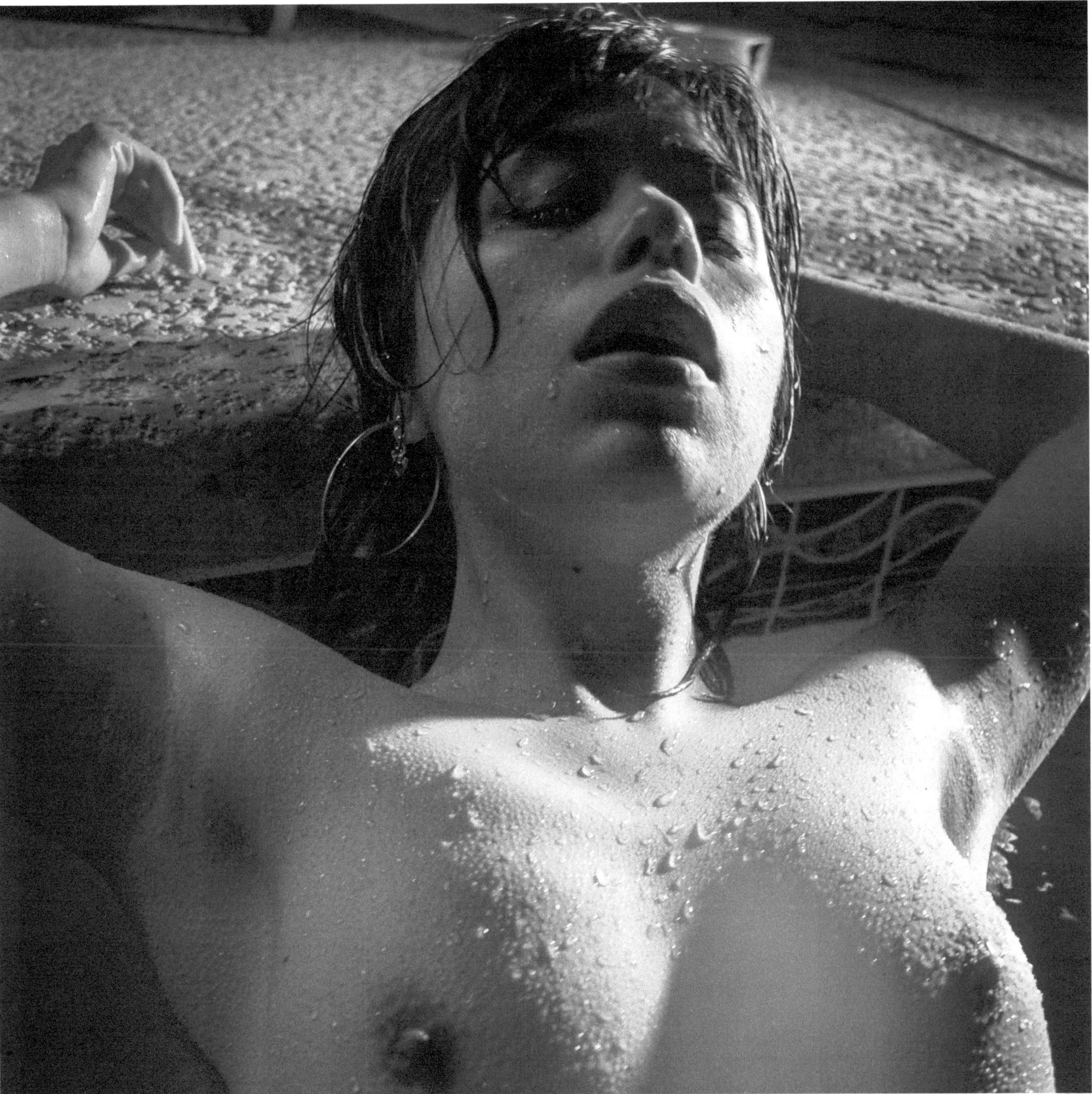

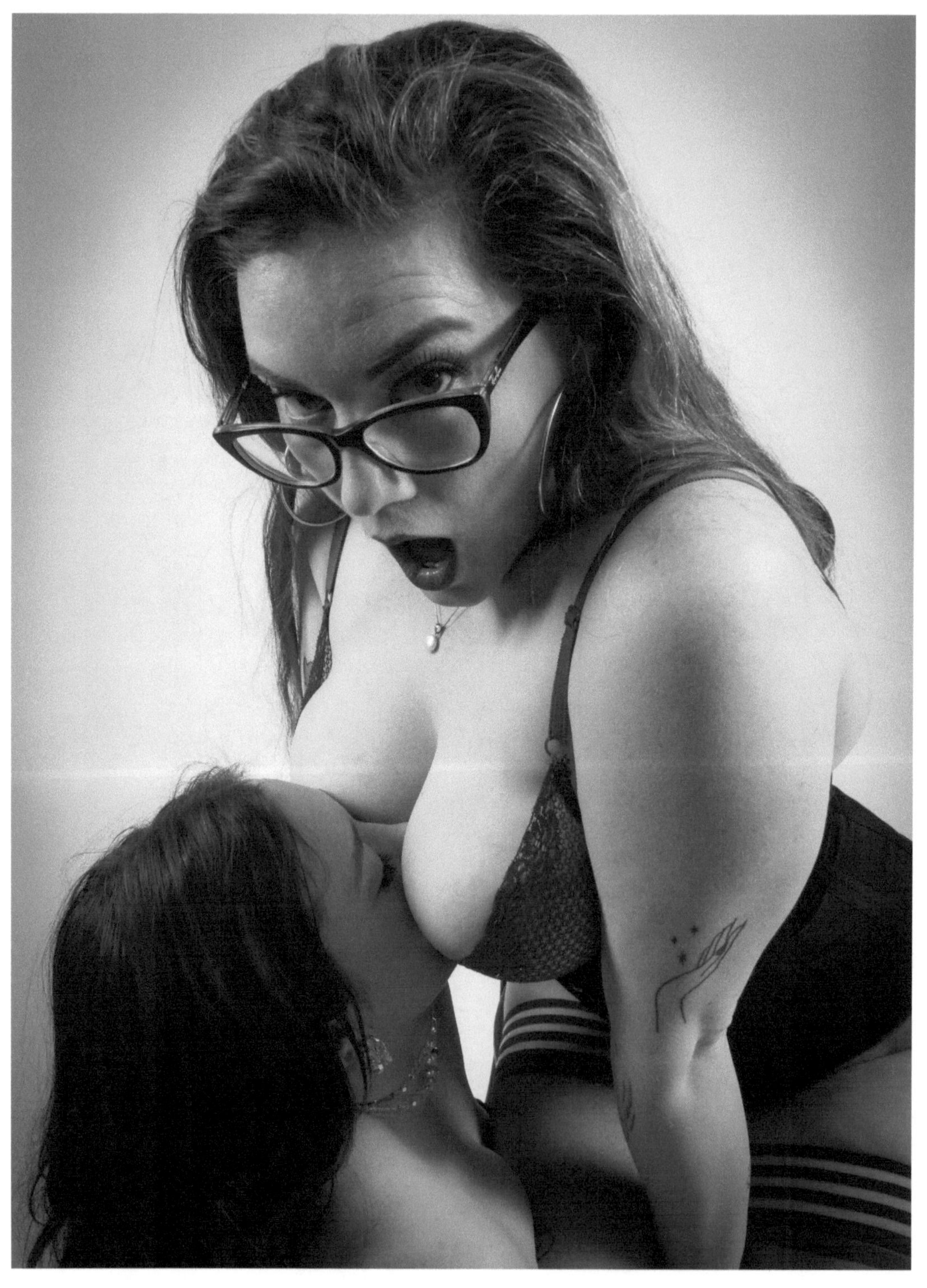

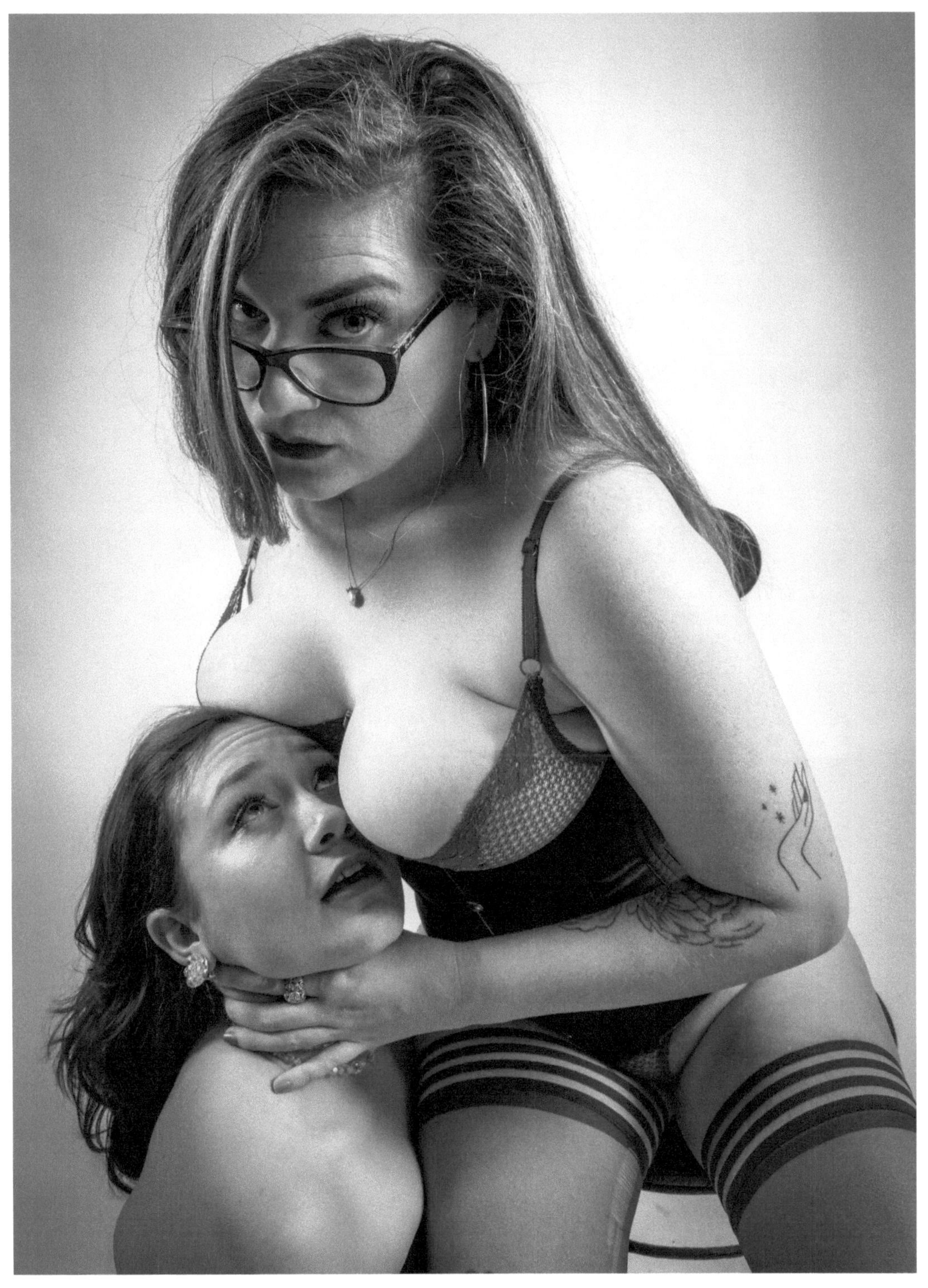

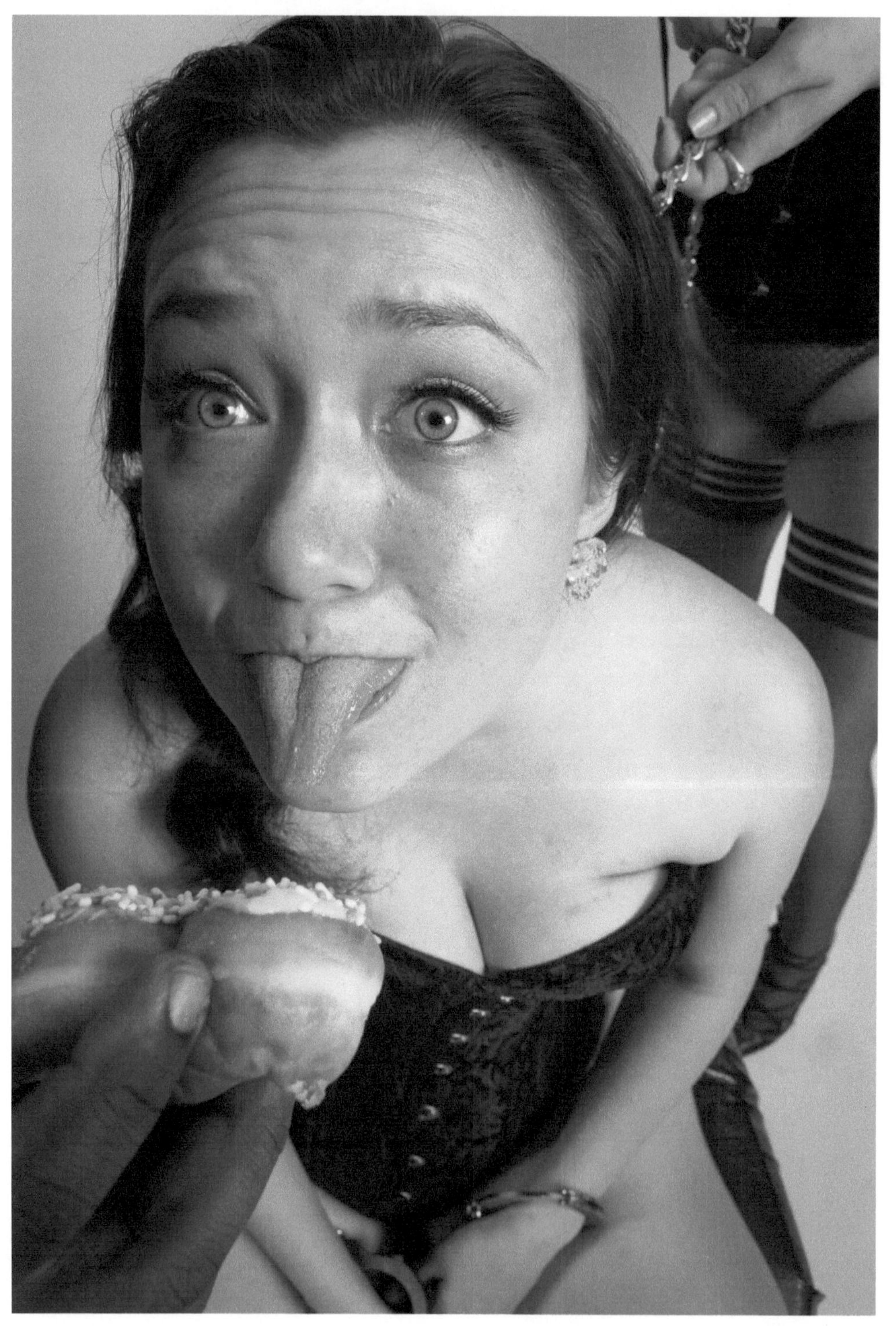

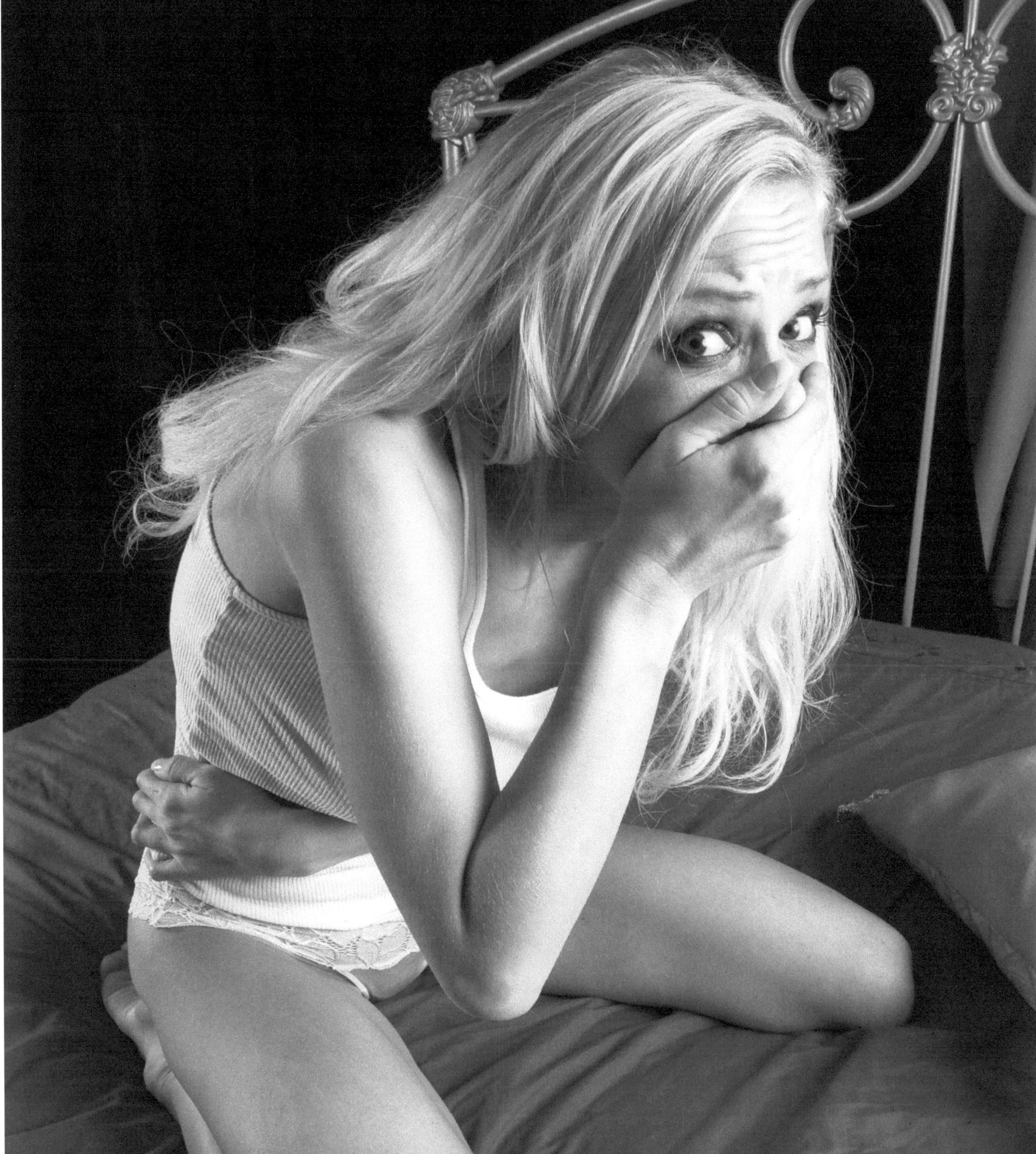

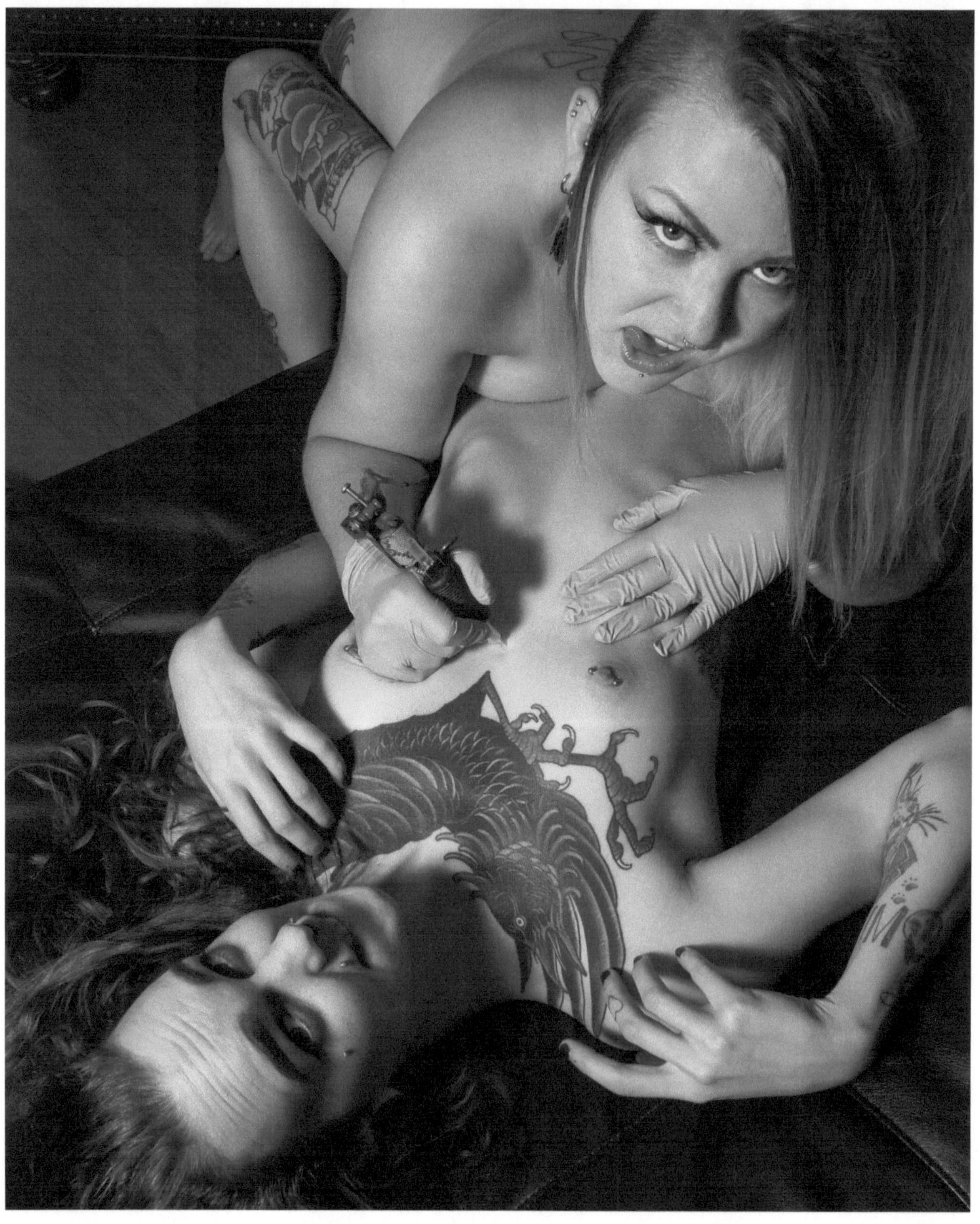

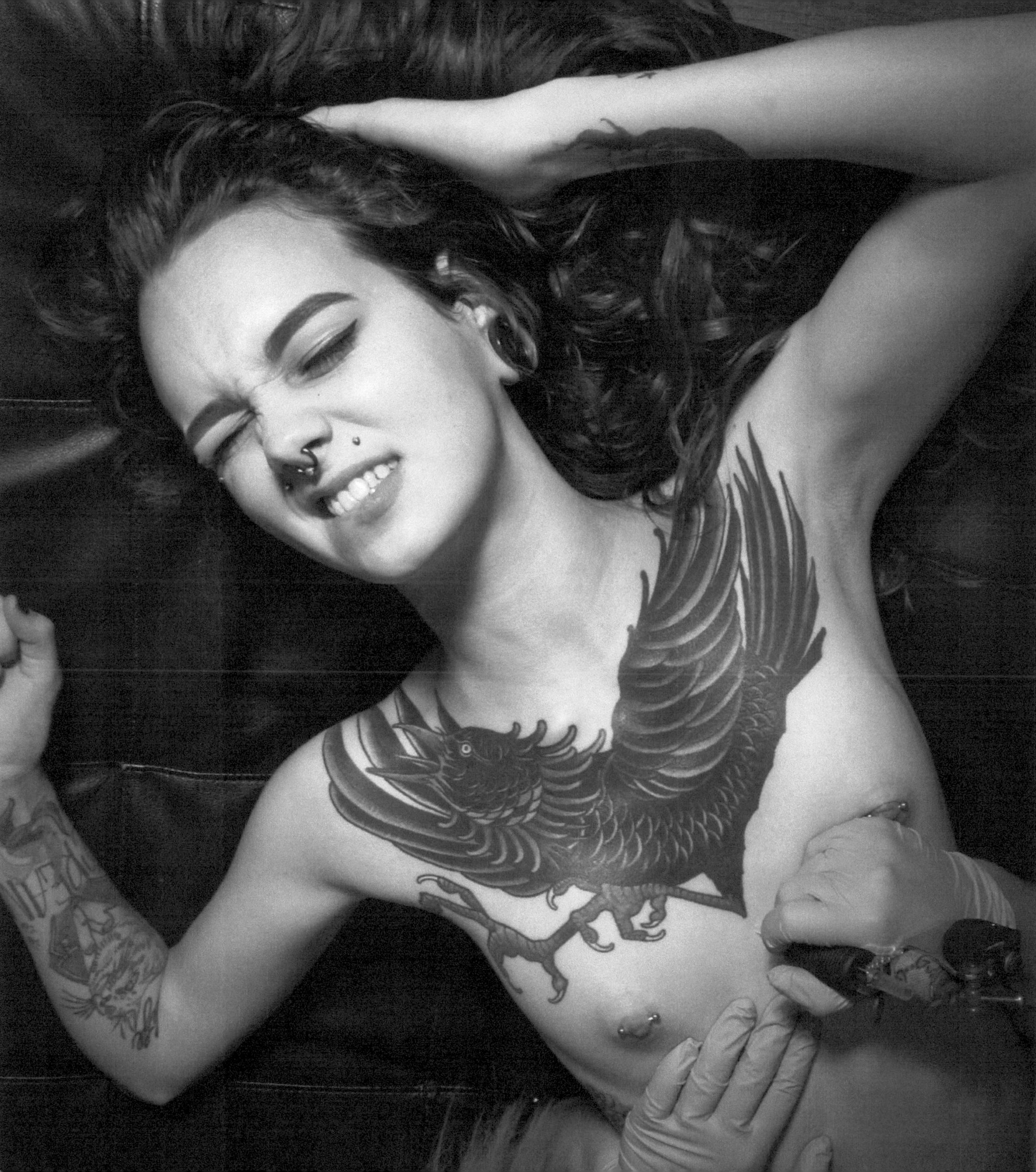

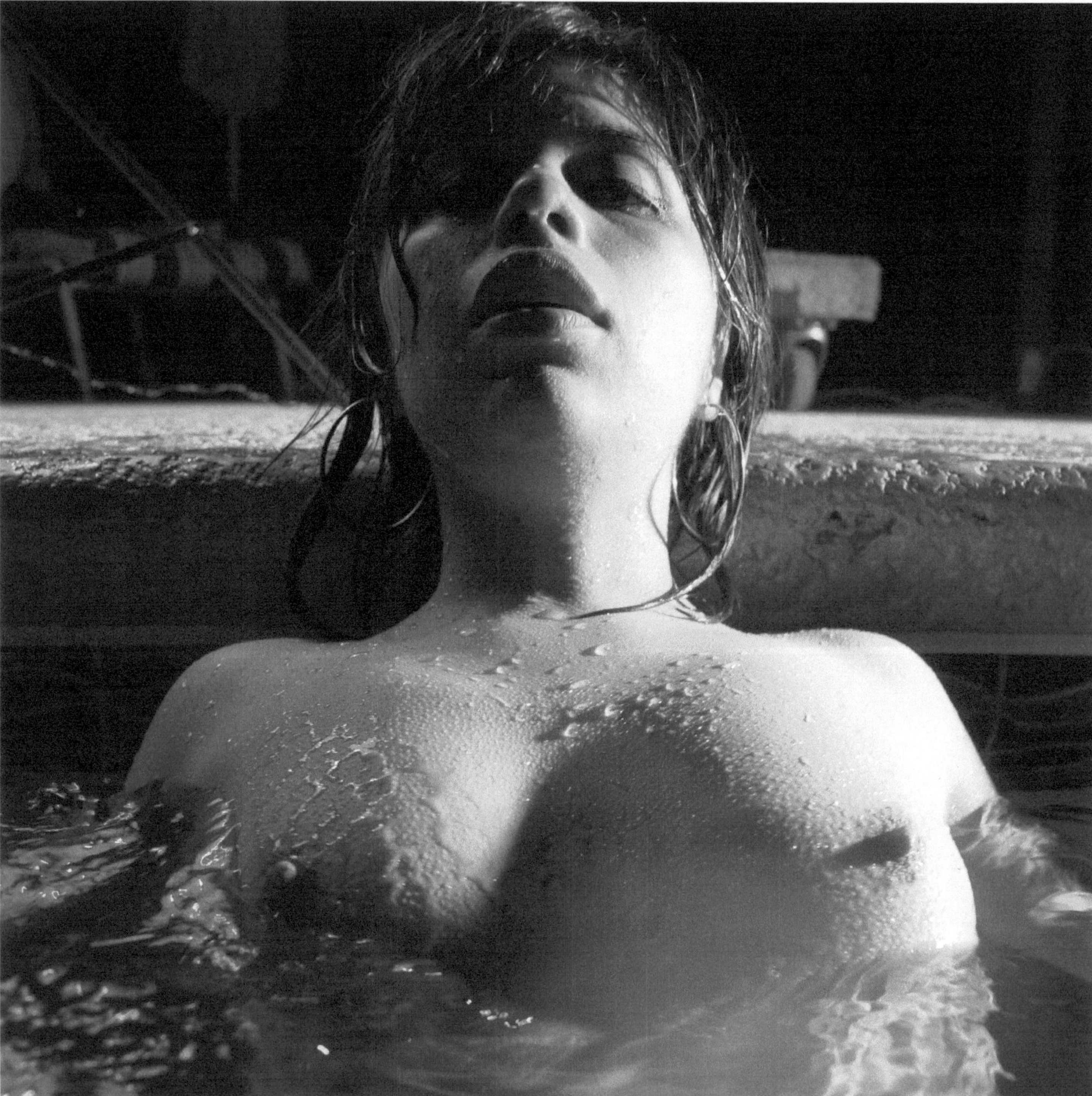

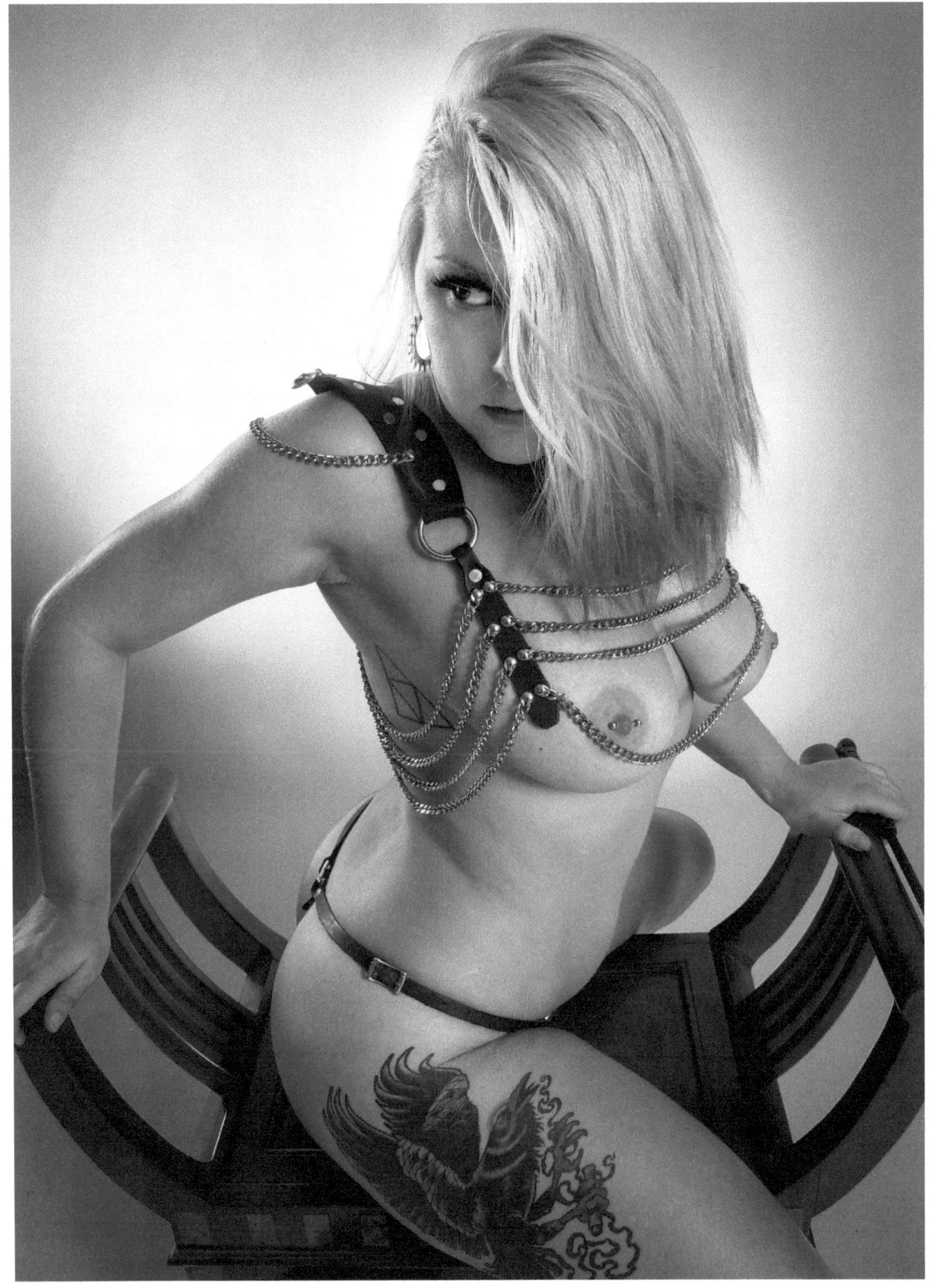

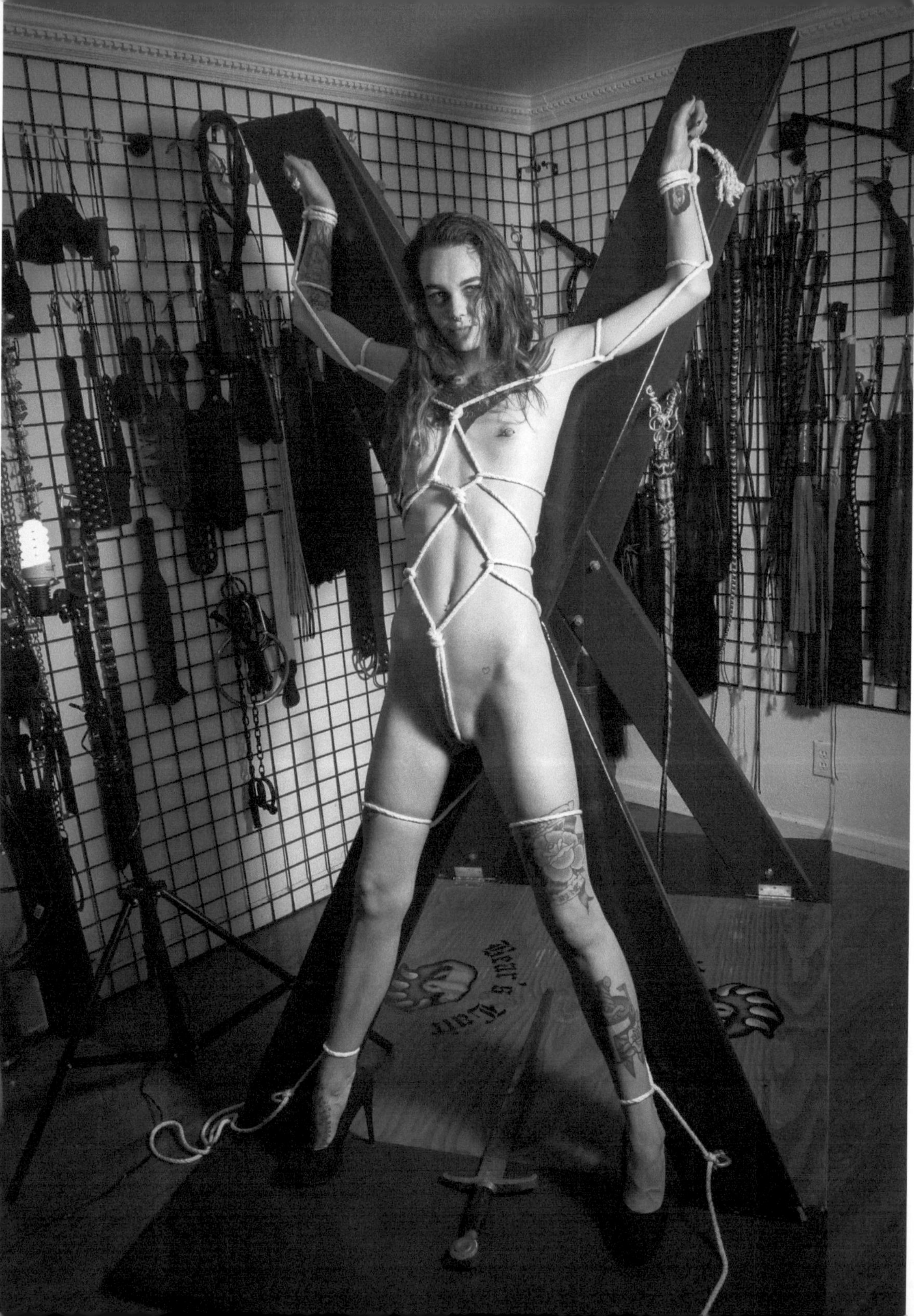
Bear's Lair

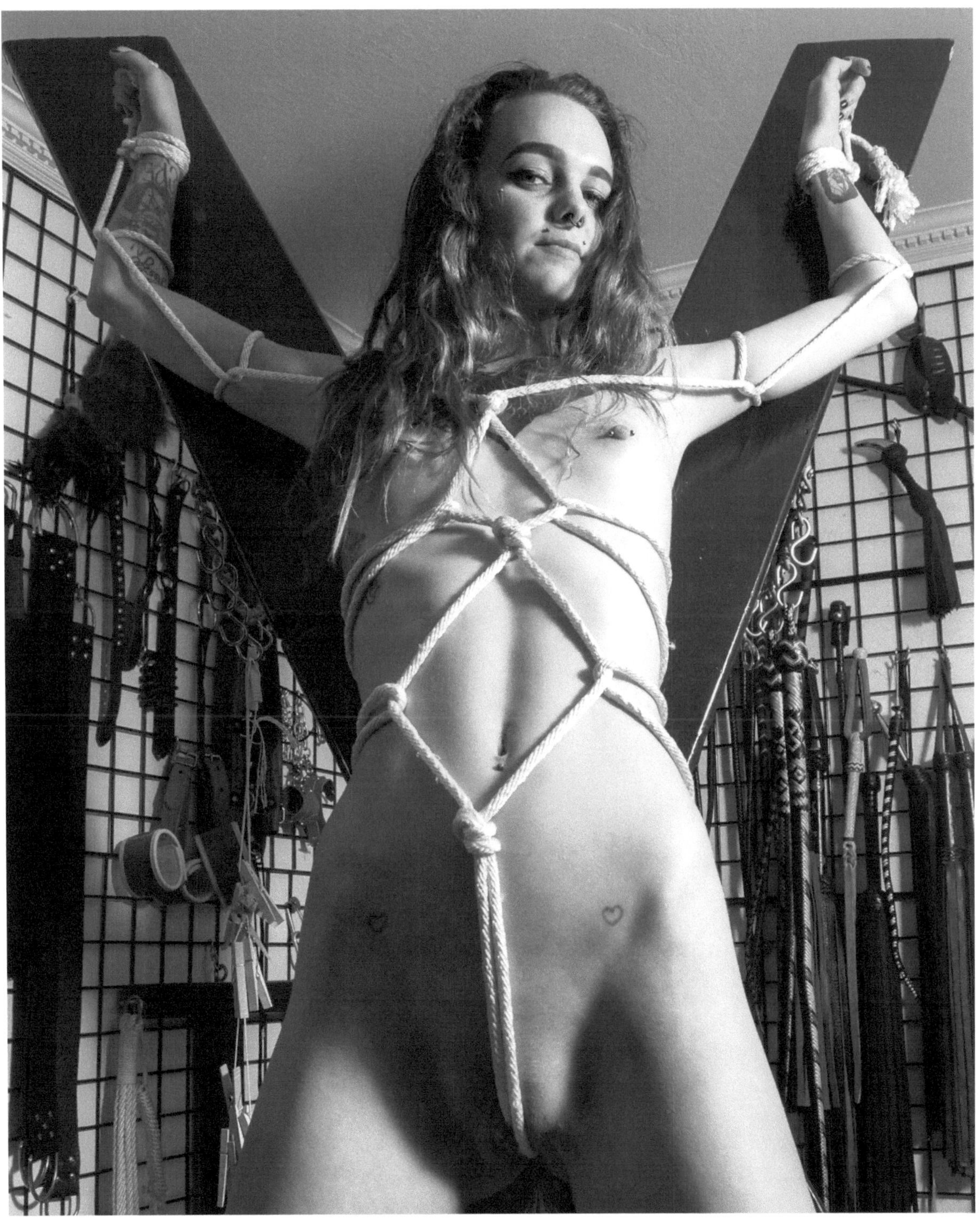

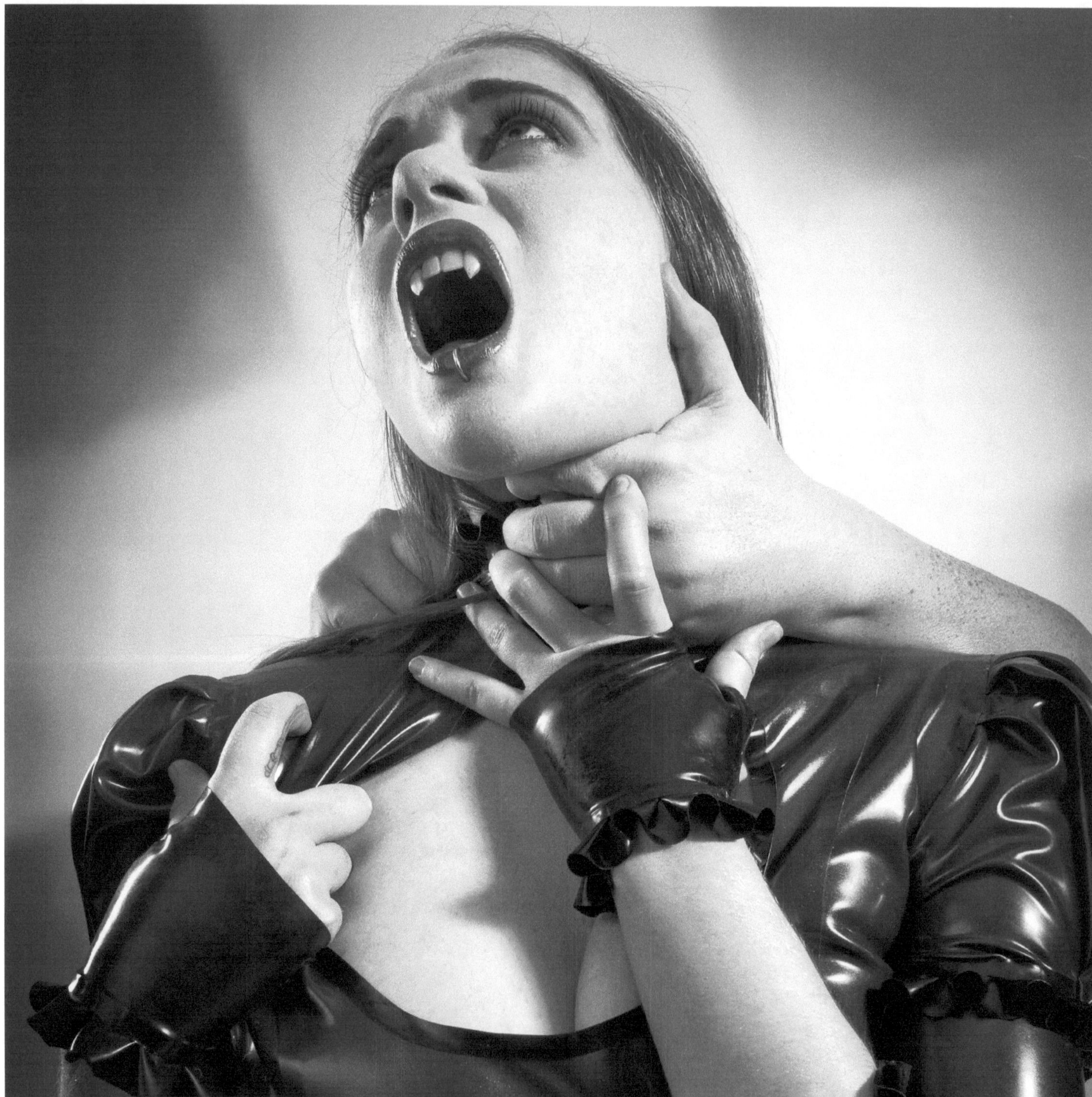

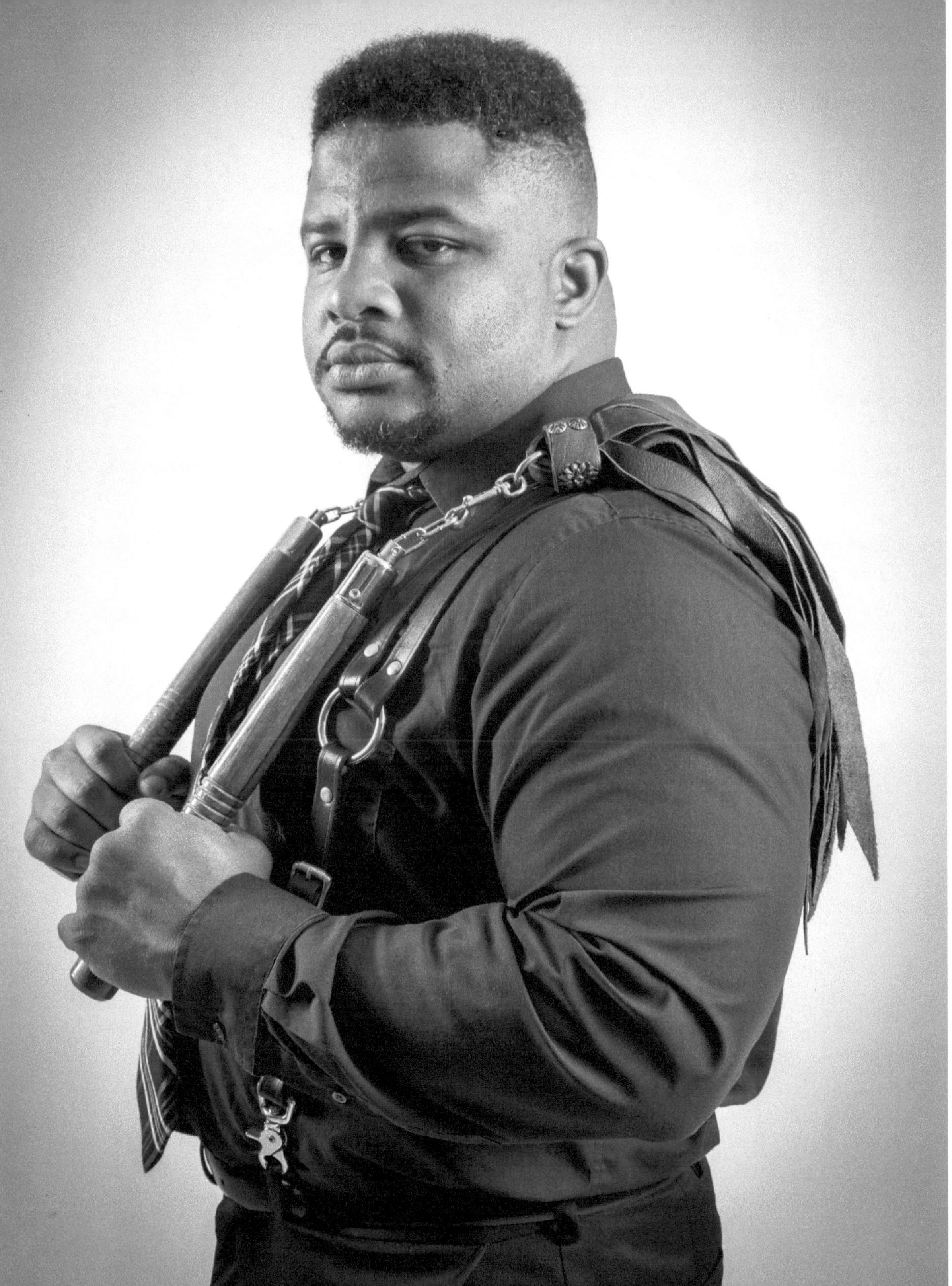

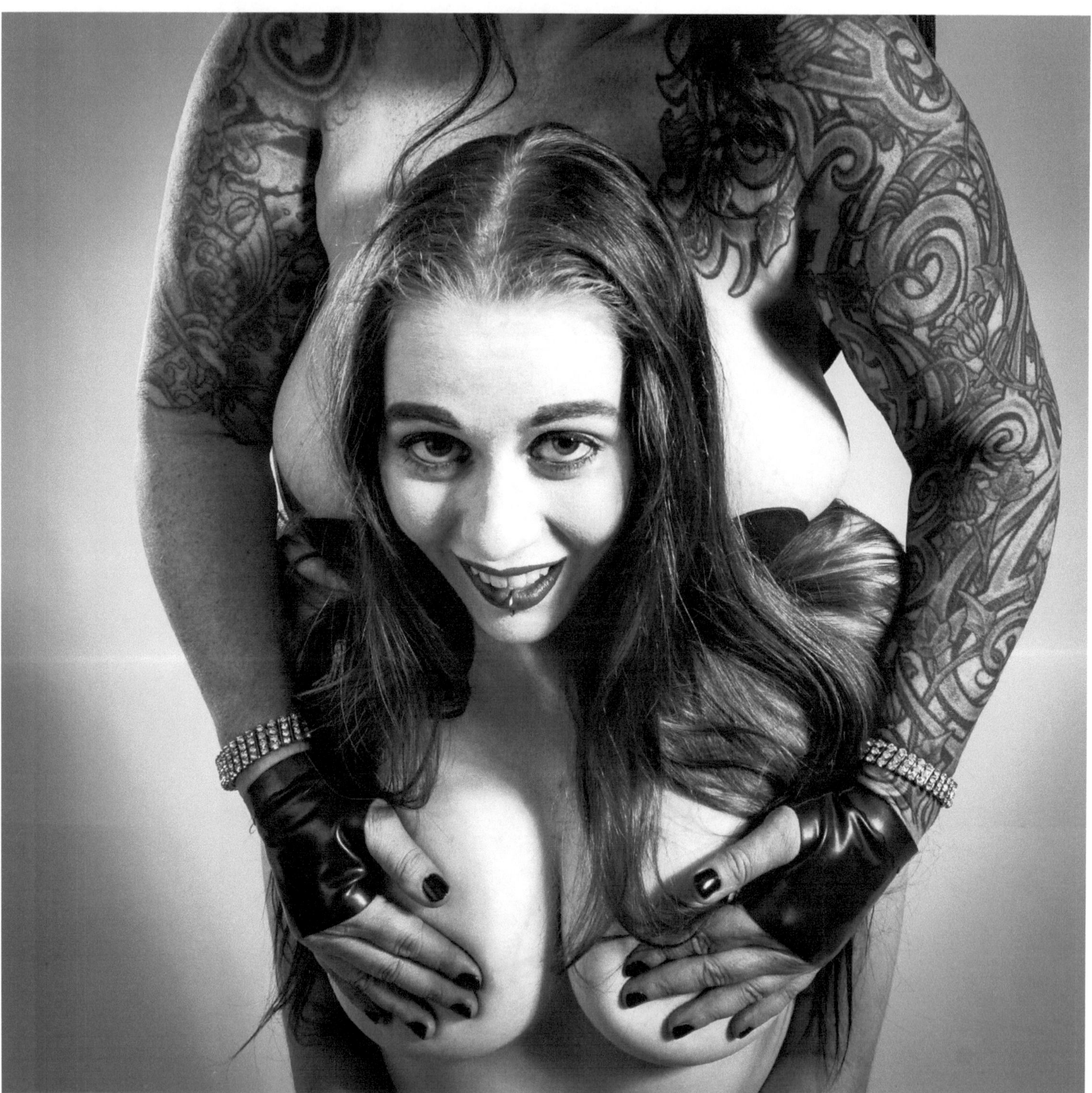

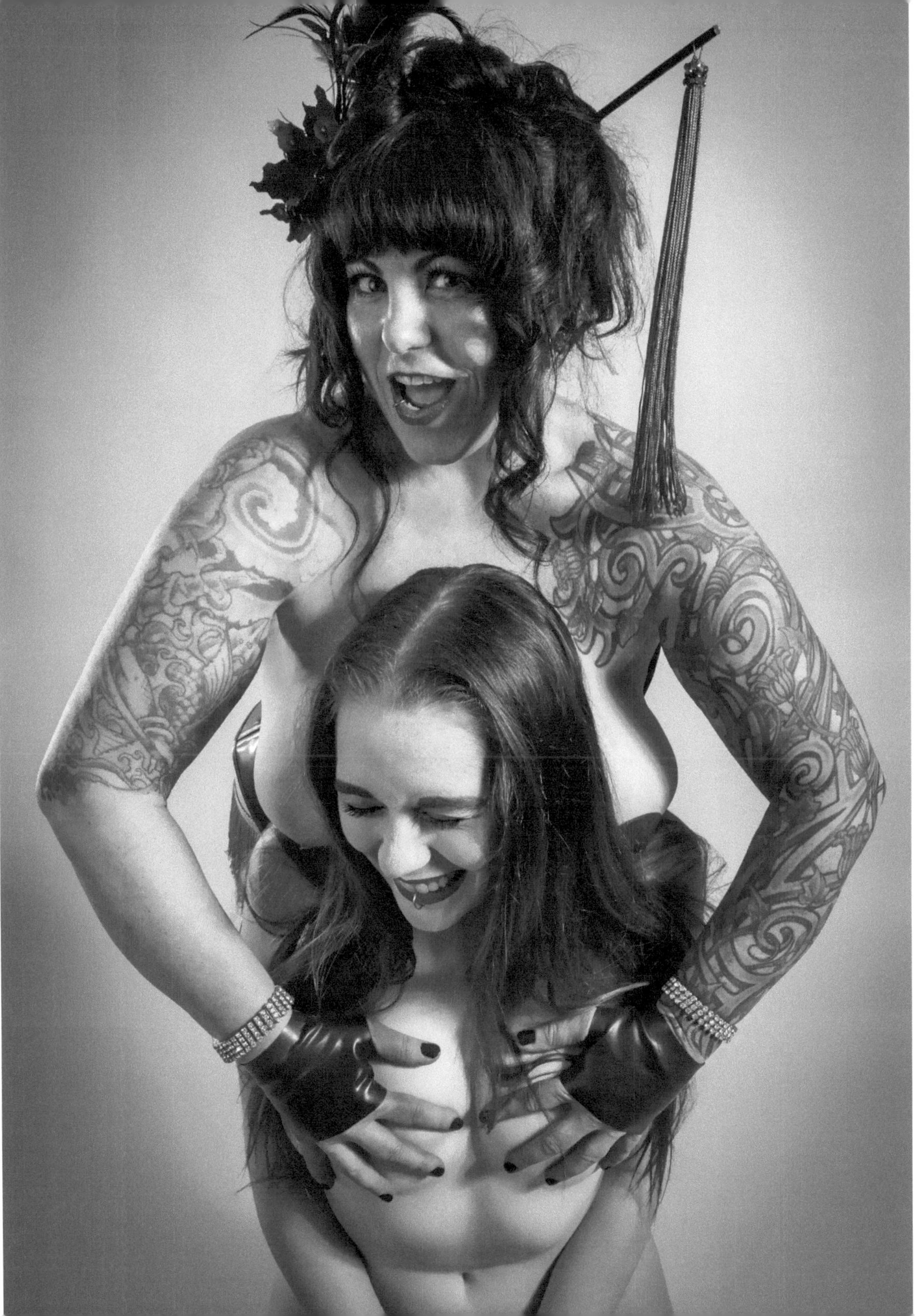

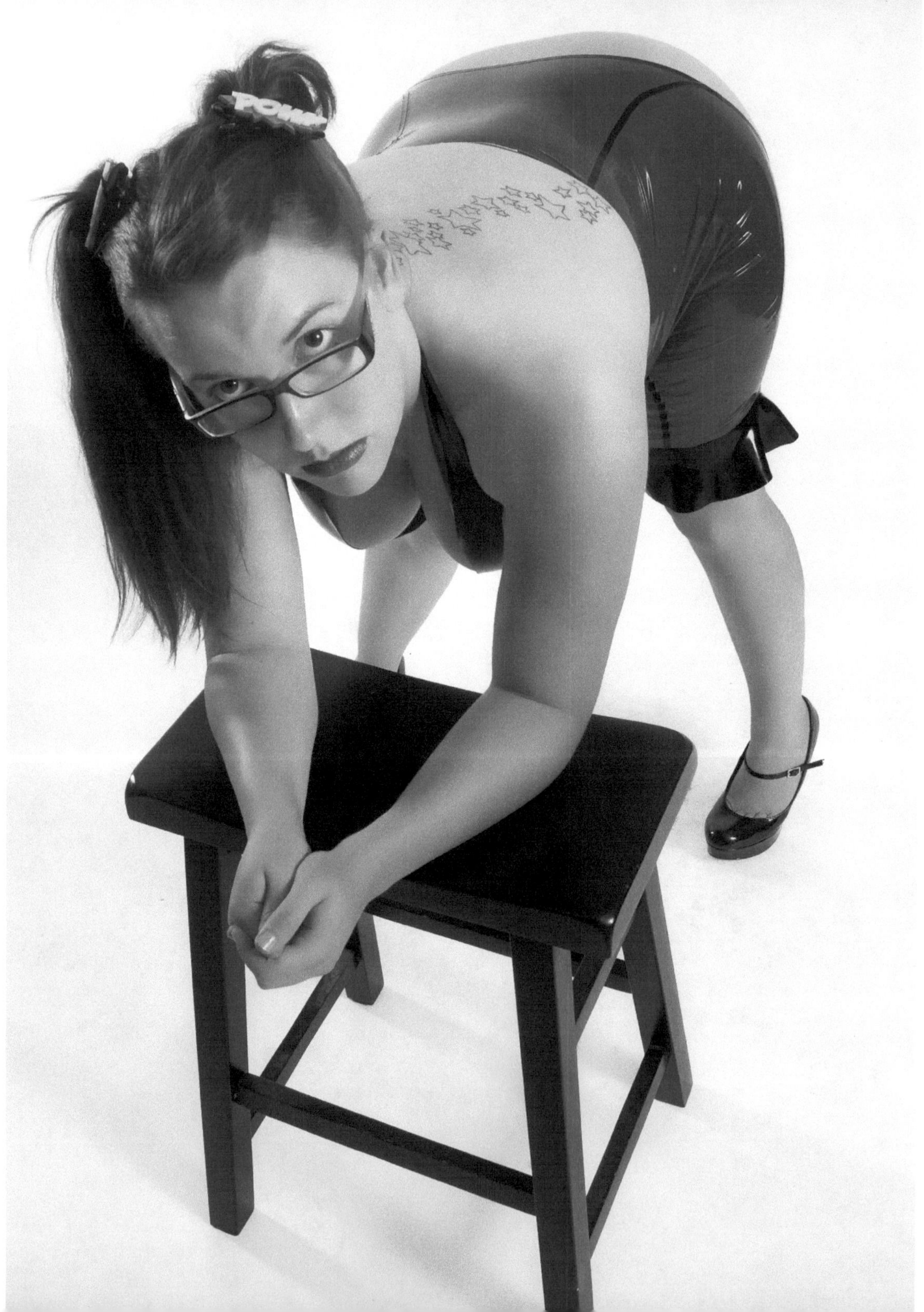

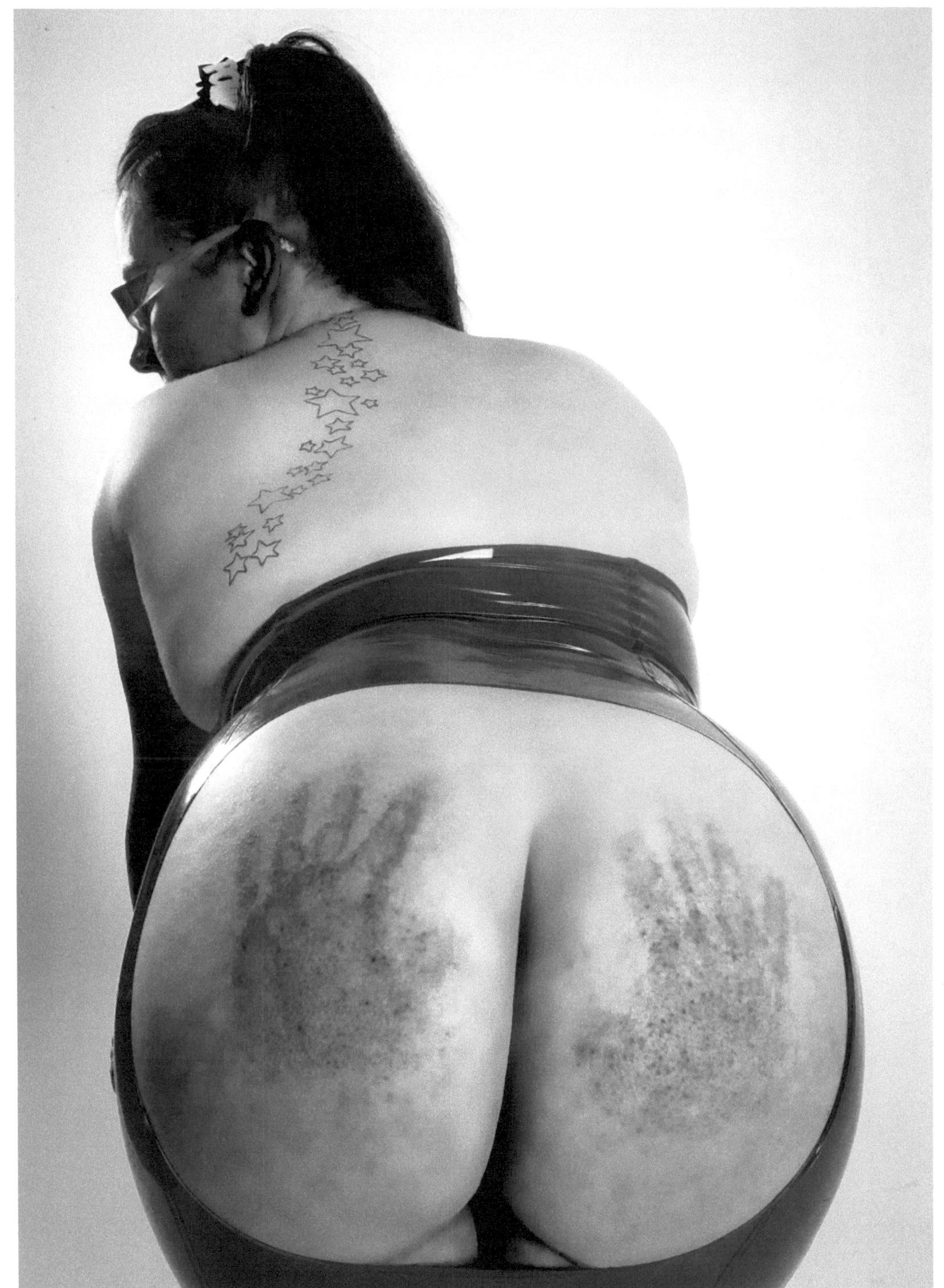

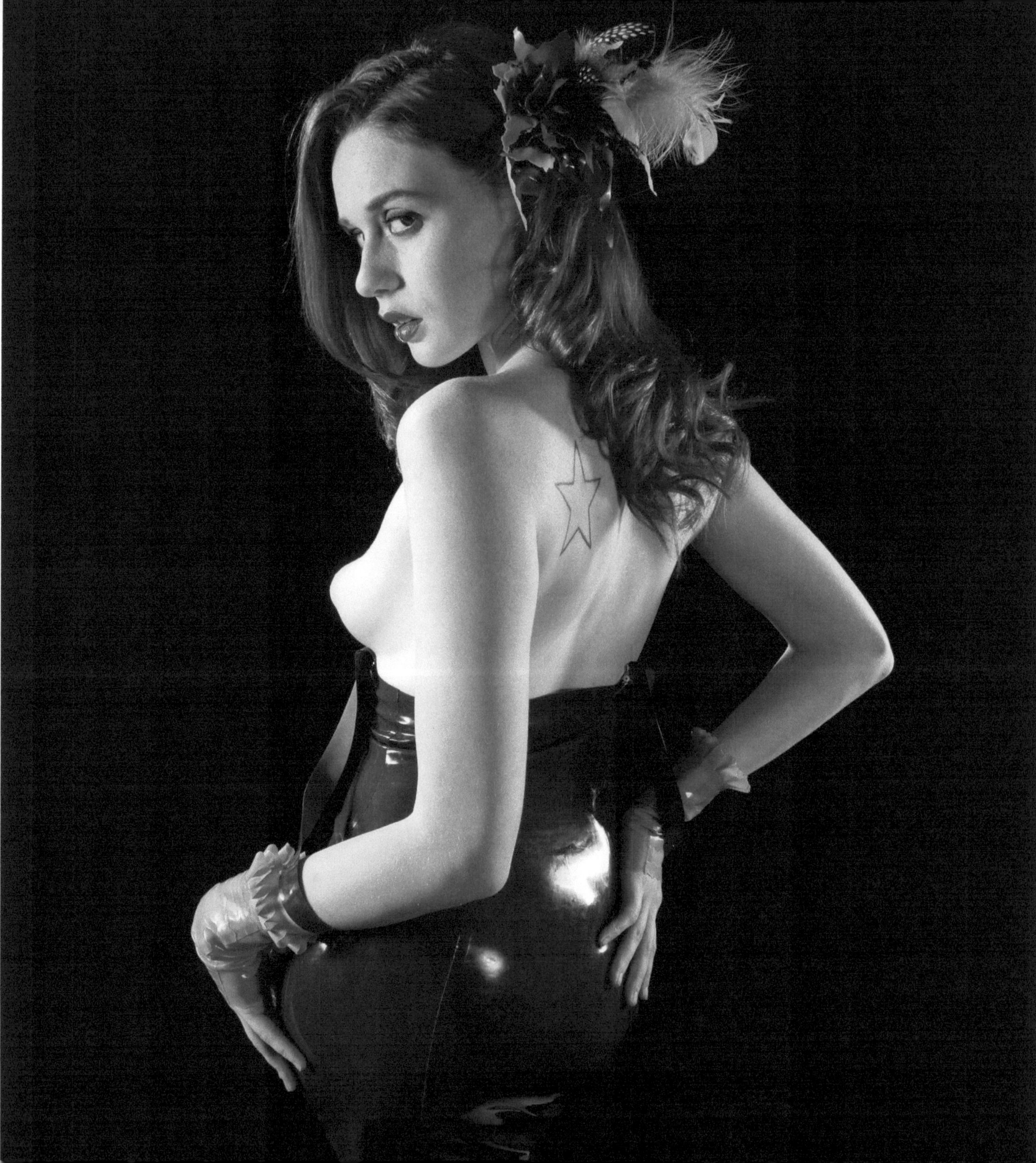

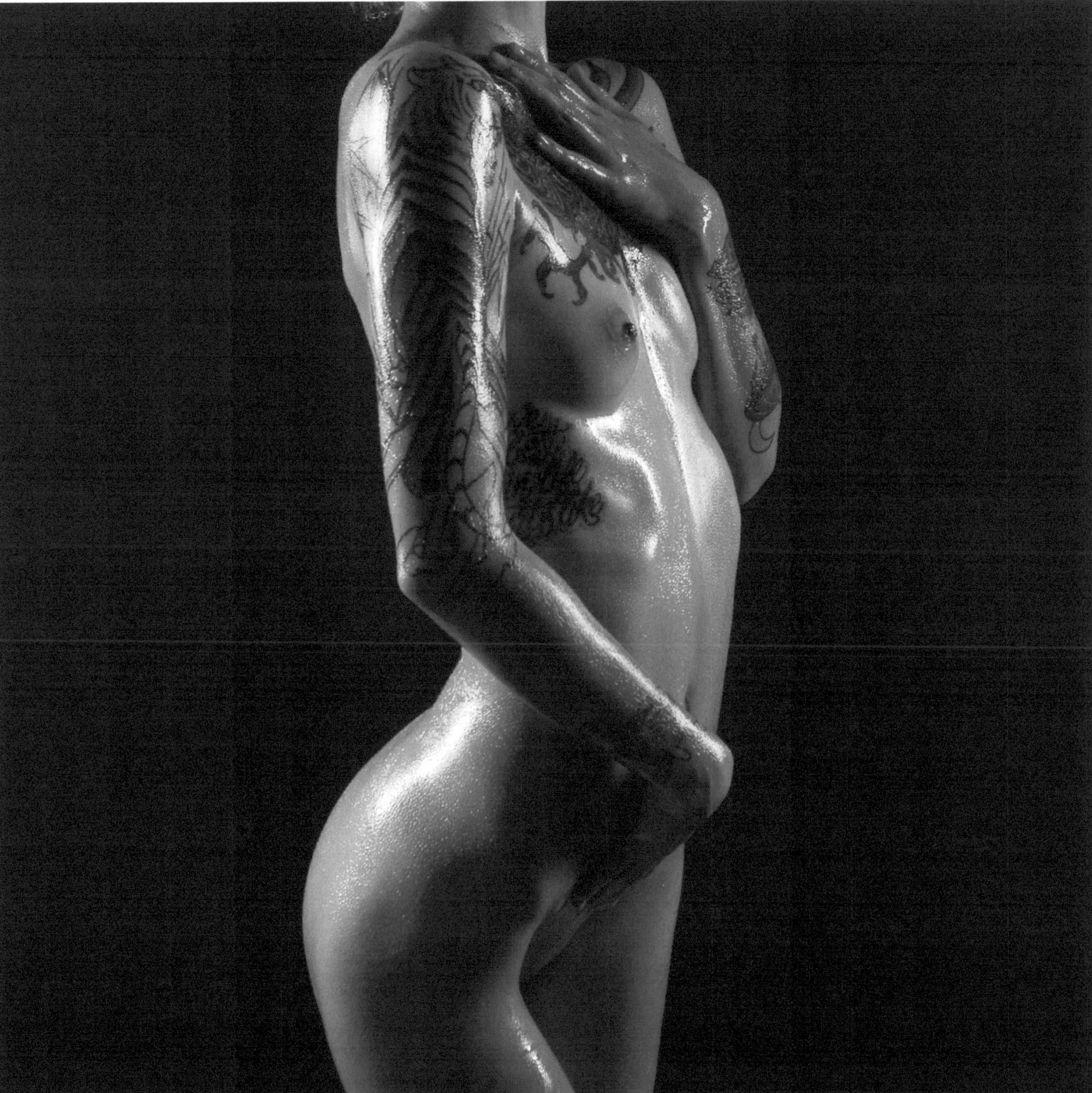

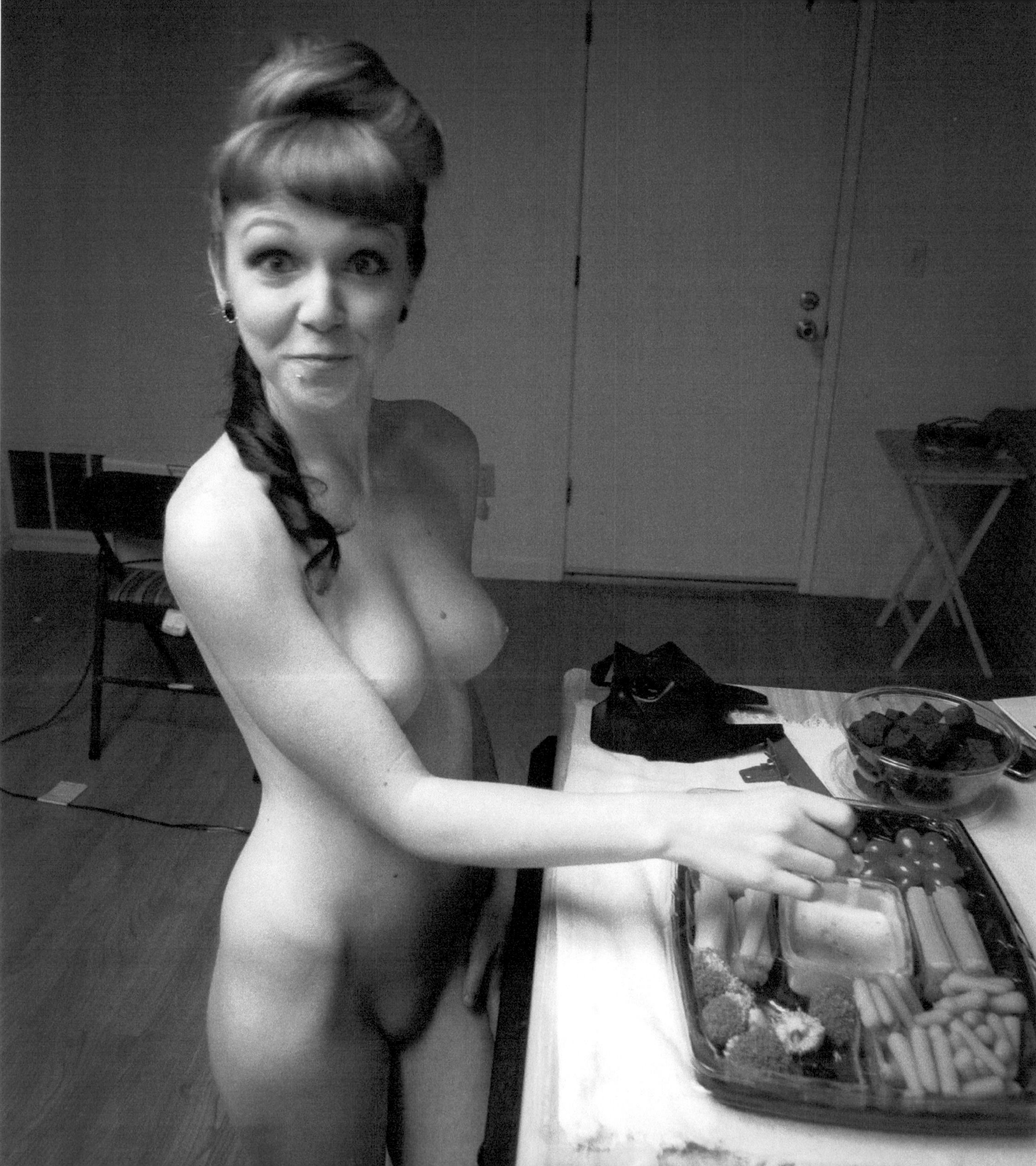

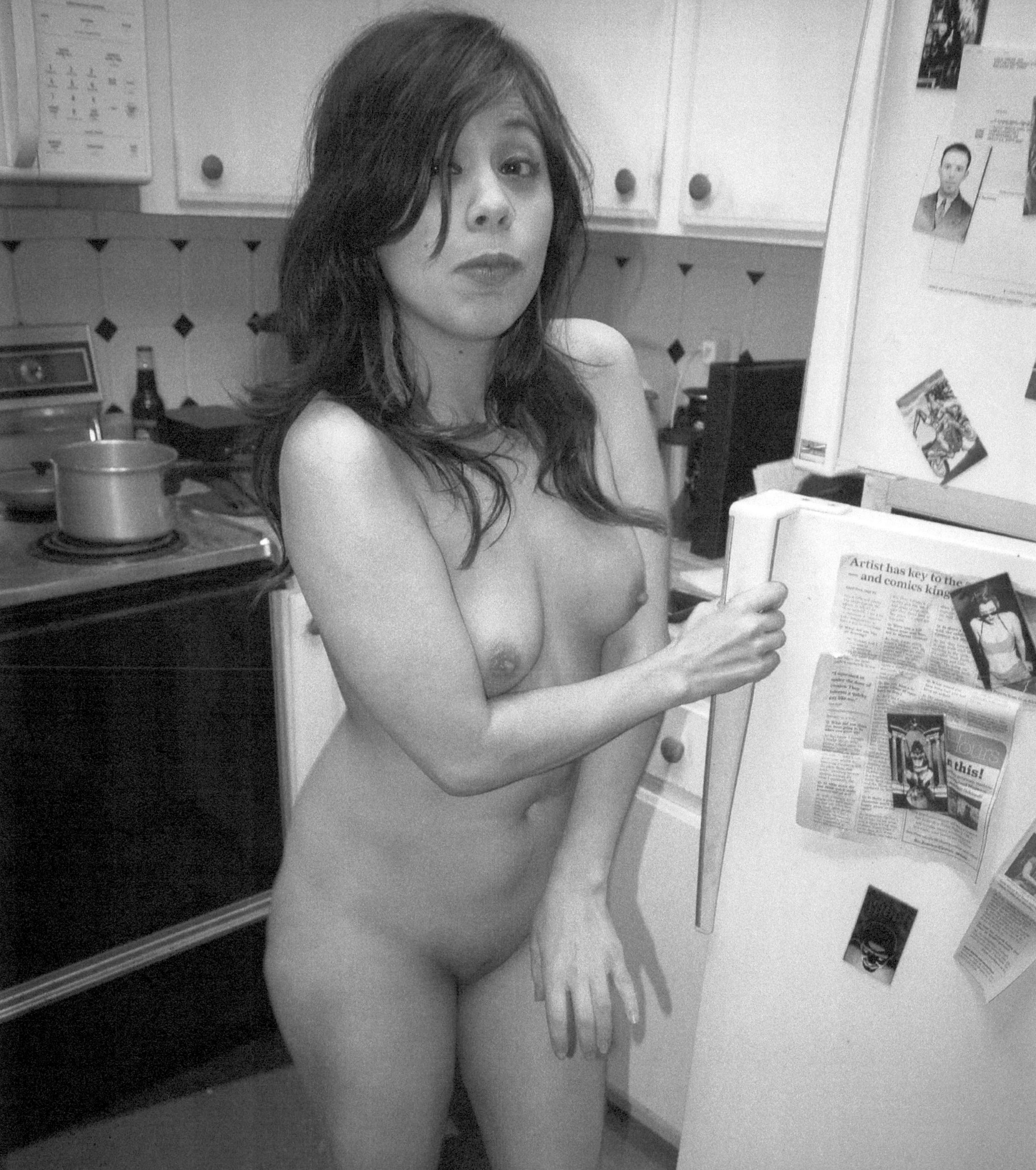
Artist has key to the
— and comics king

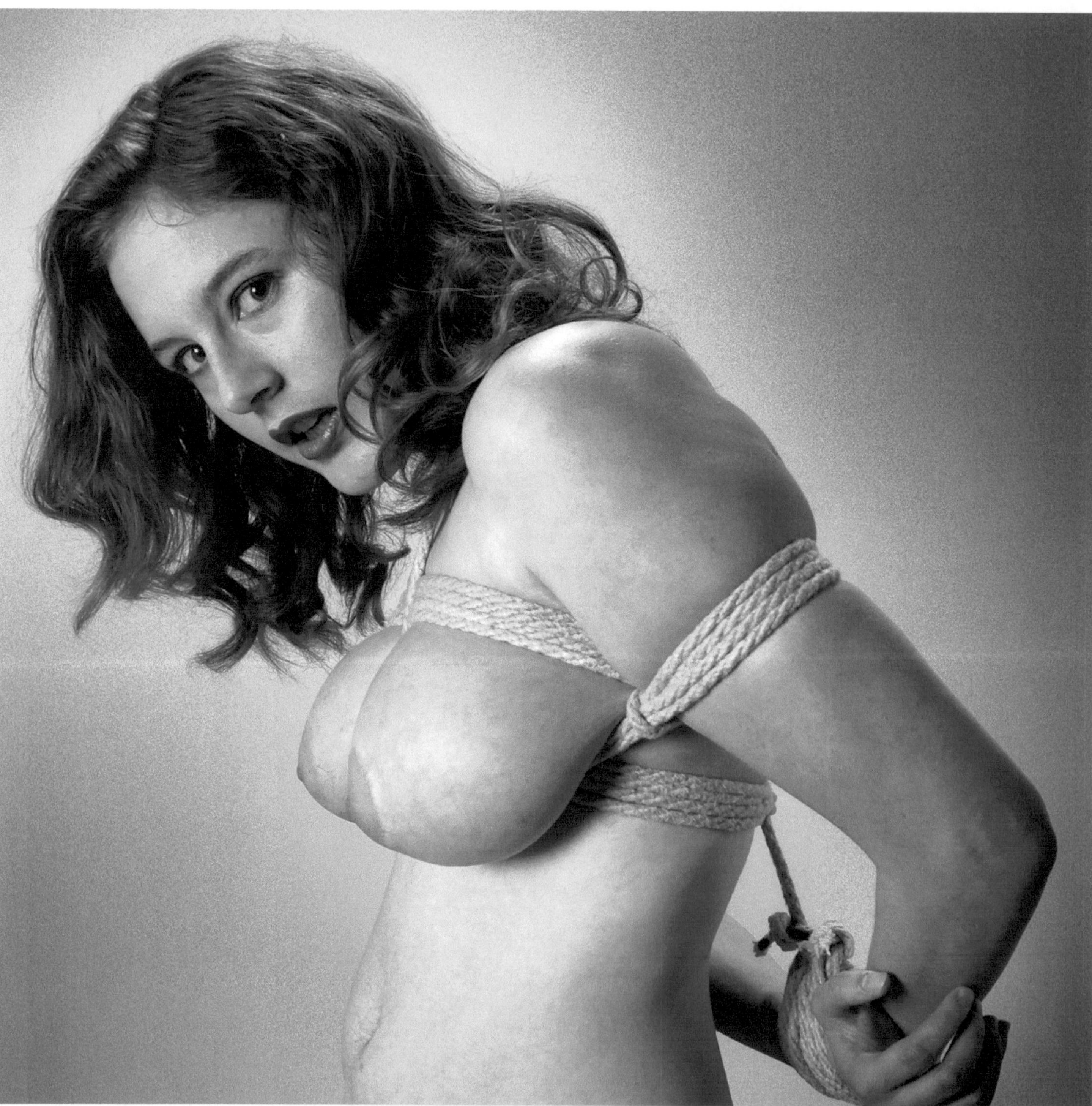

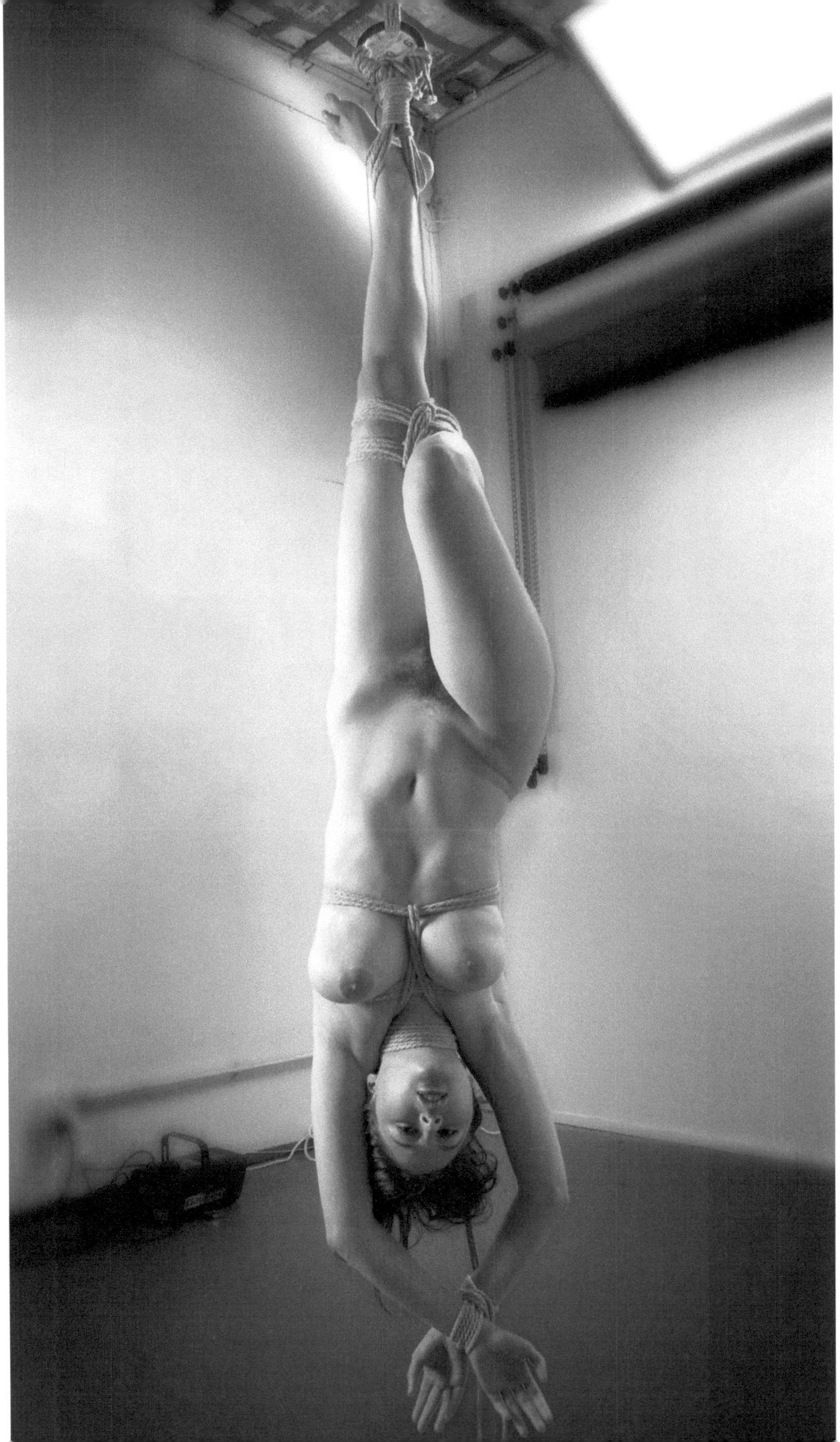

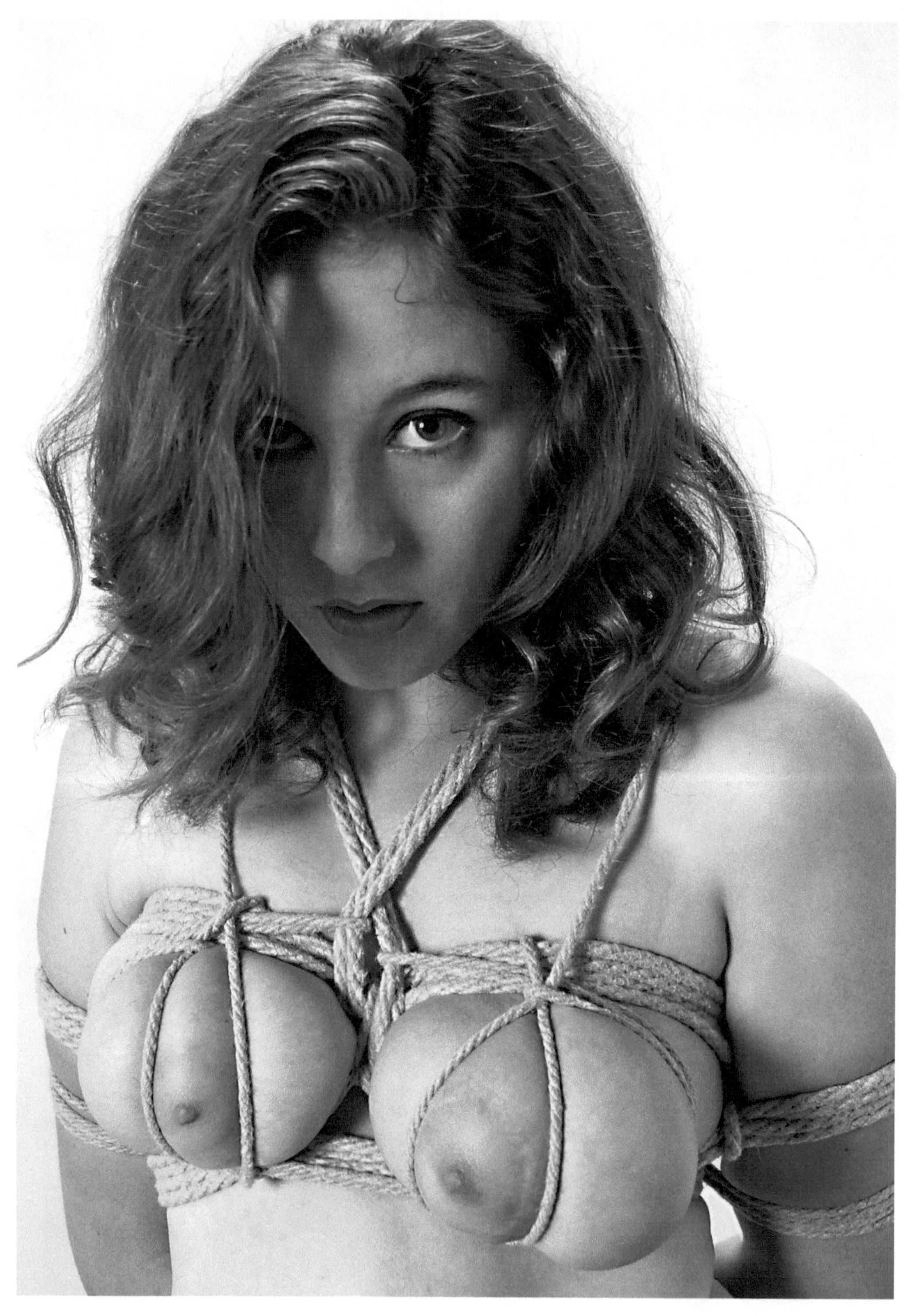

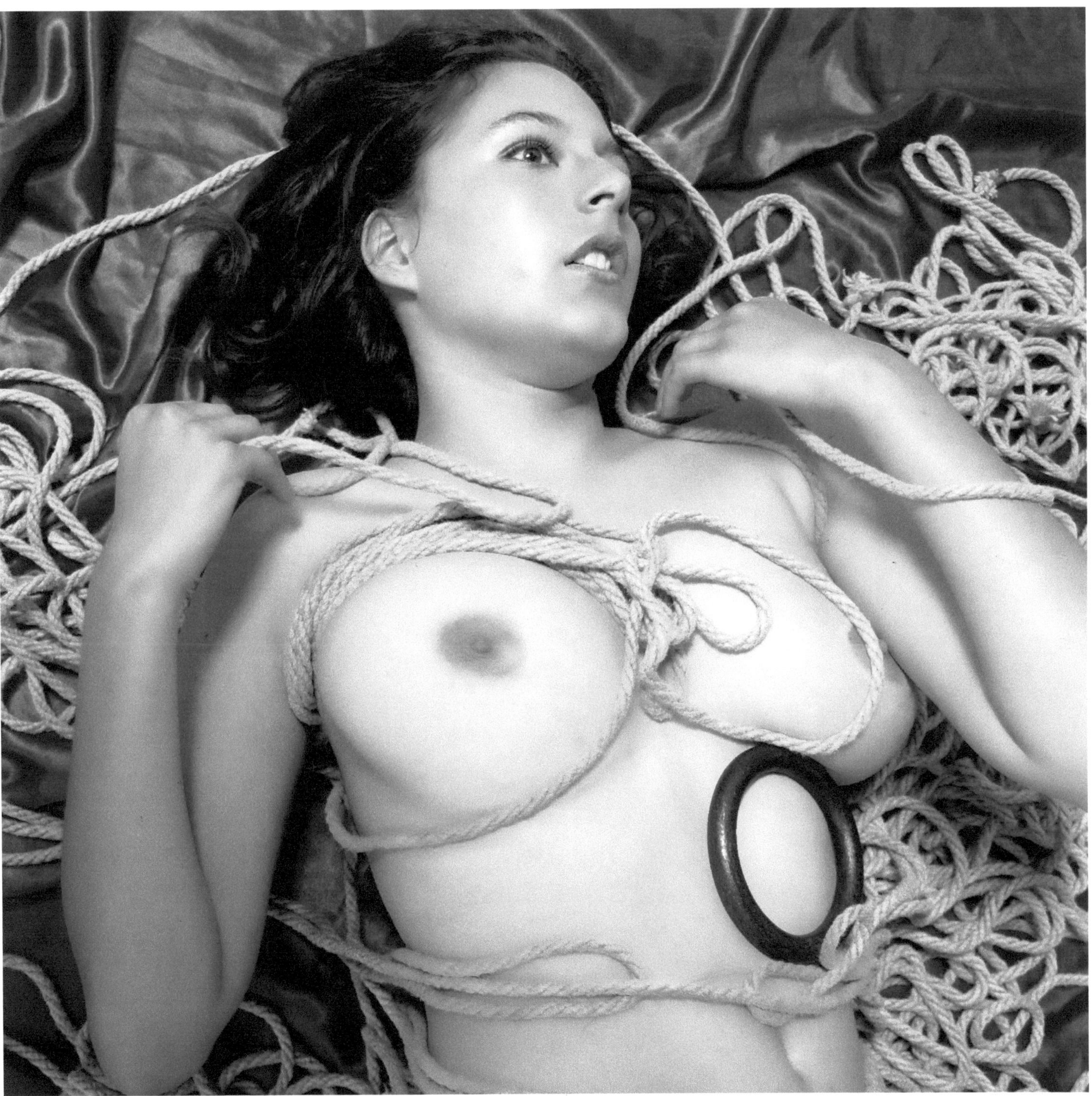

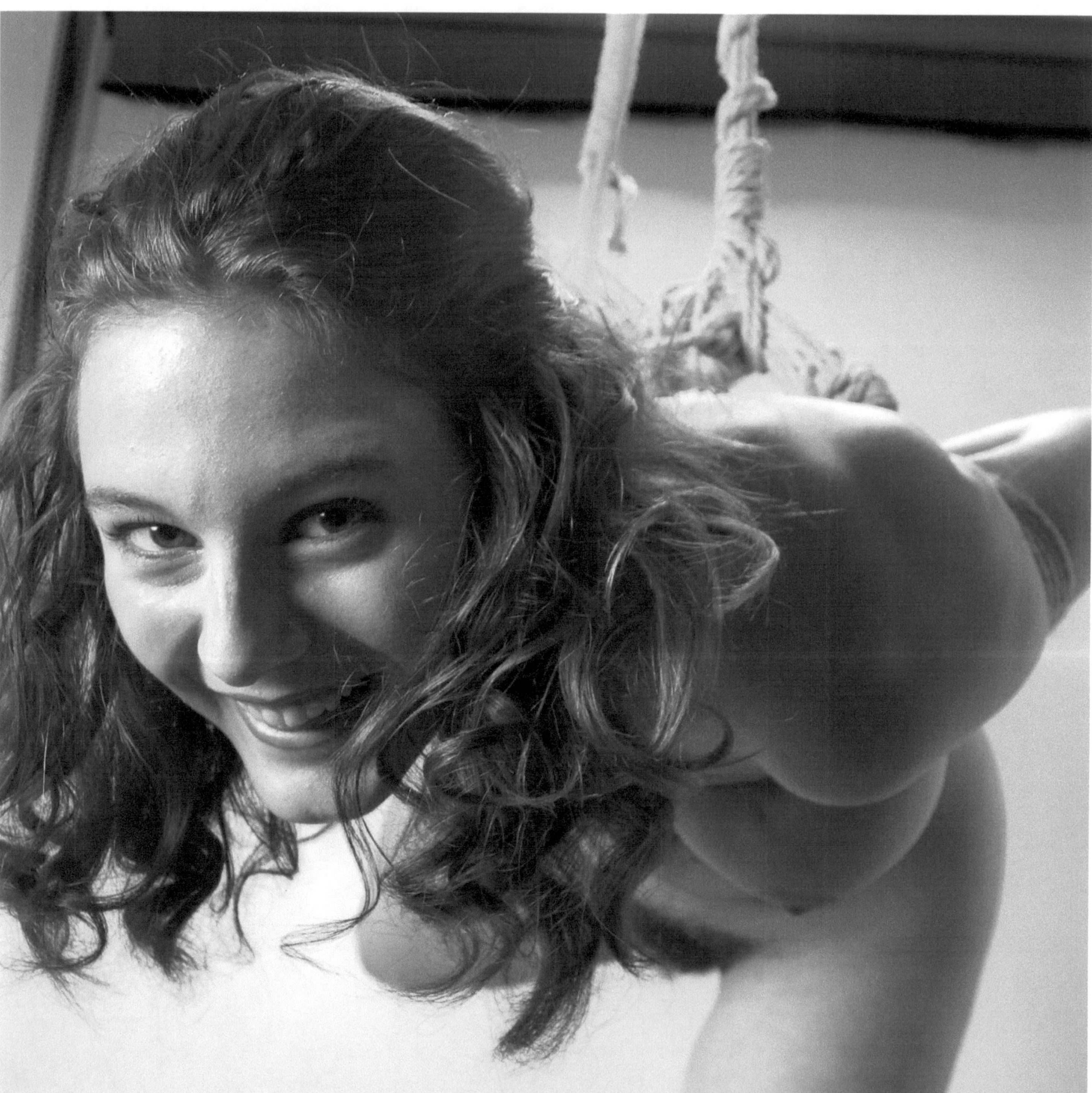

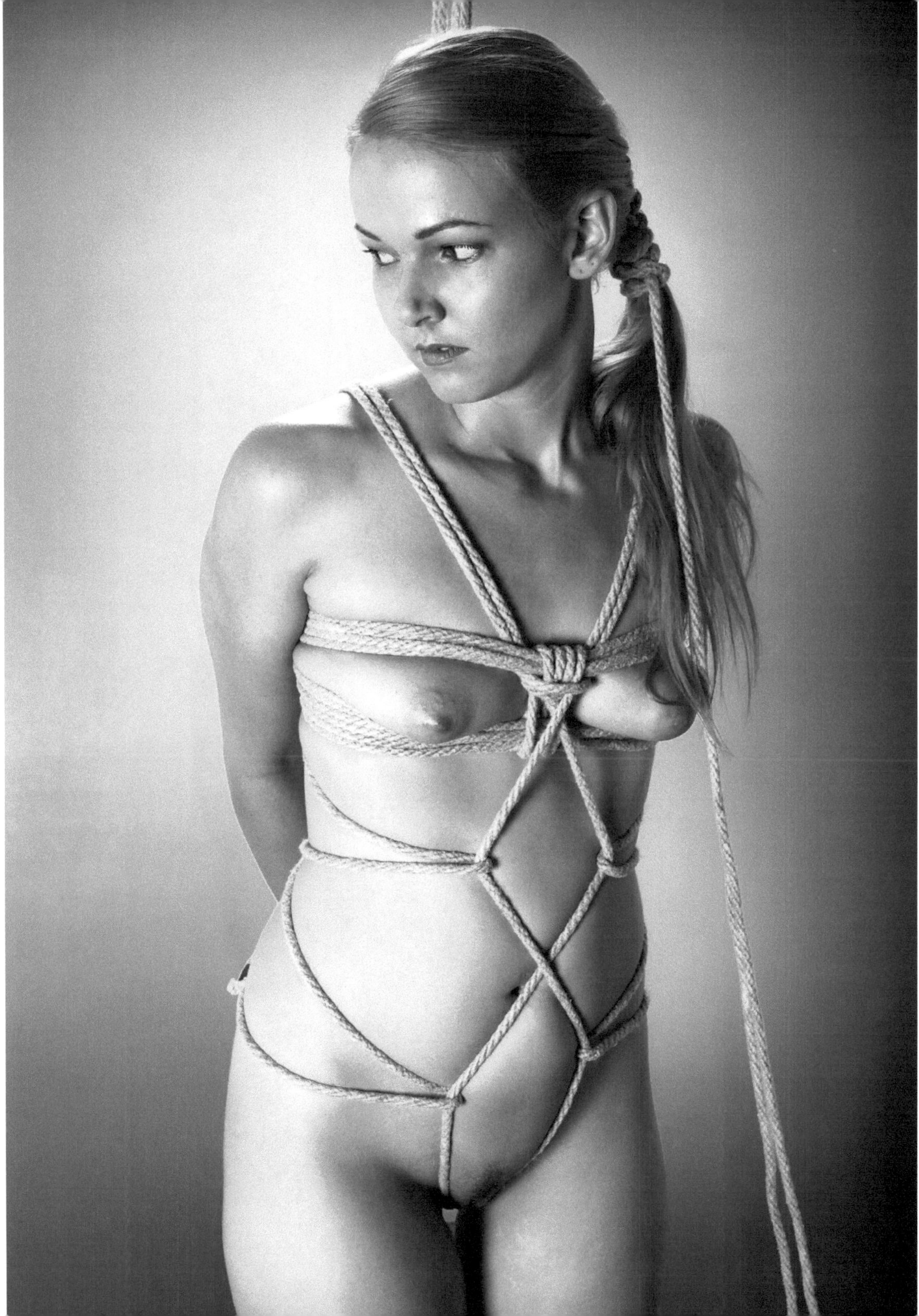

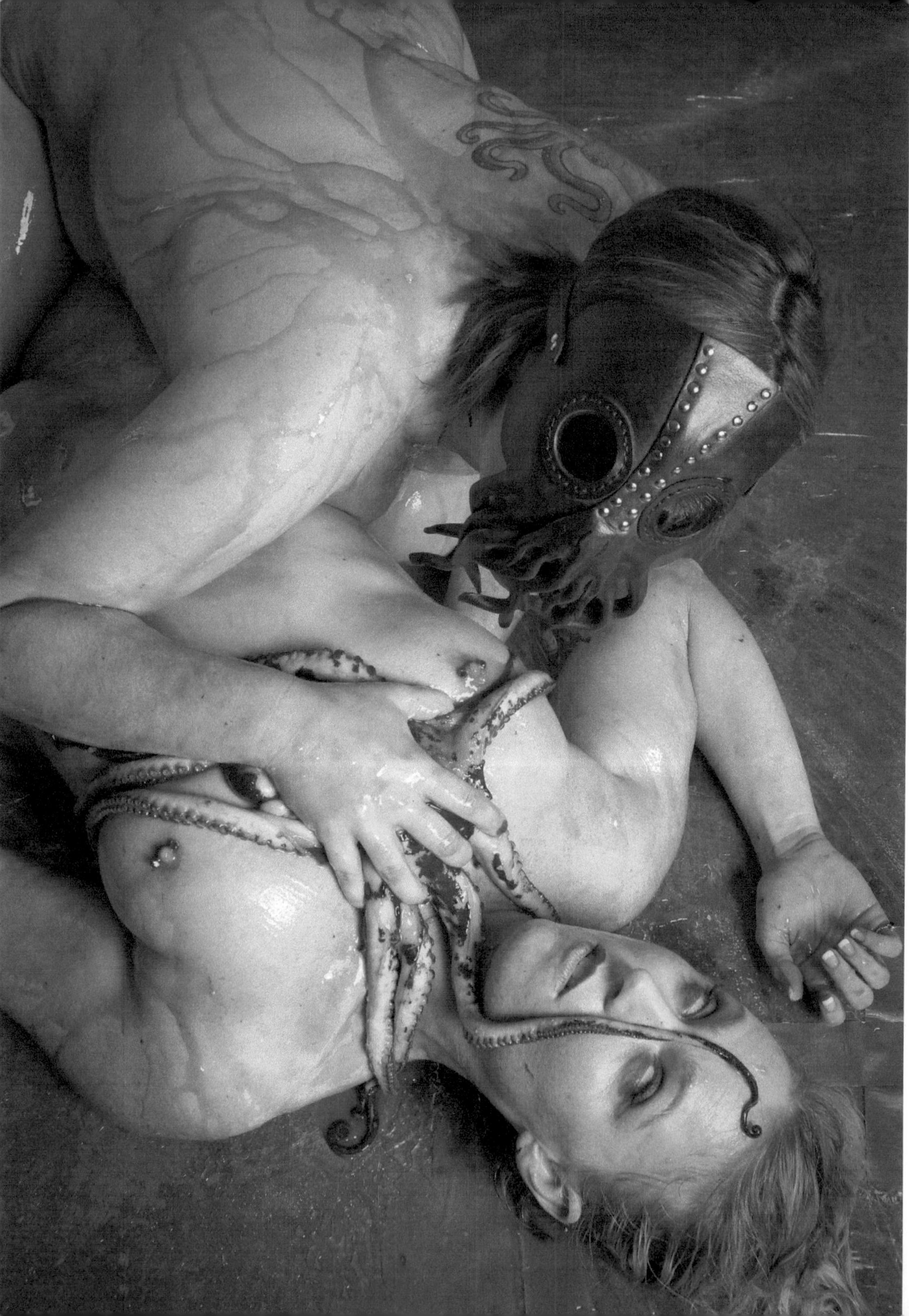

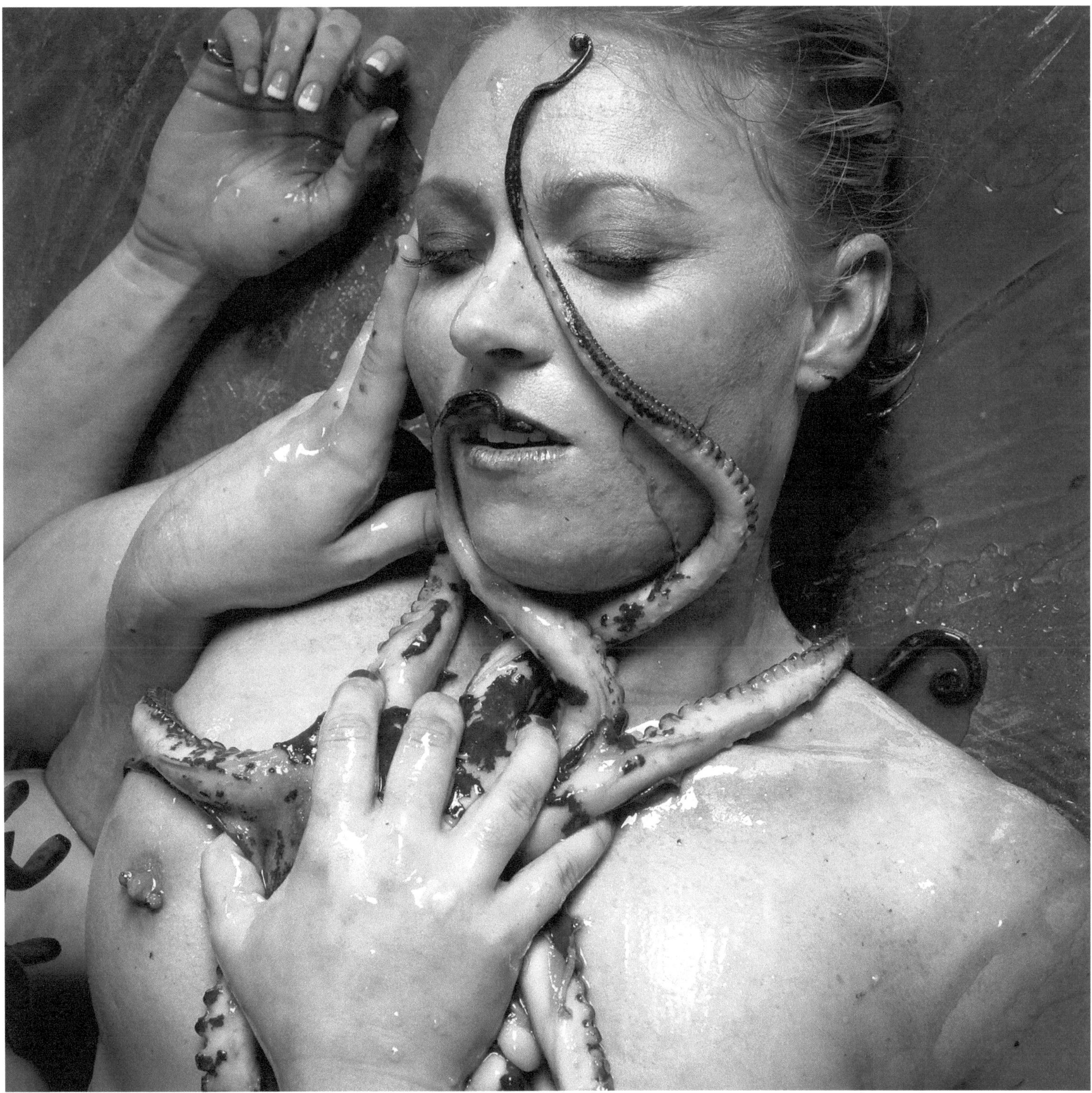

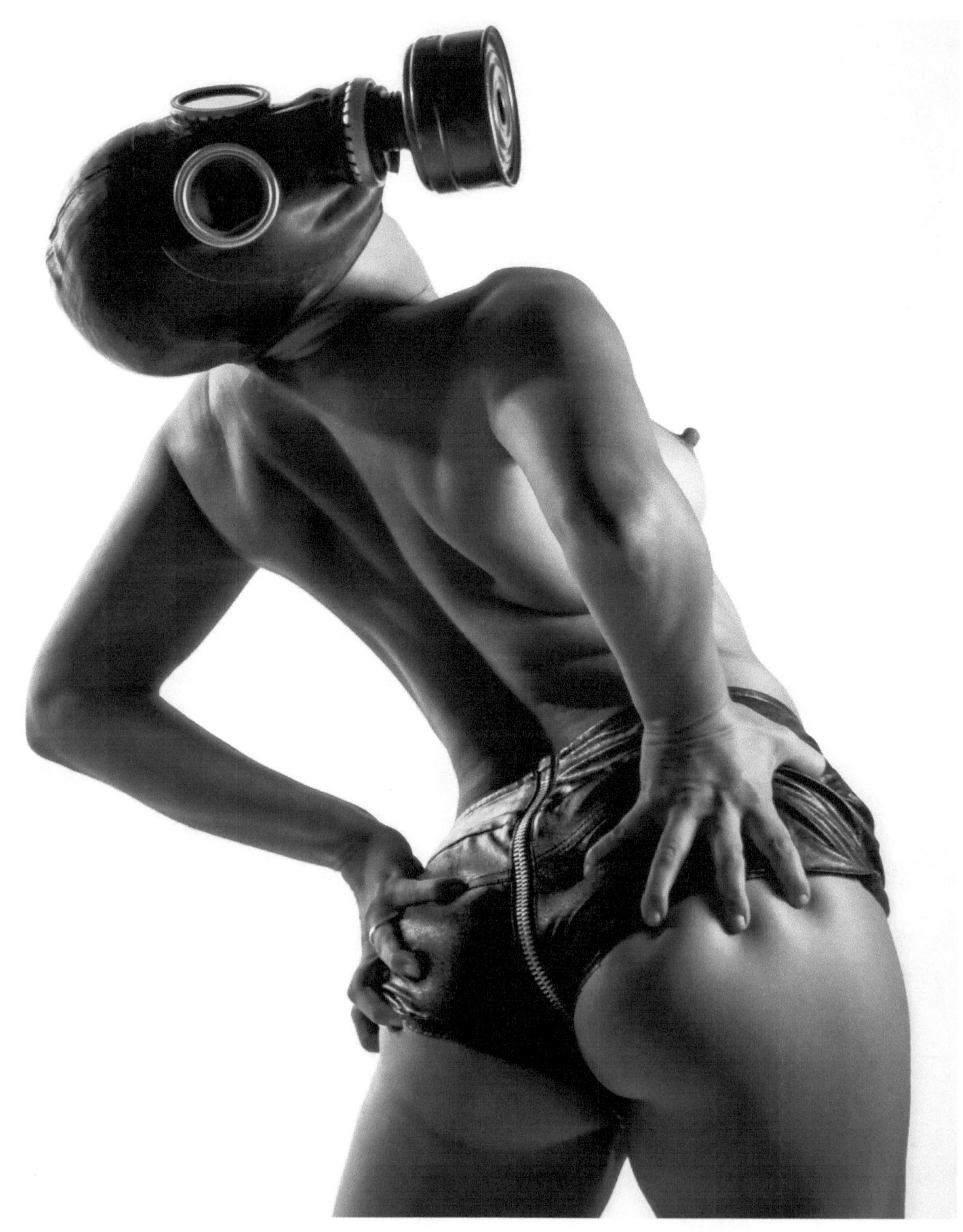

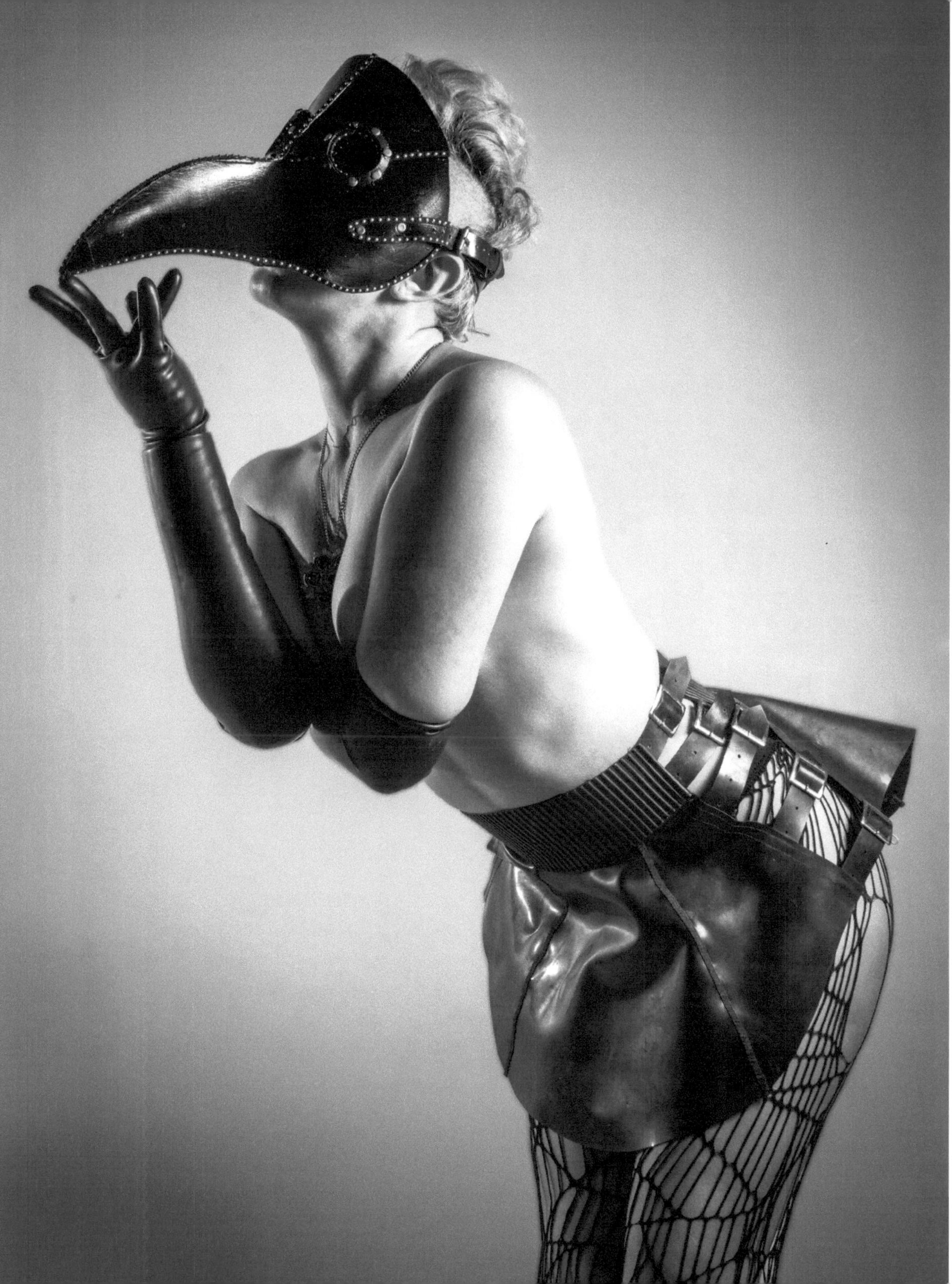

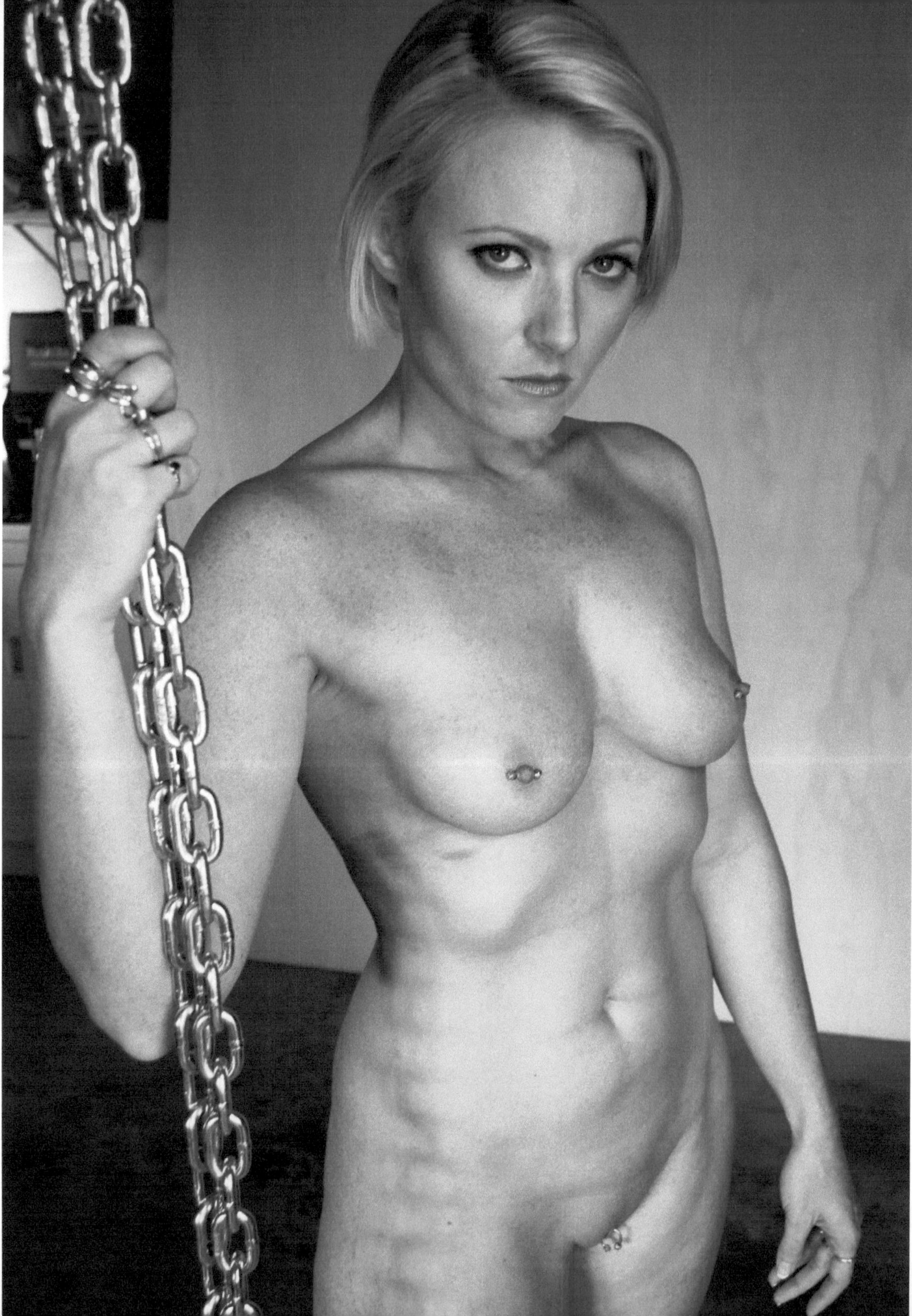

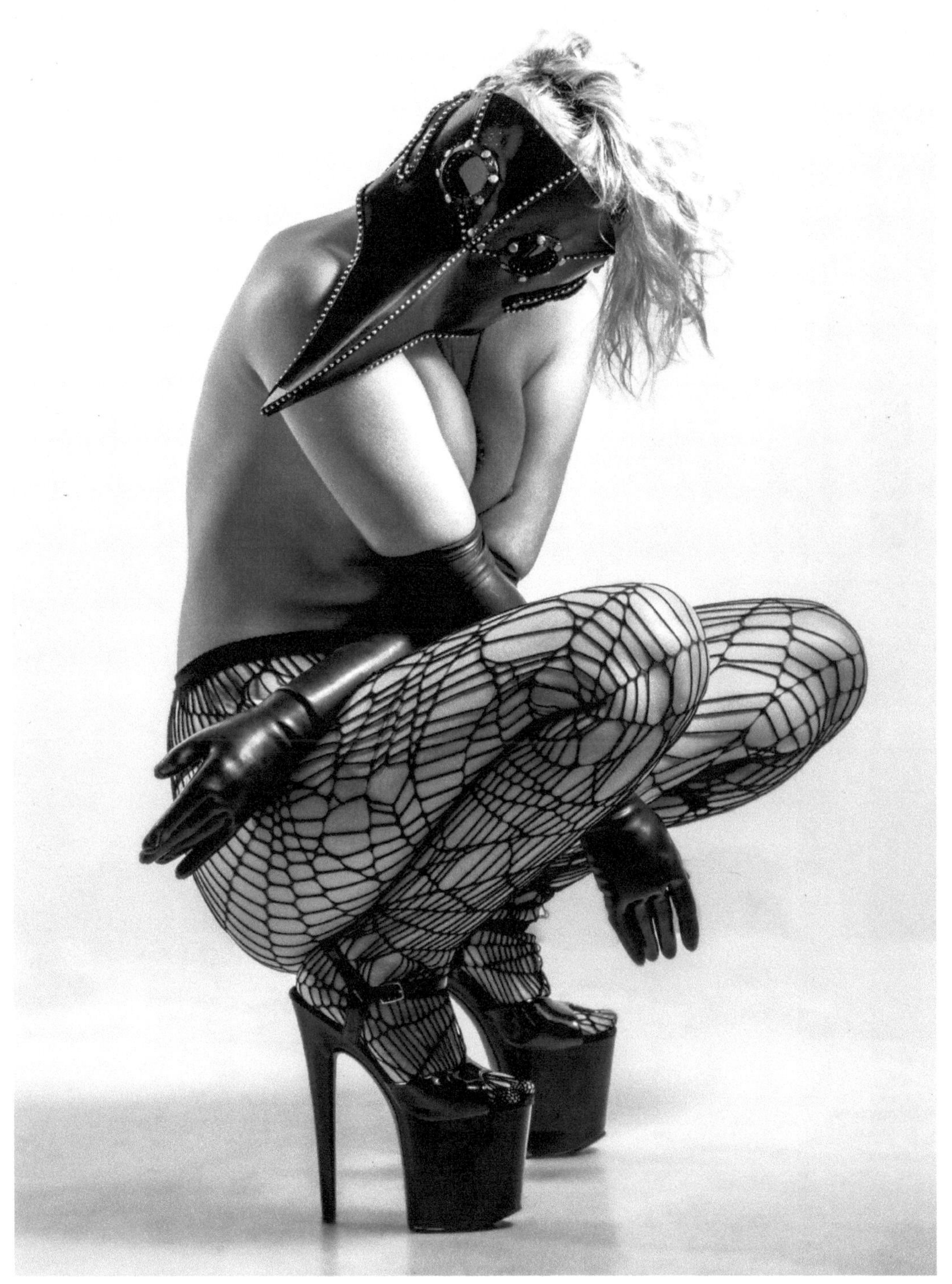

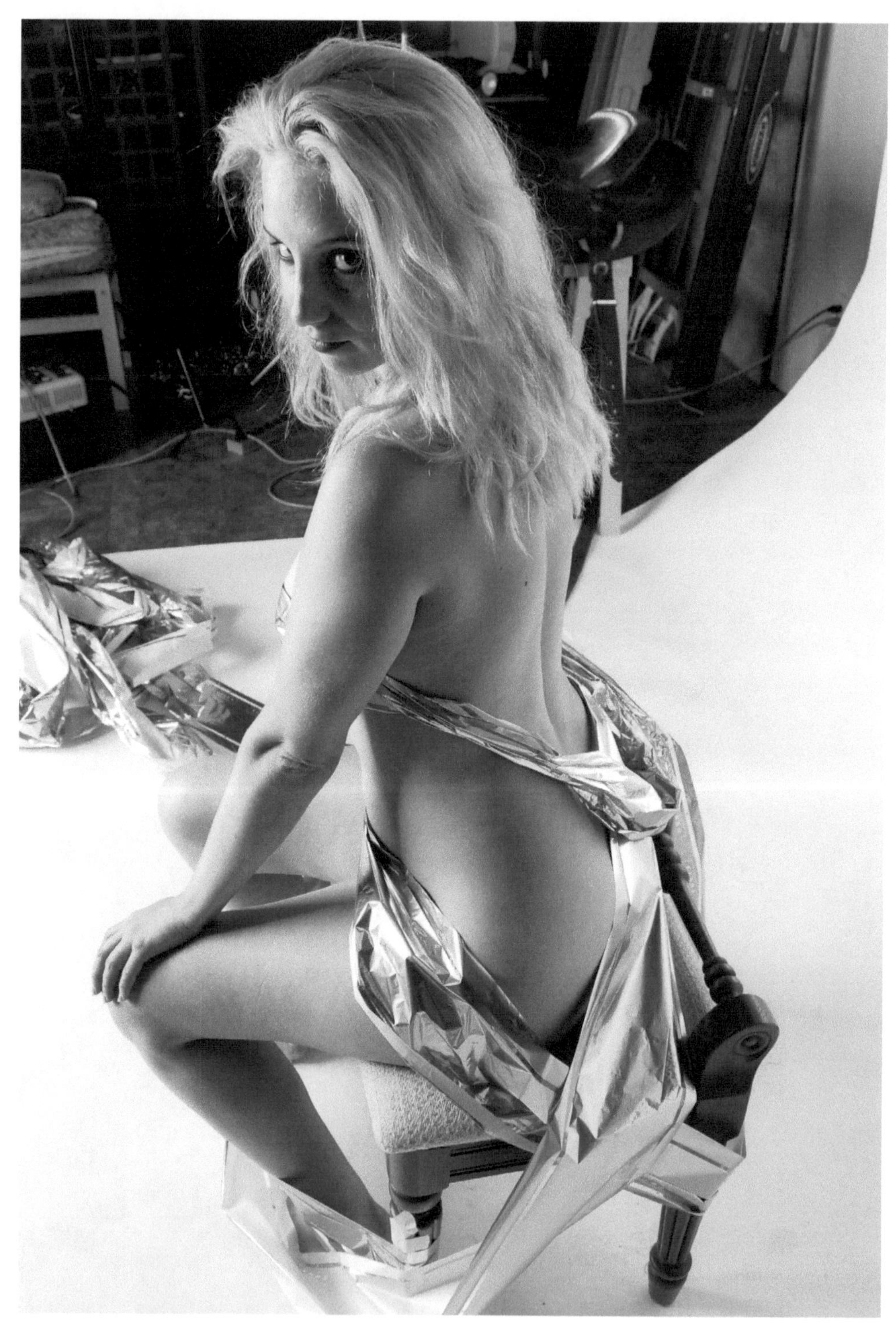

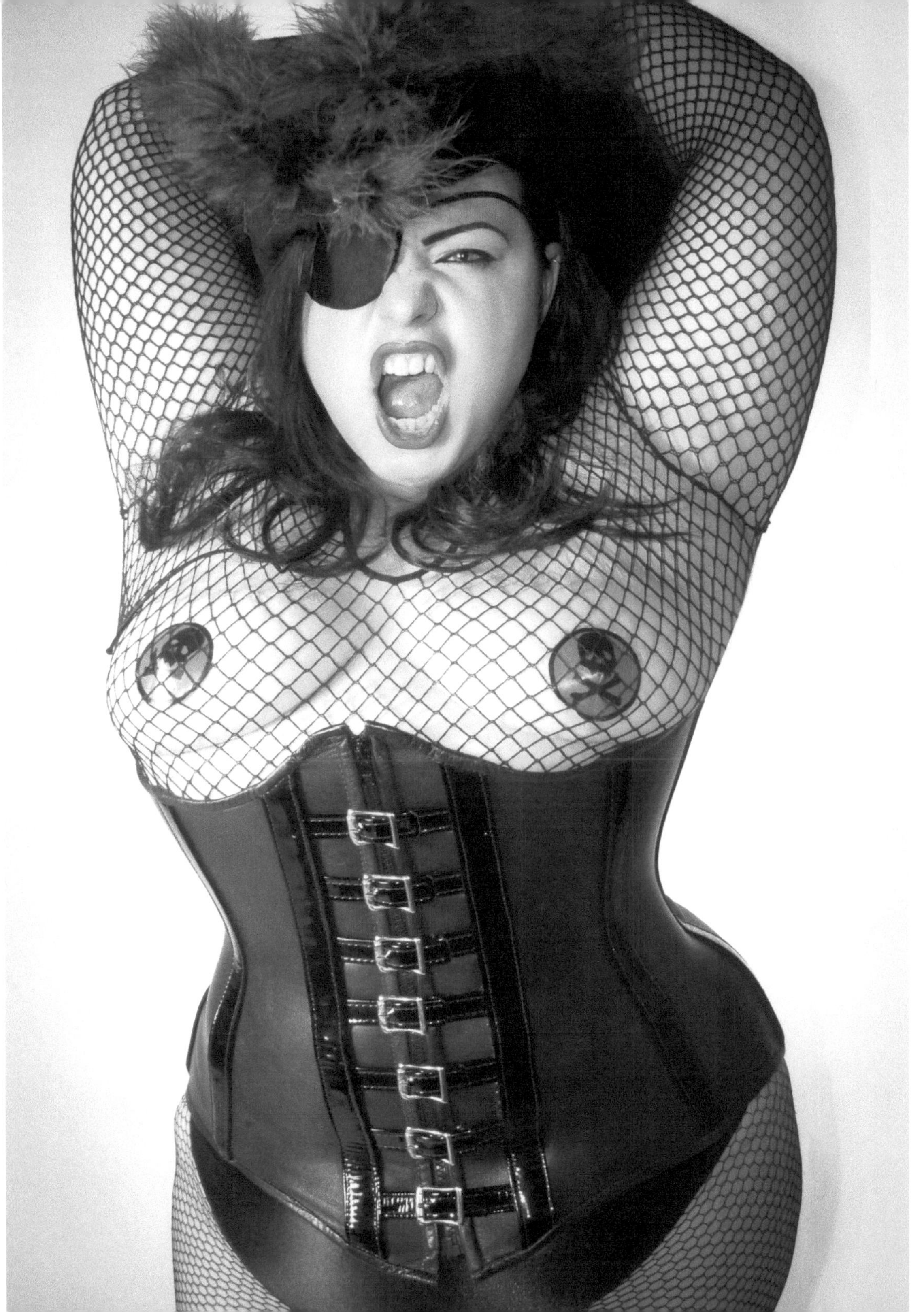

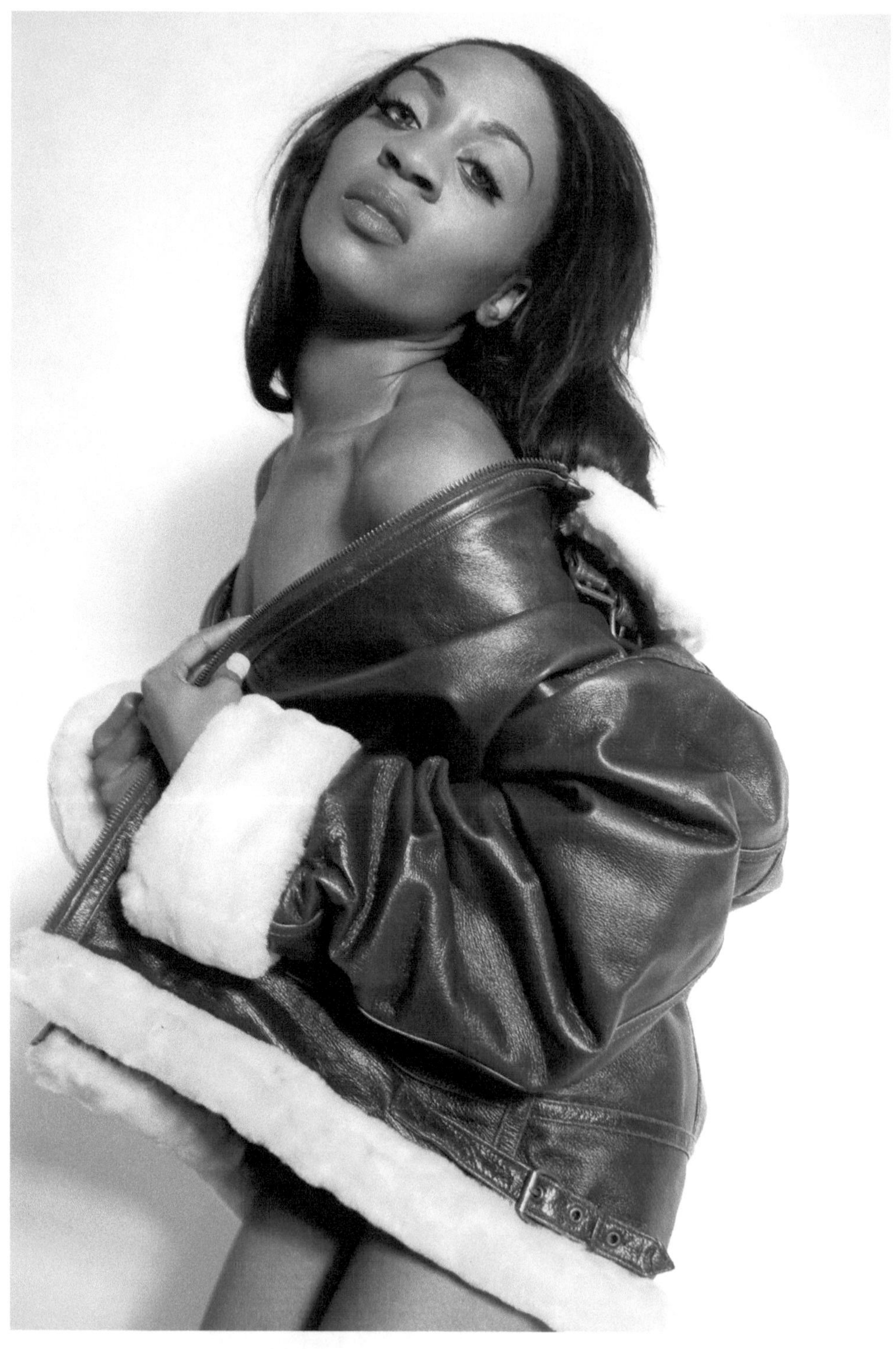

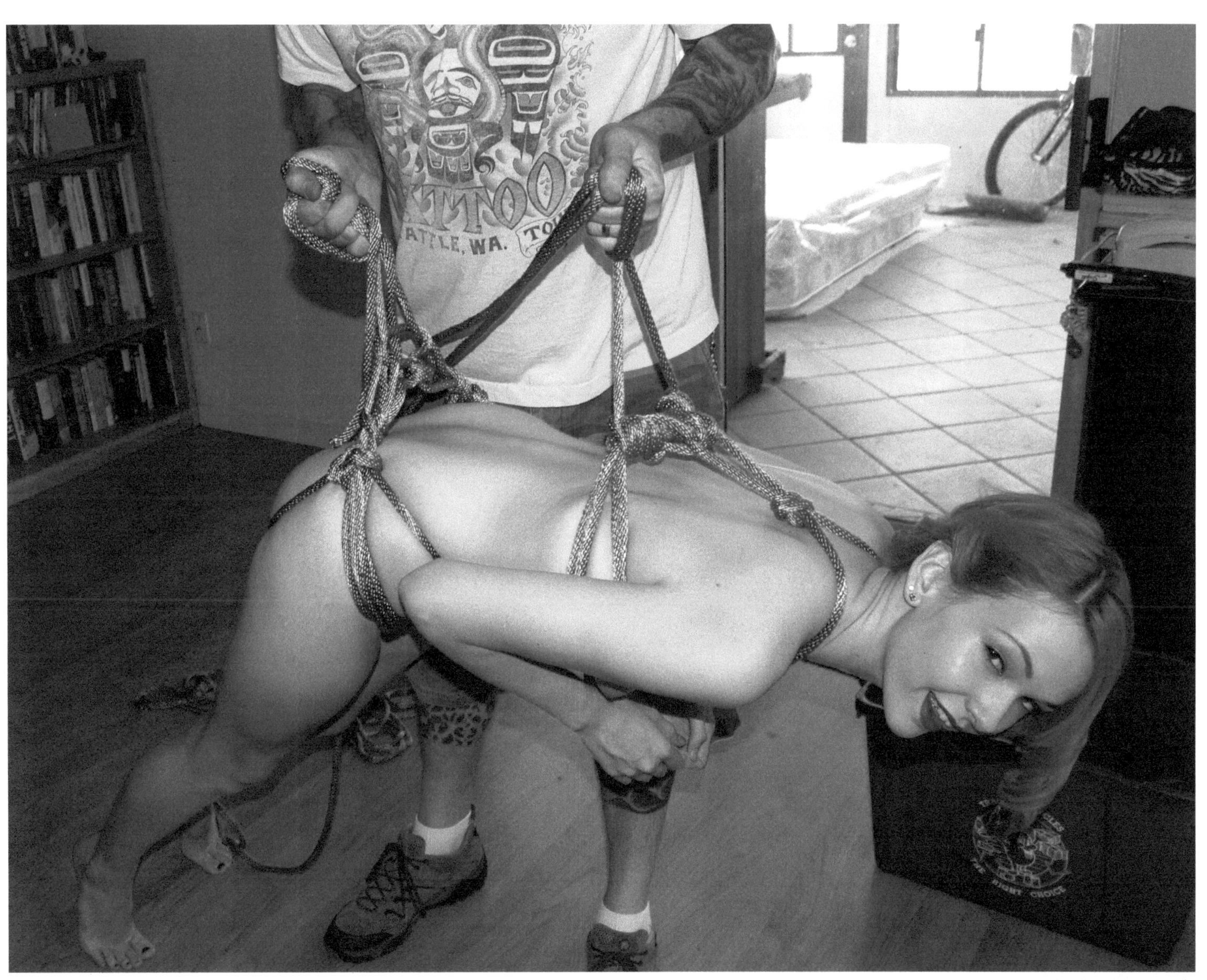

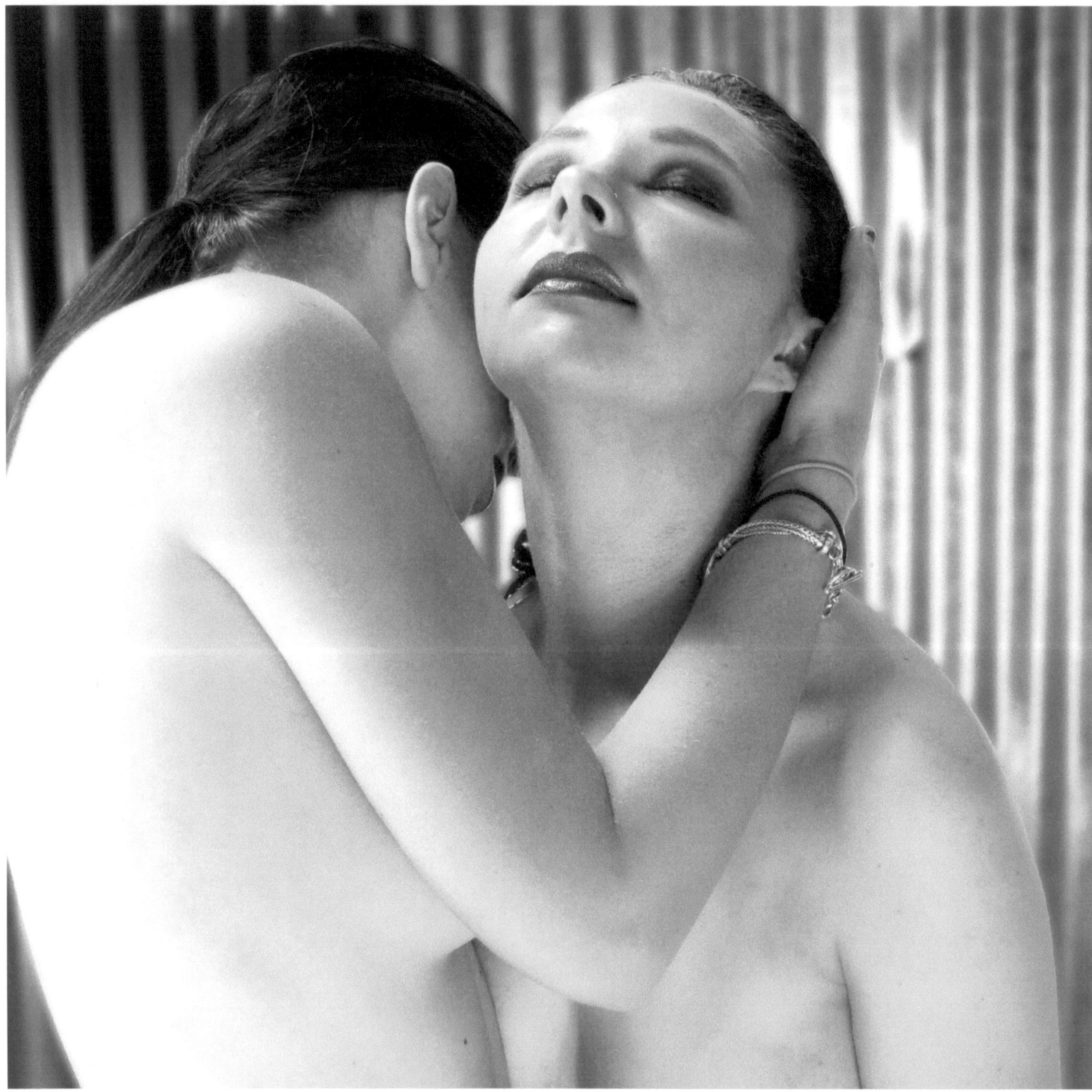

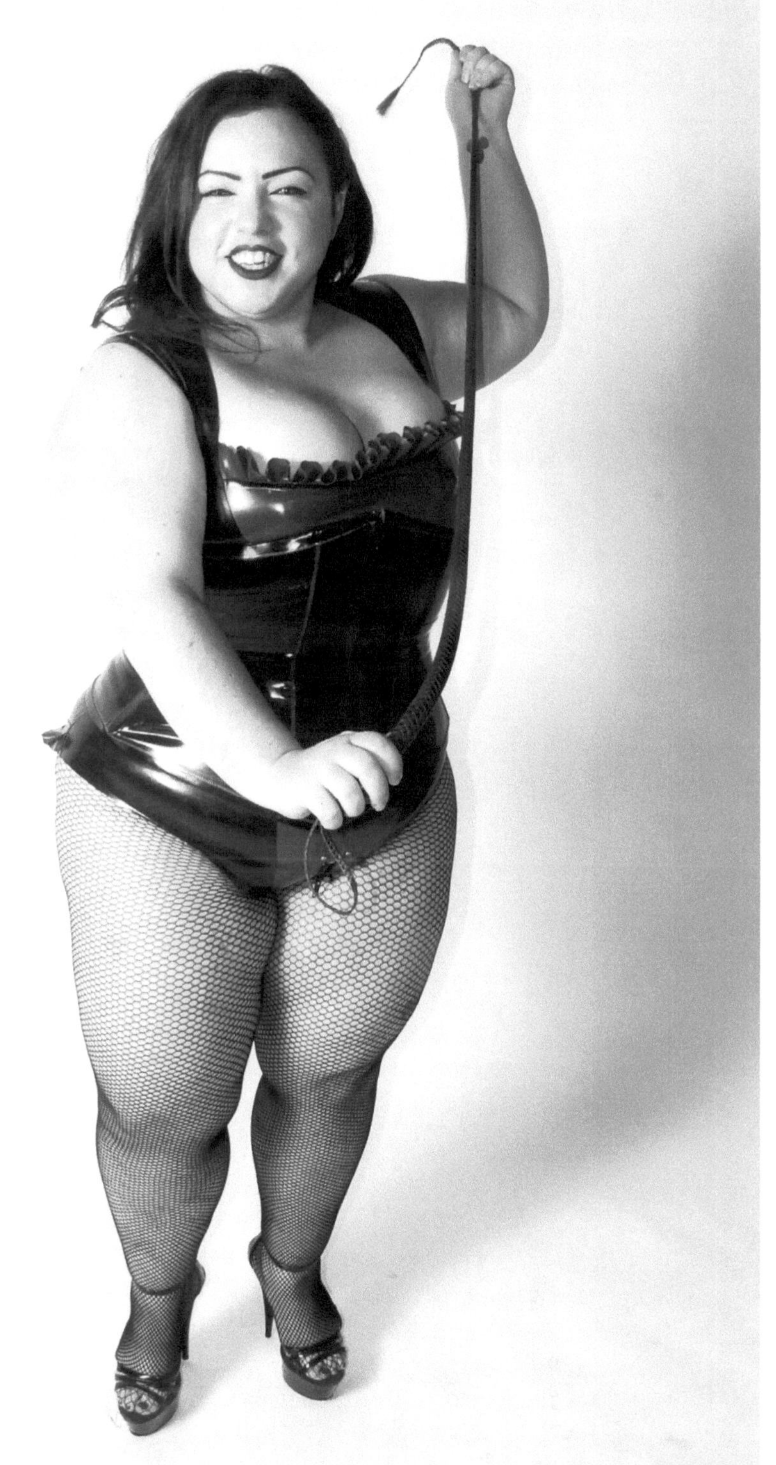

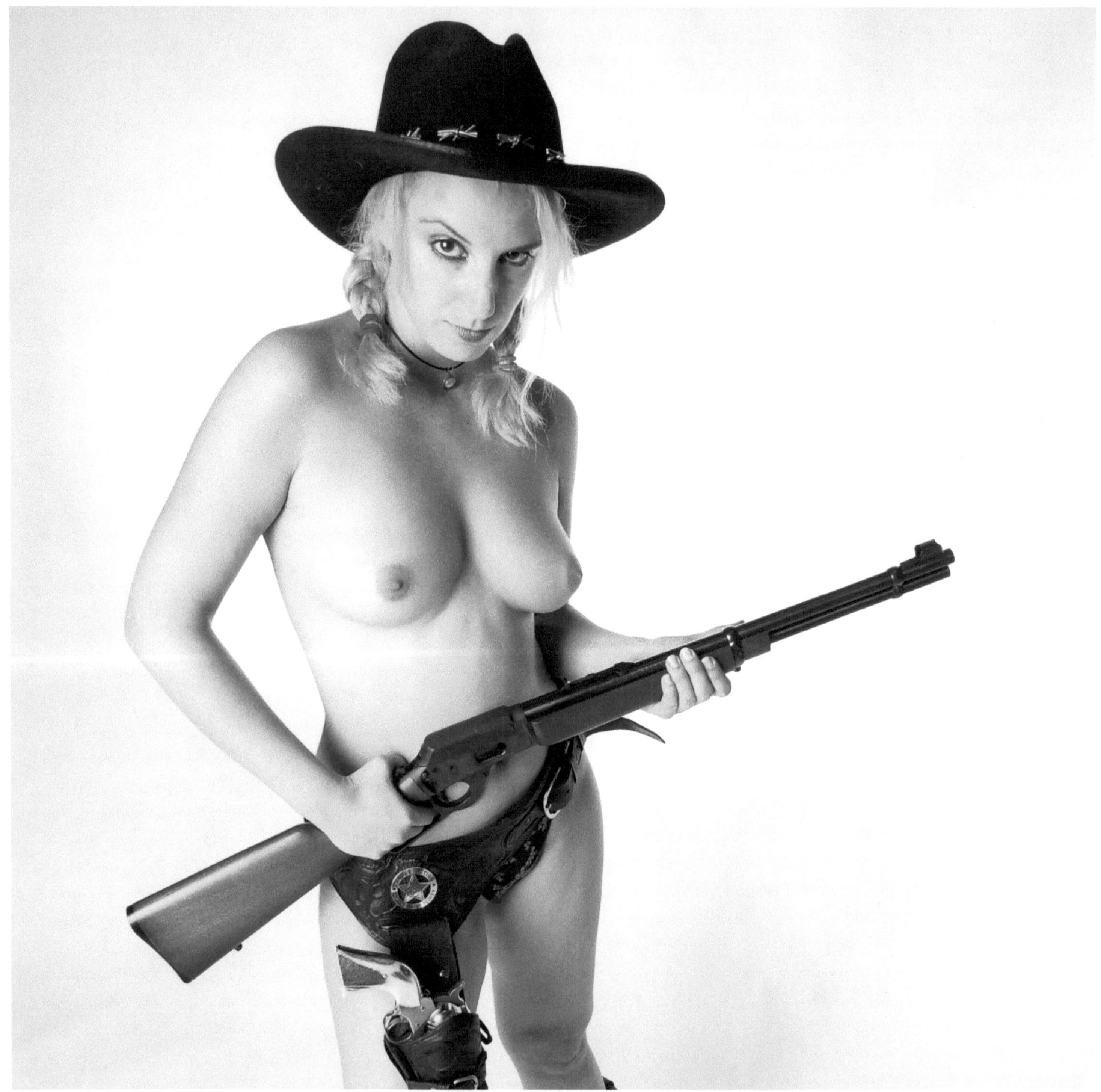

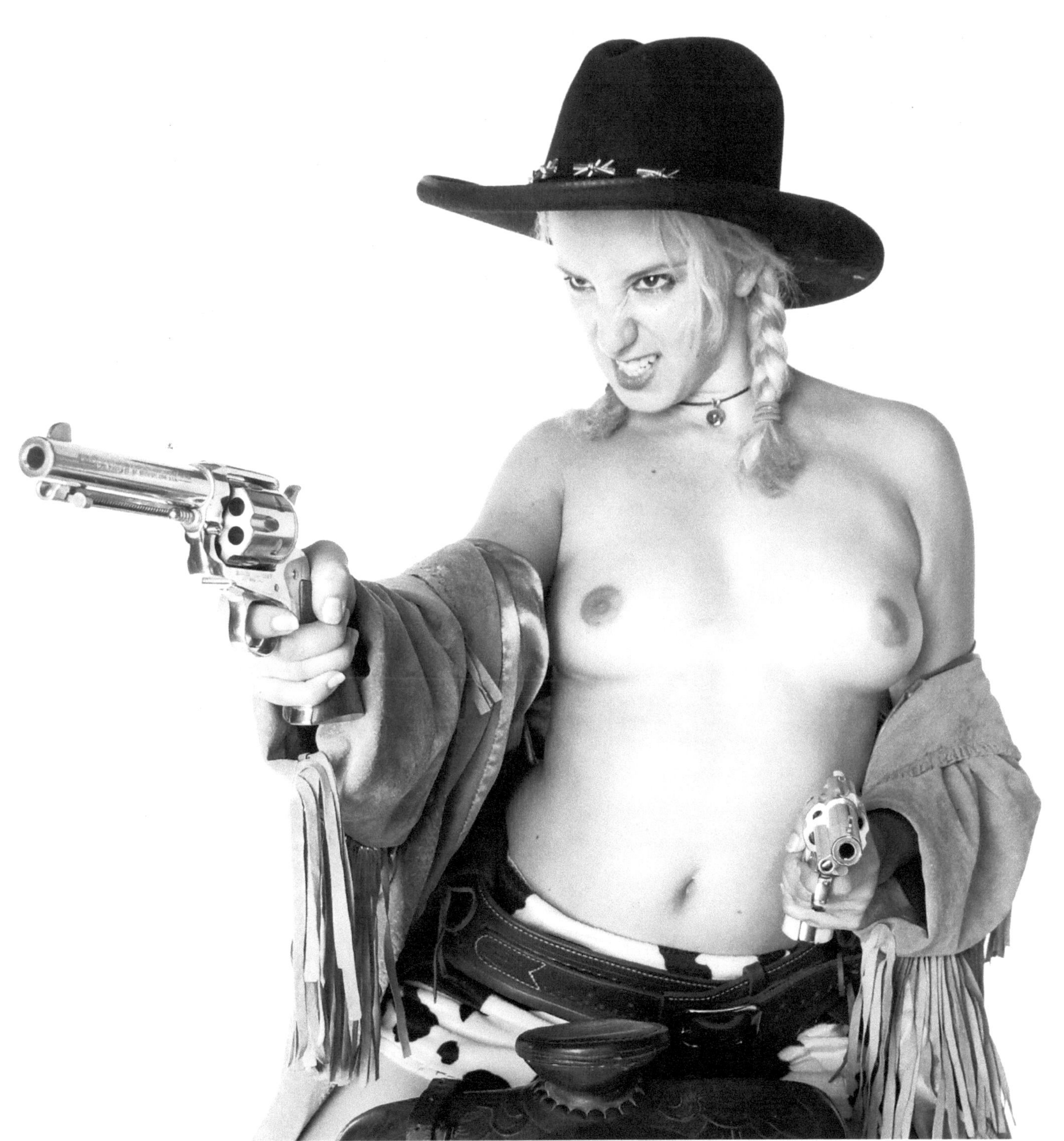

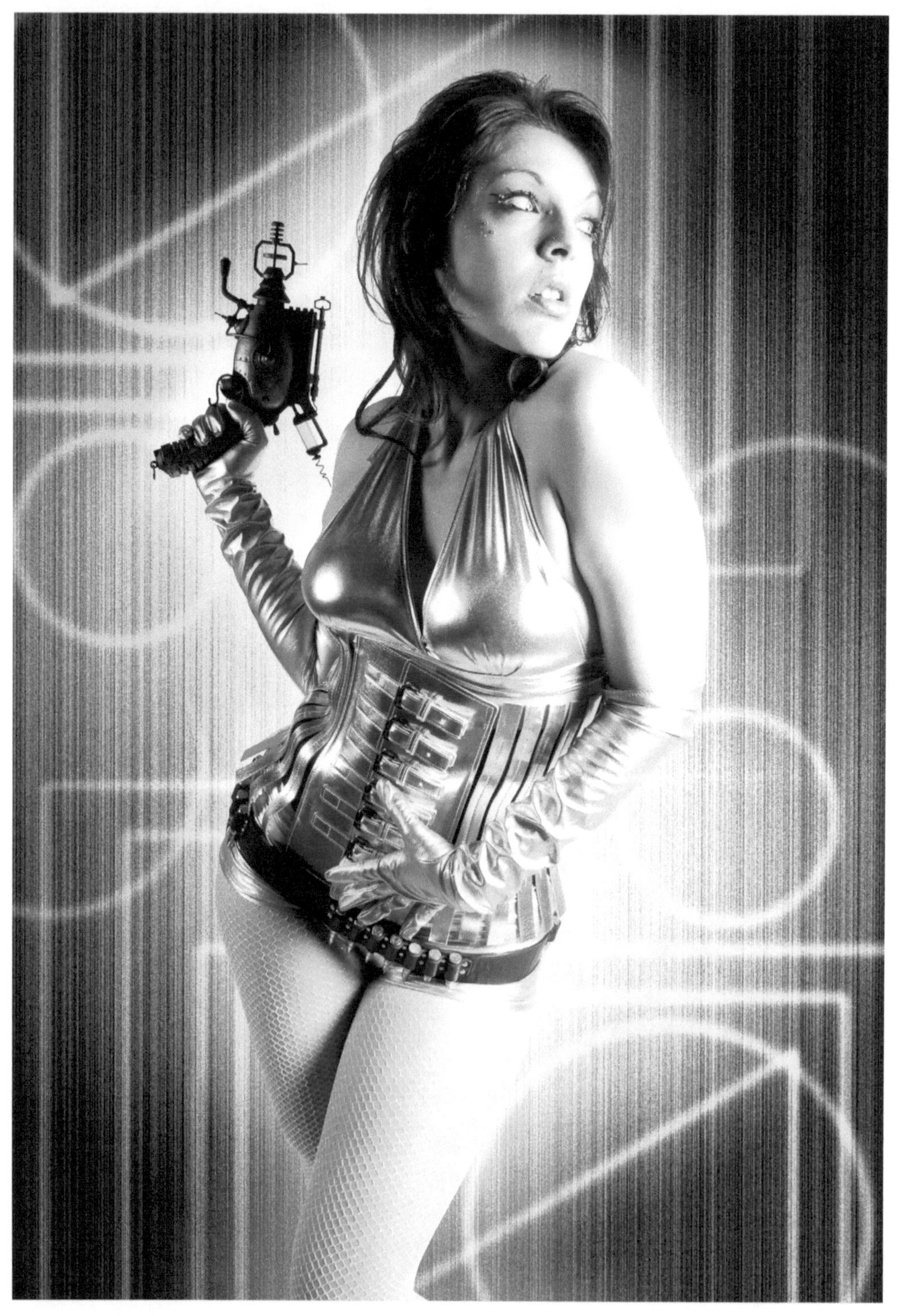

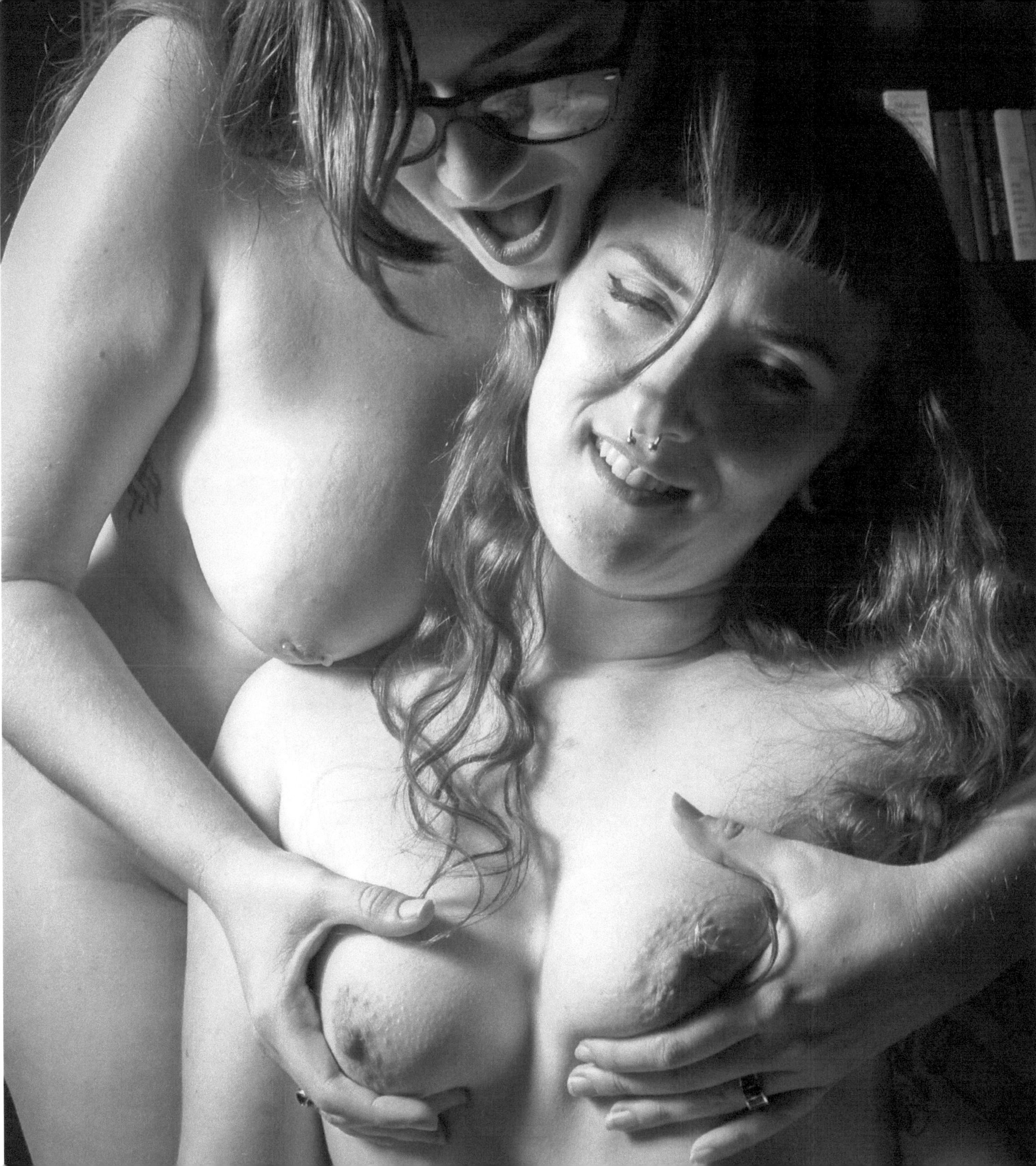

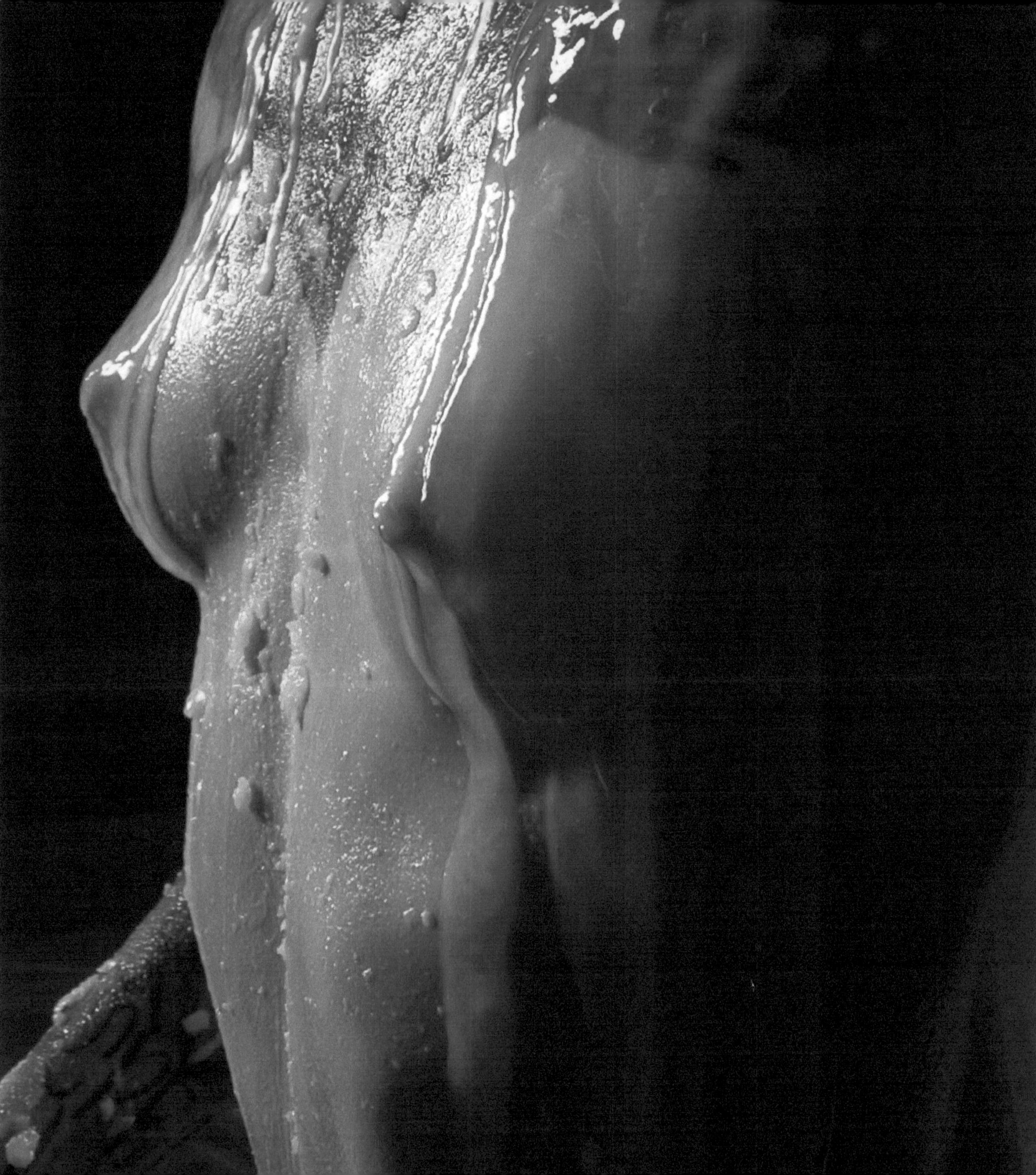

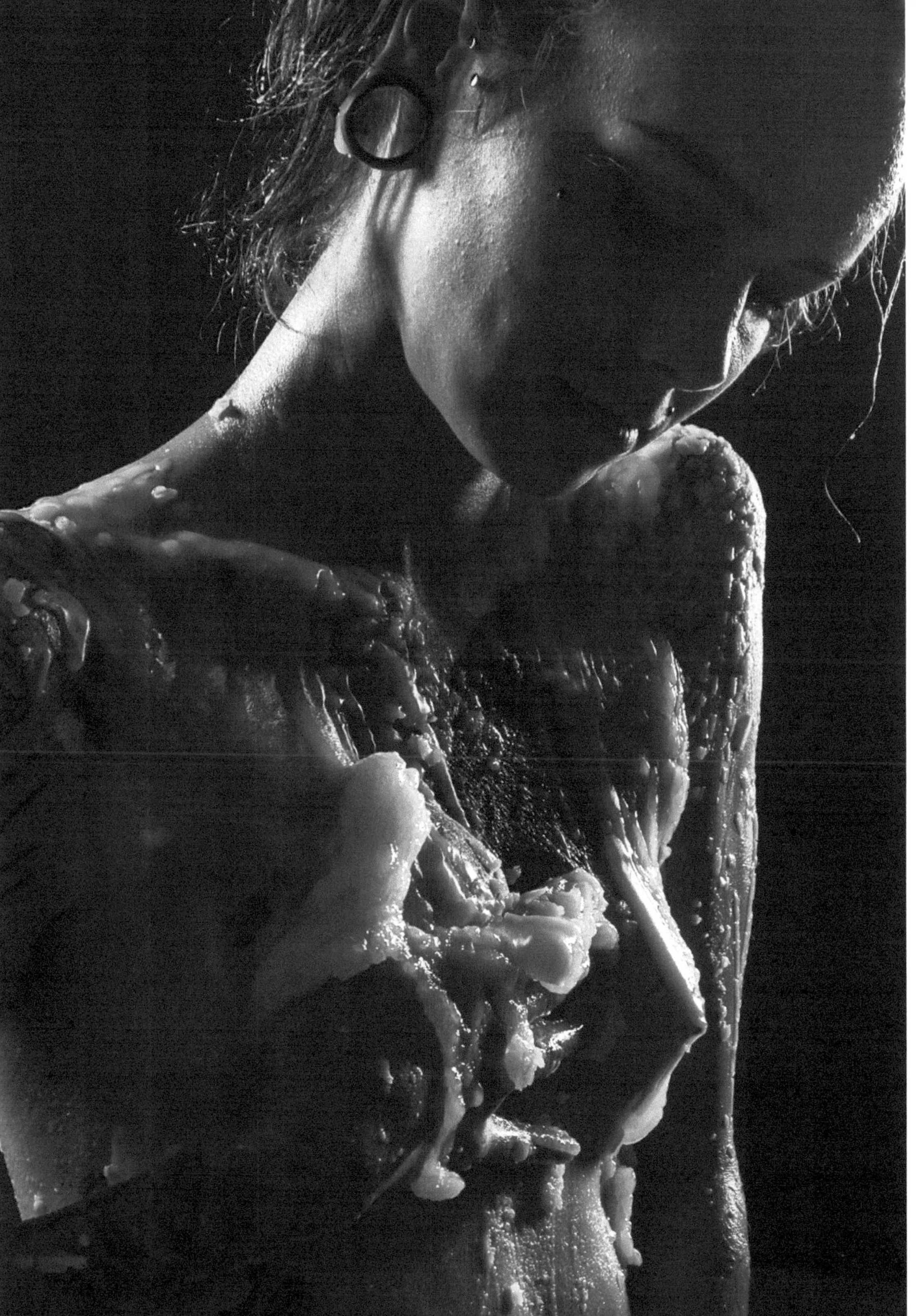

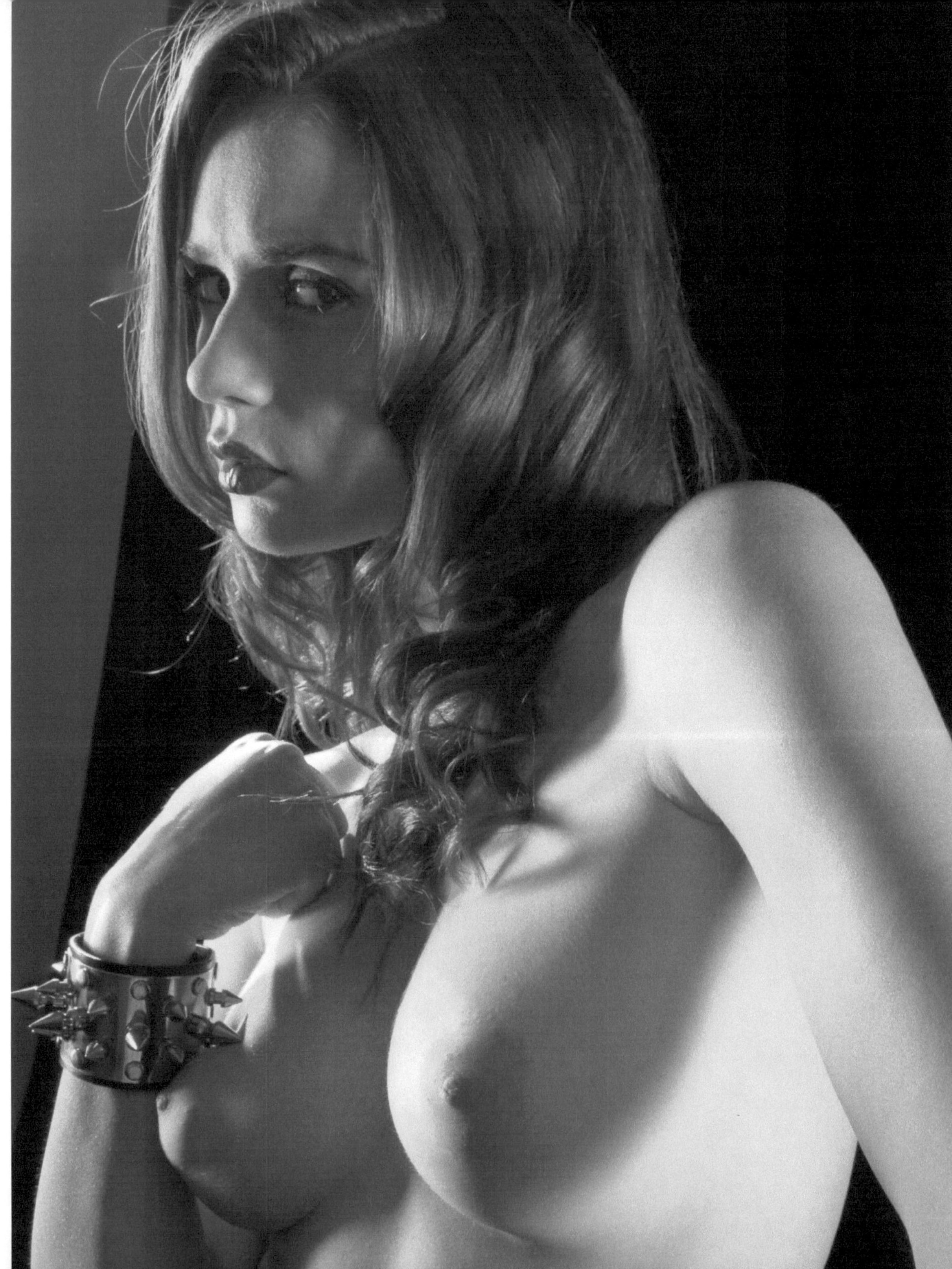

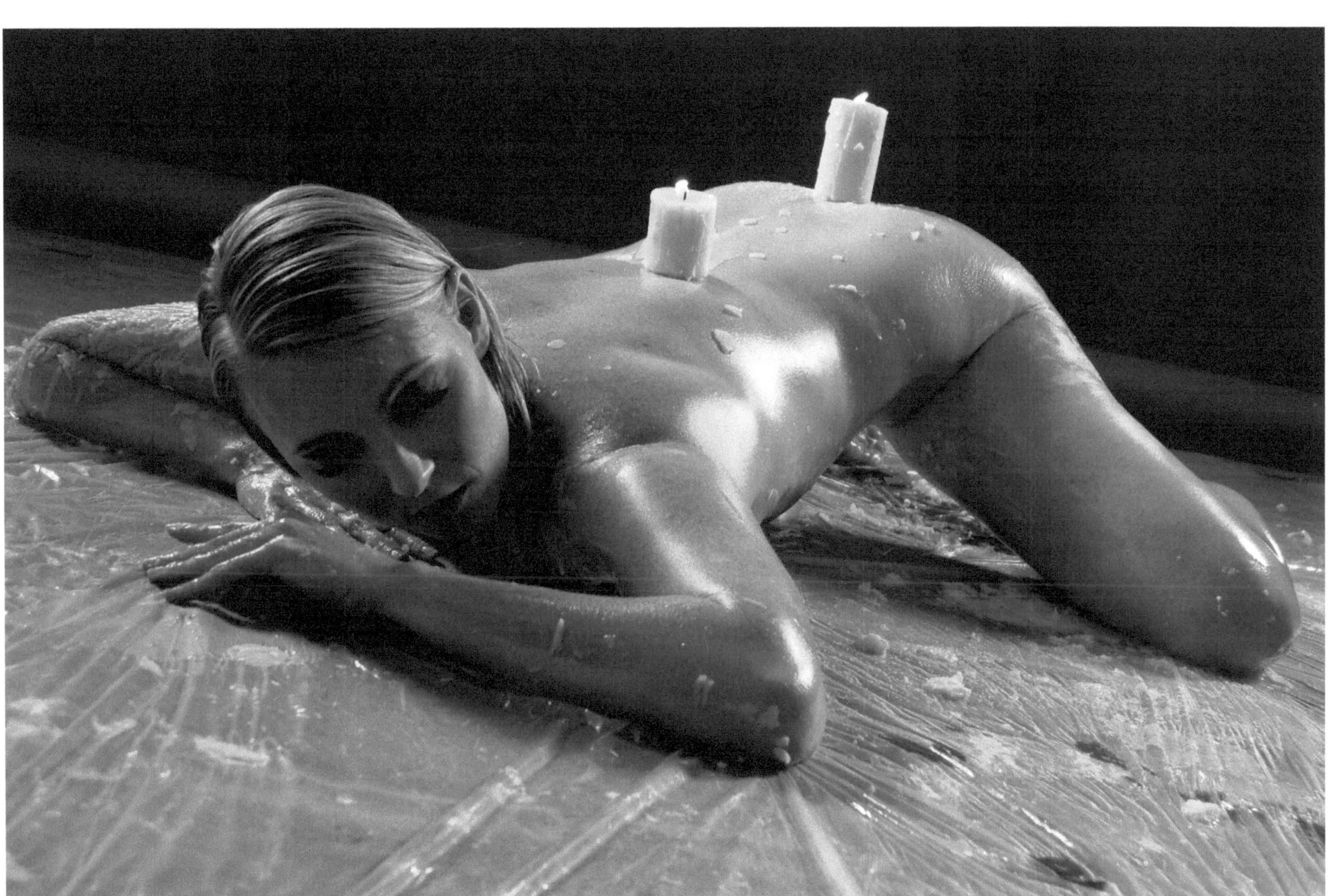

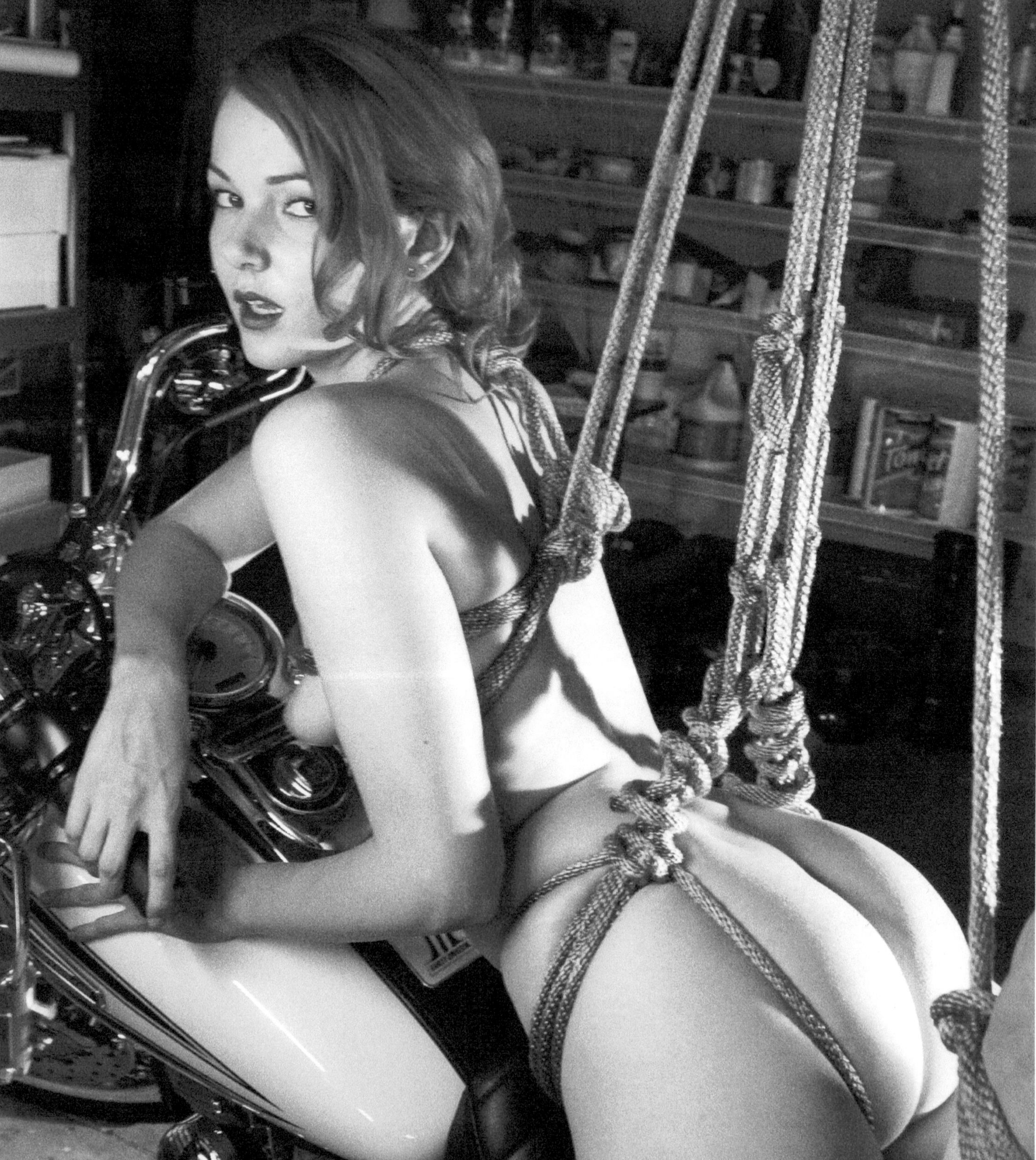

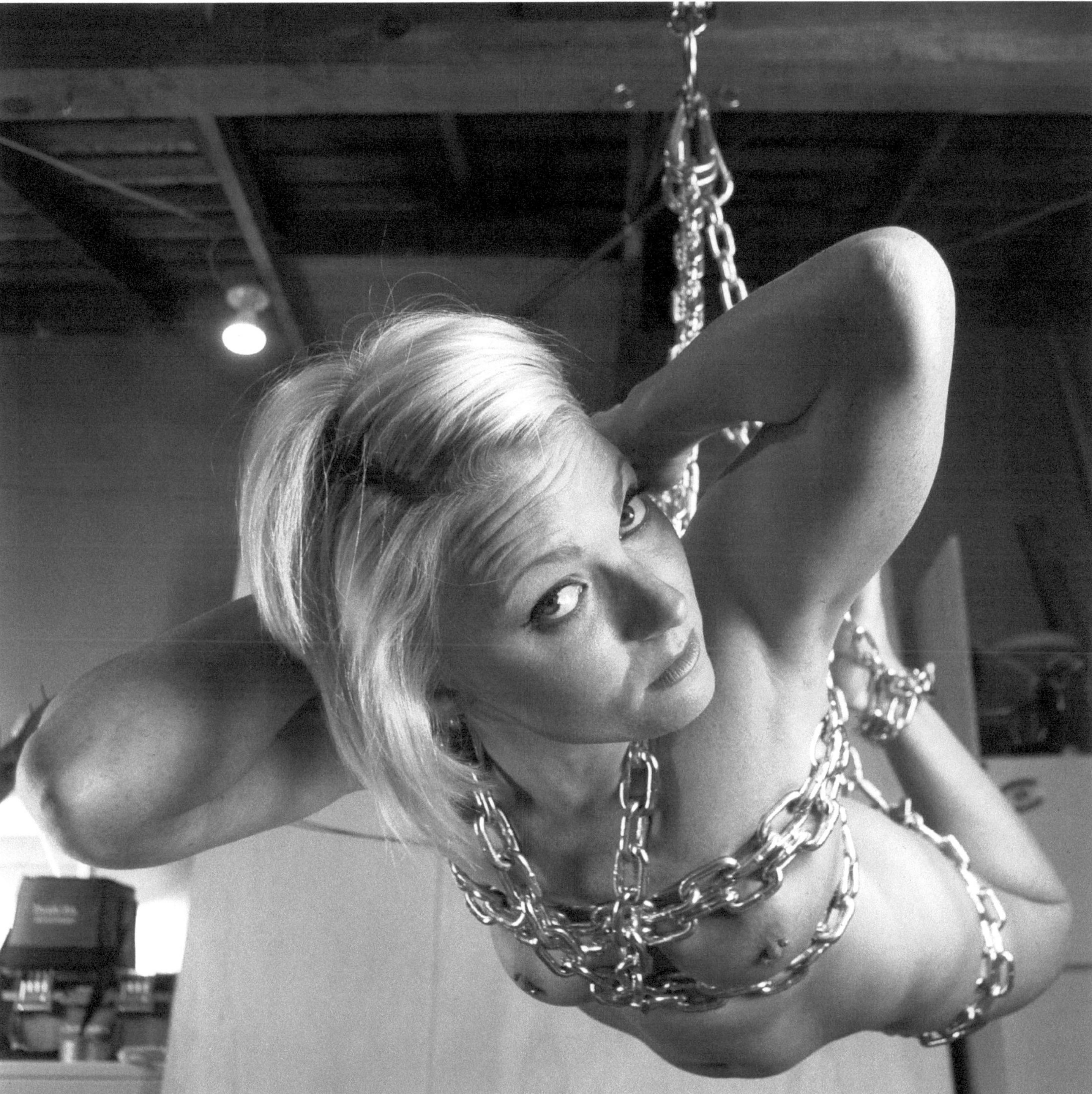

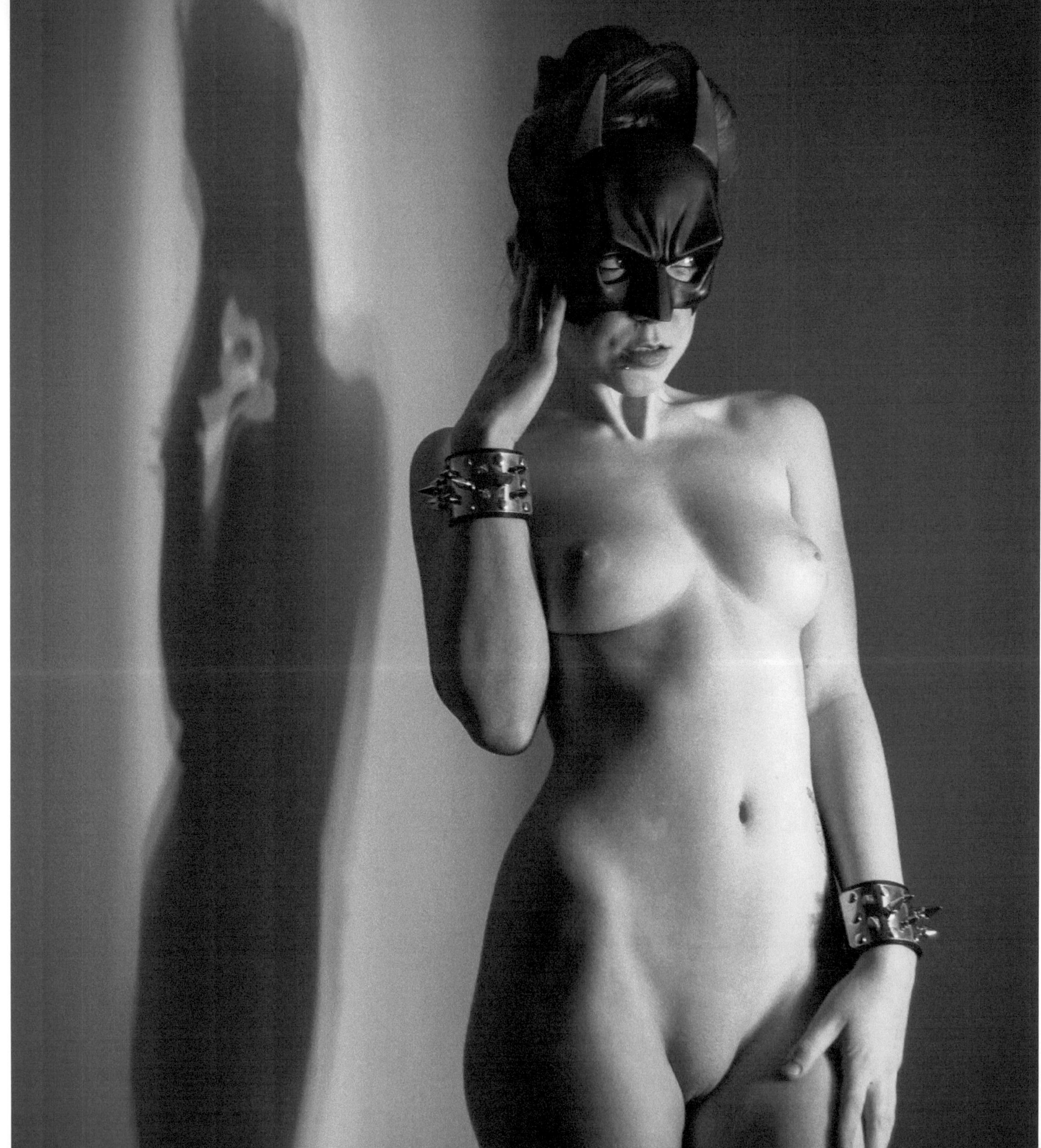

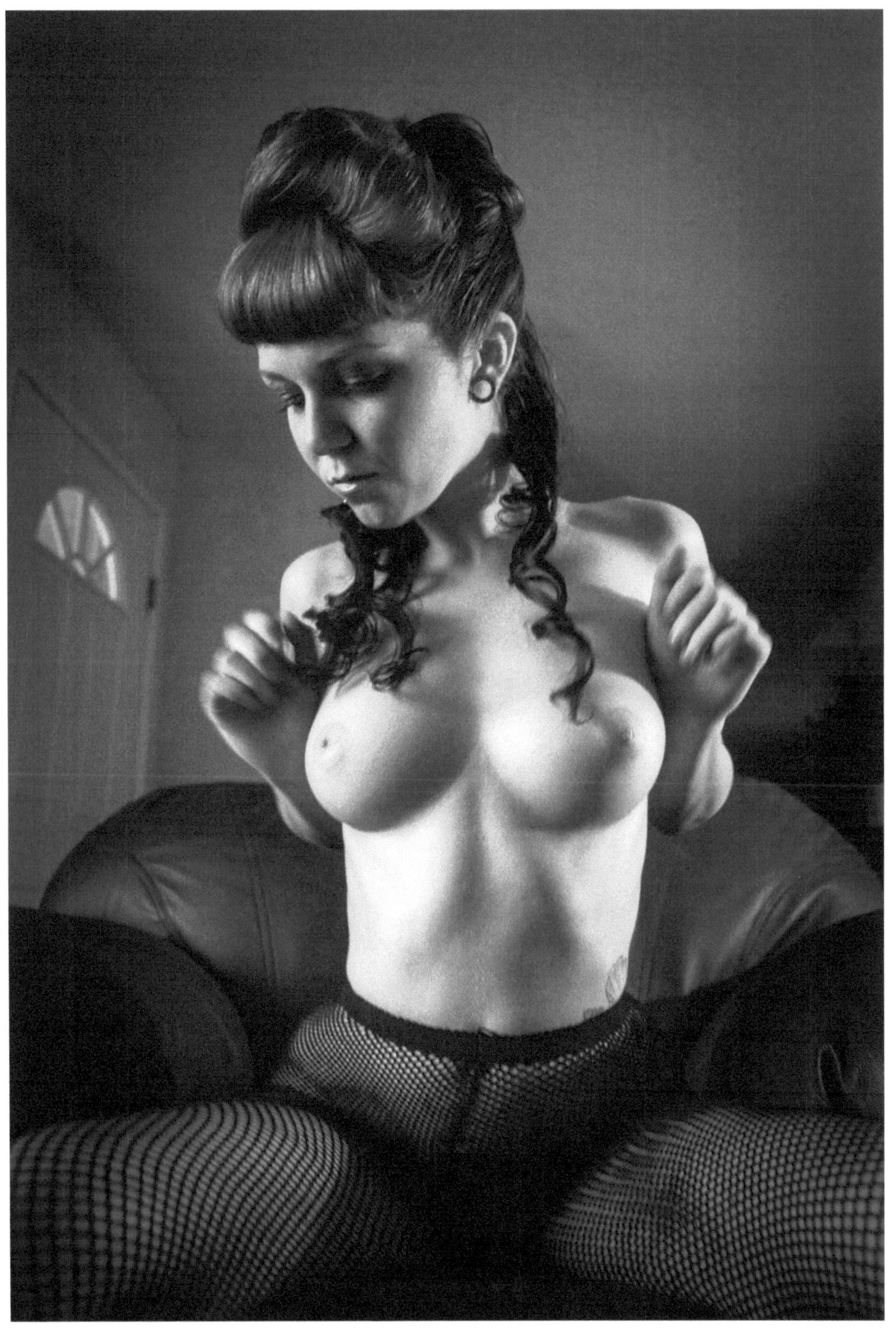

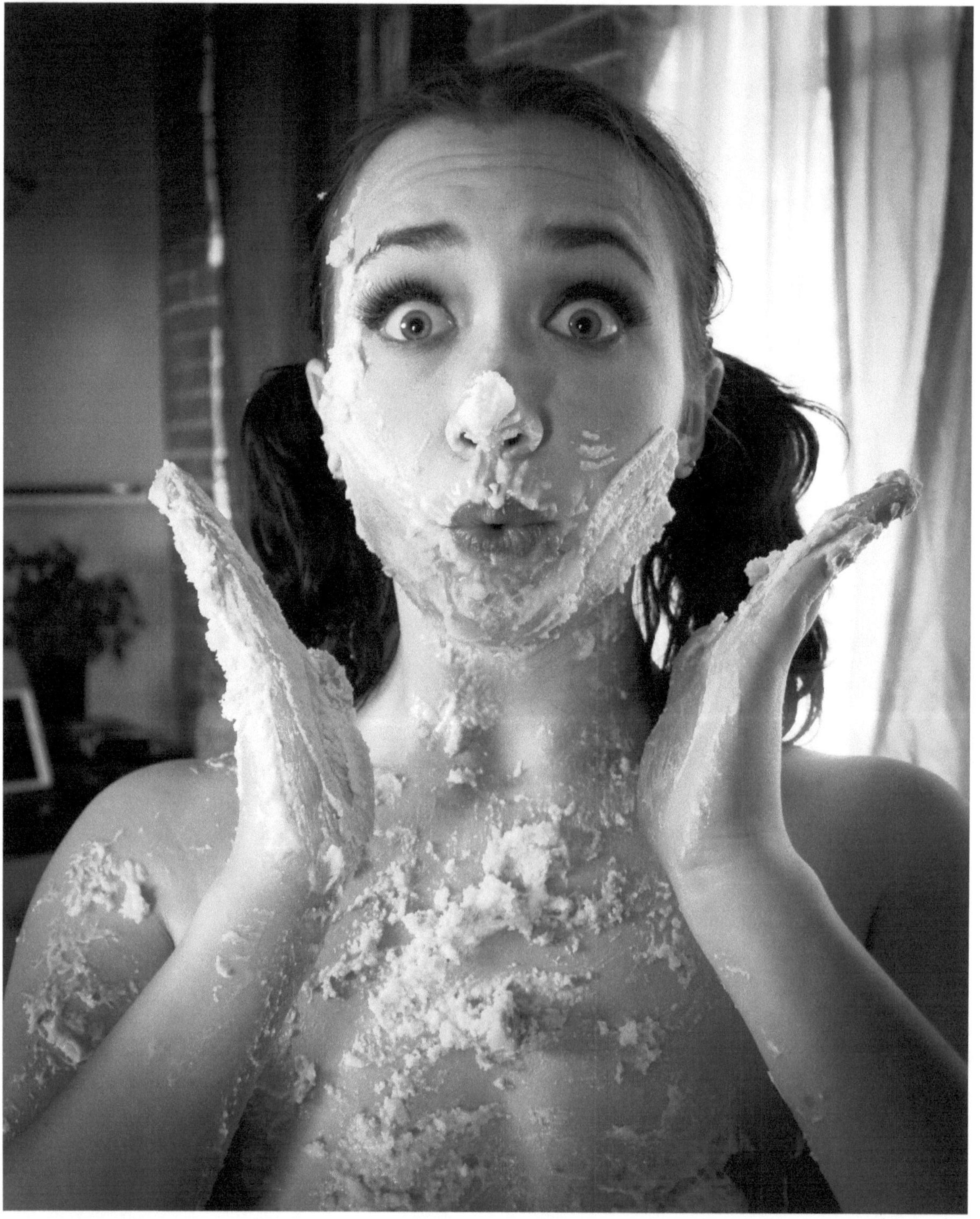

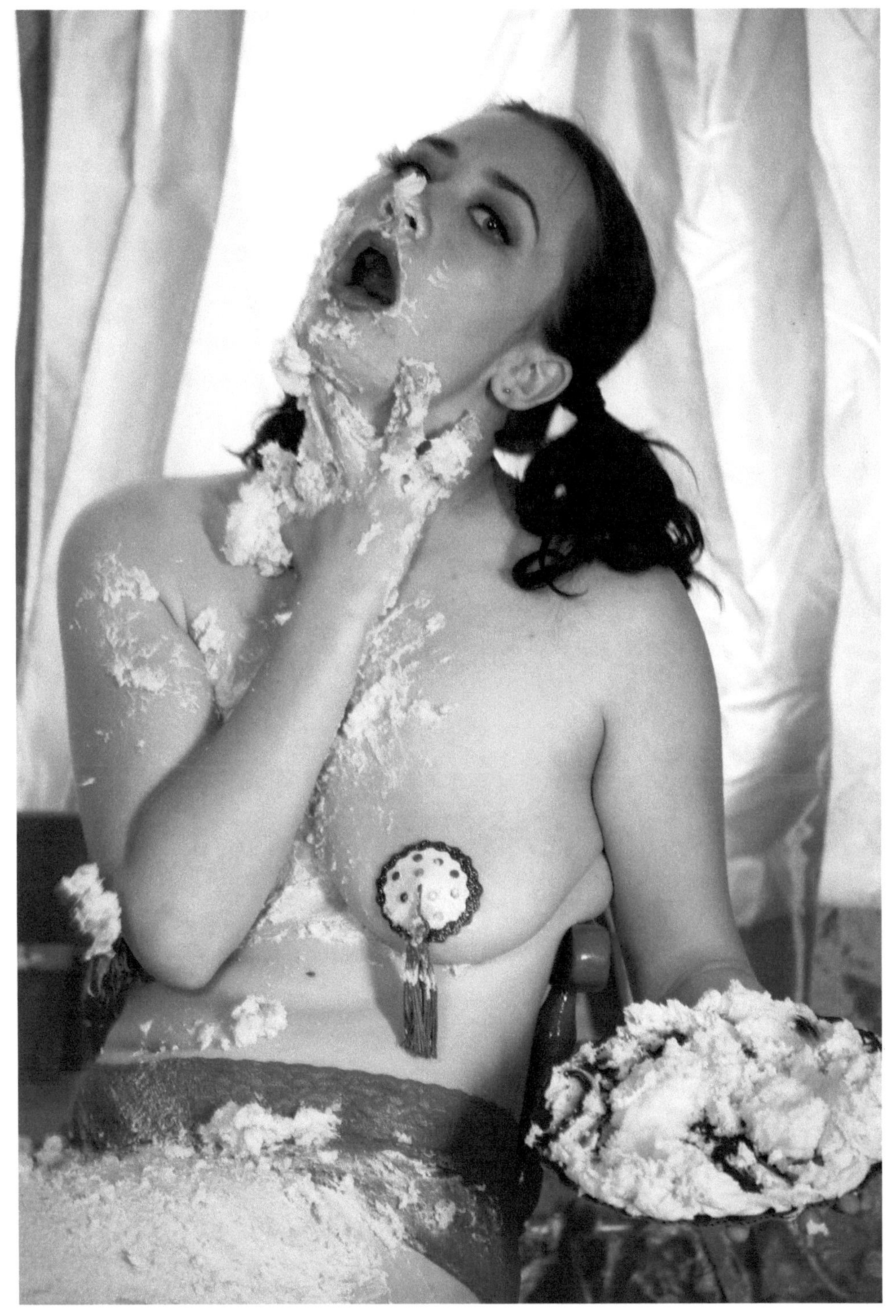

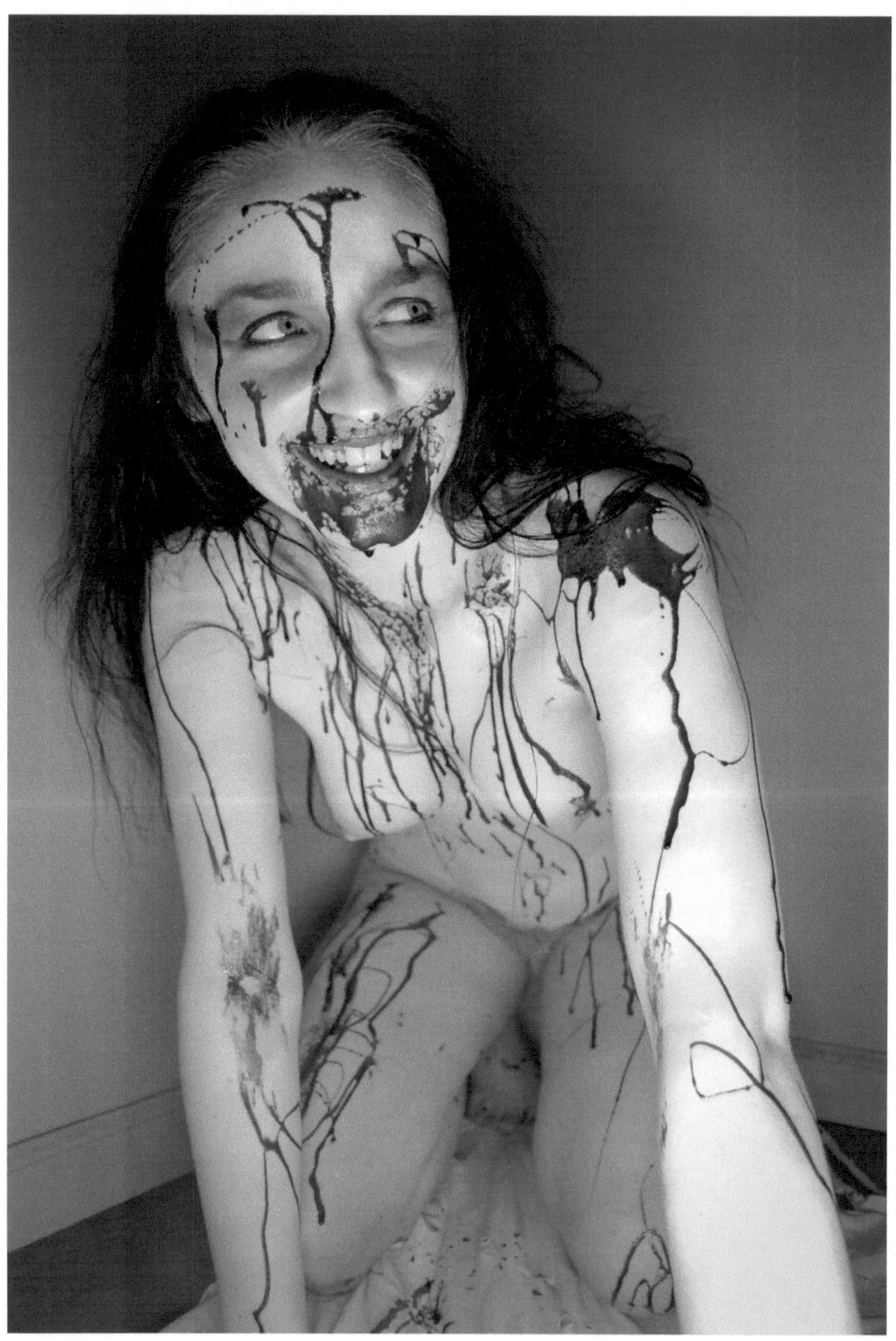

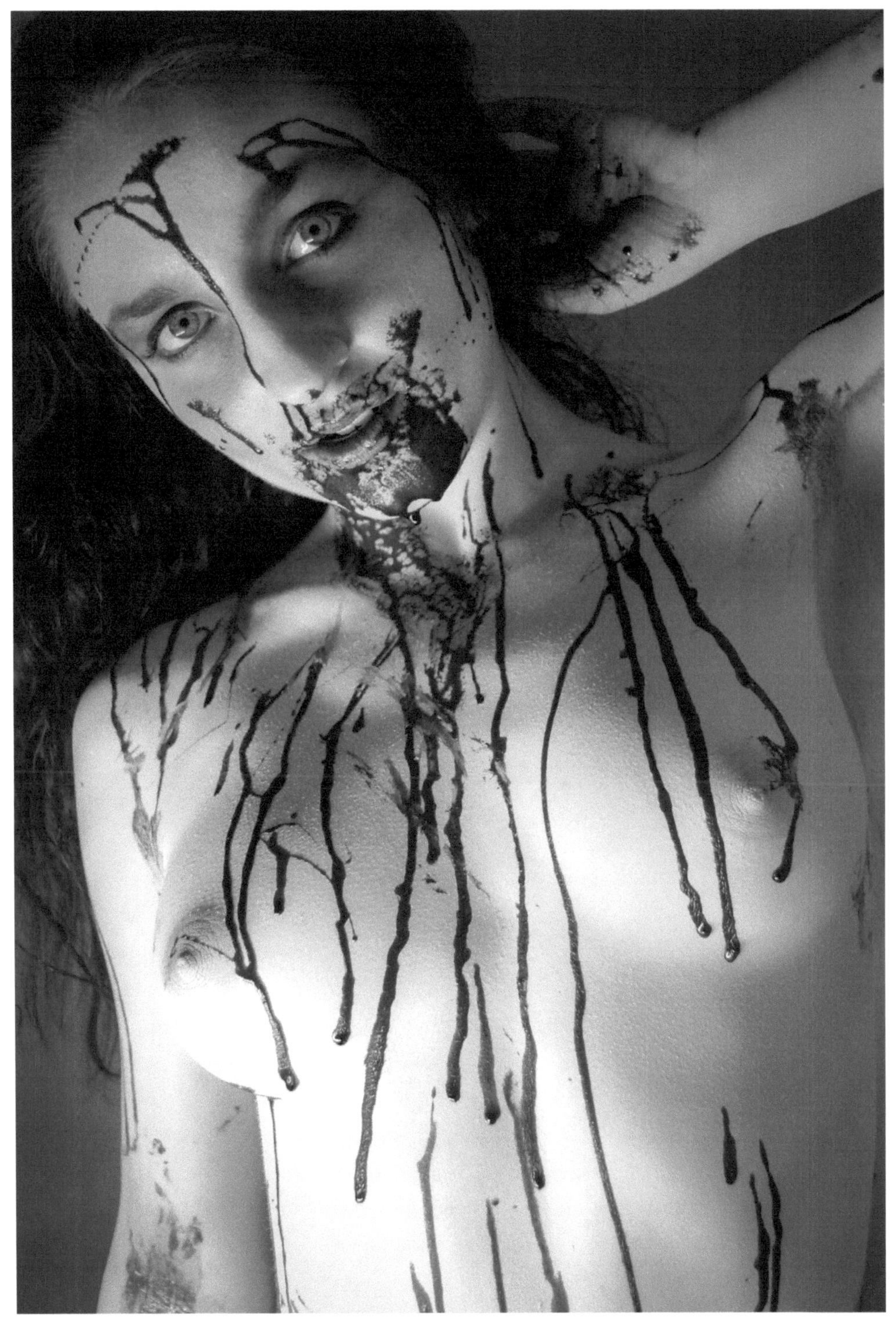

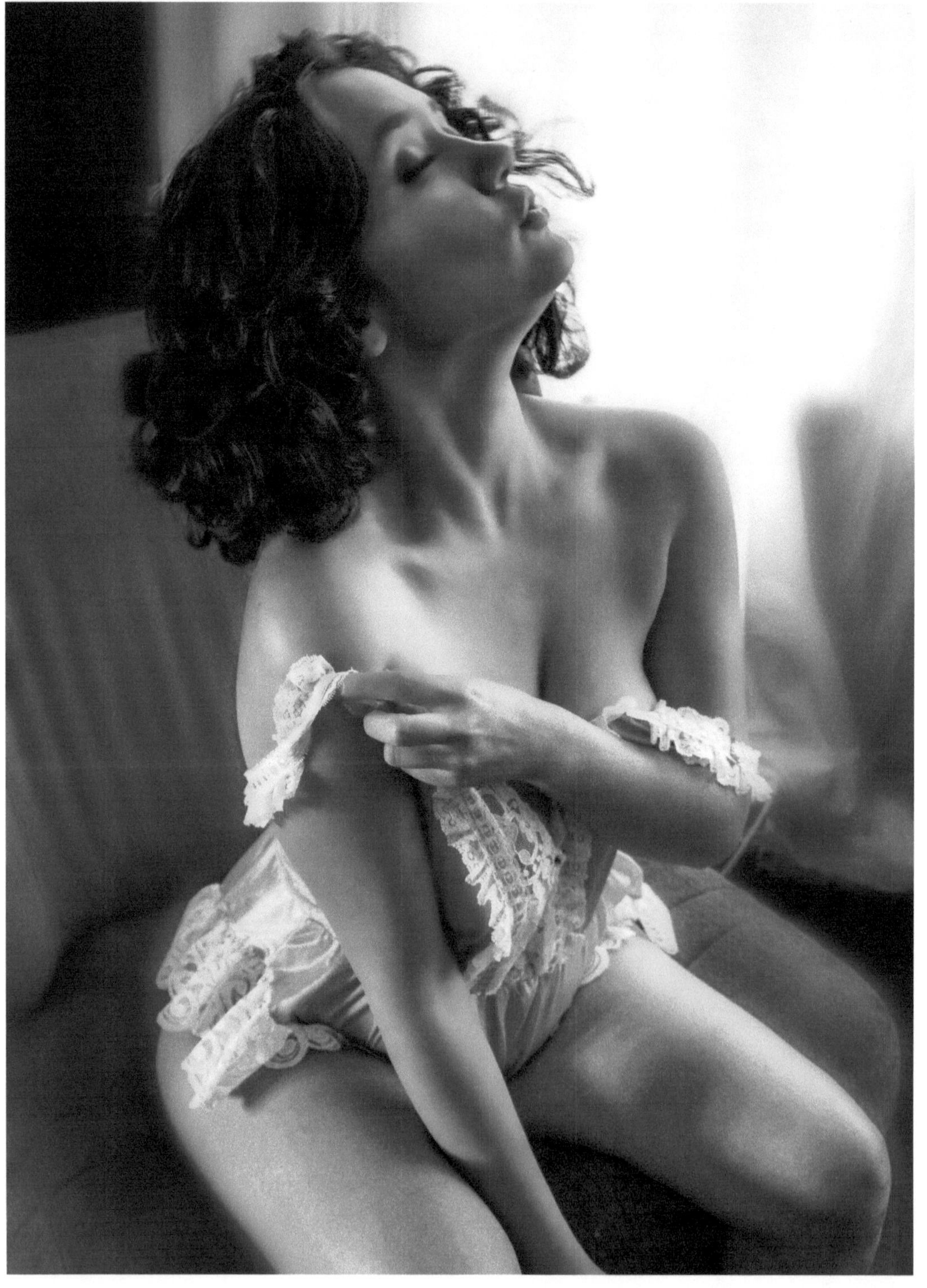

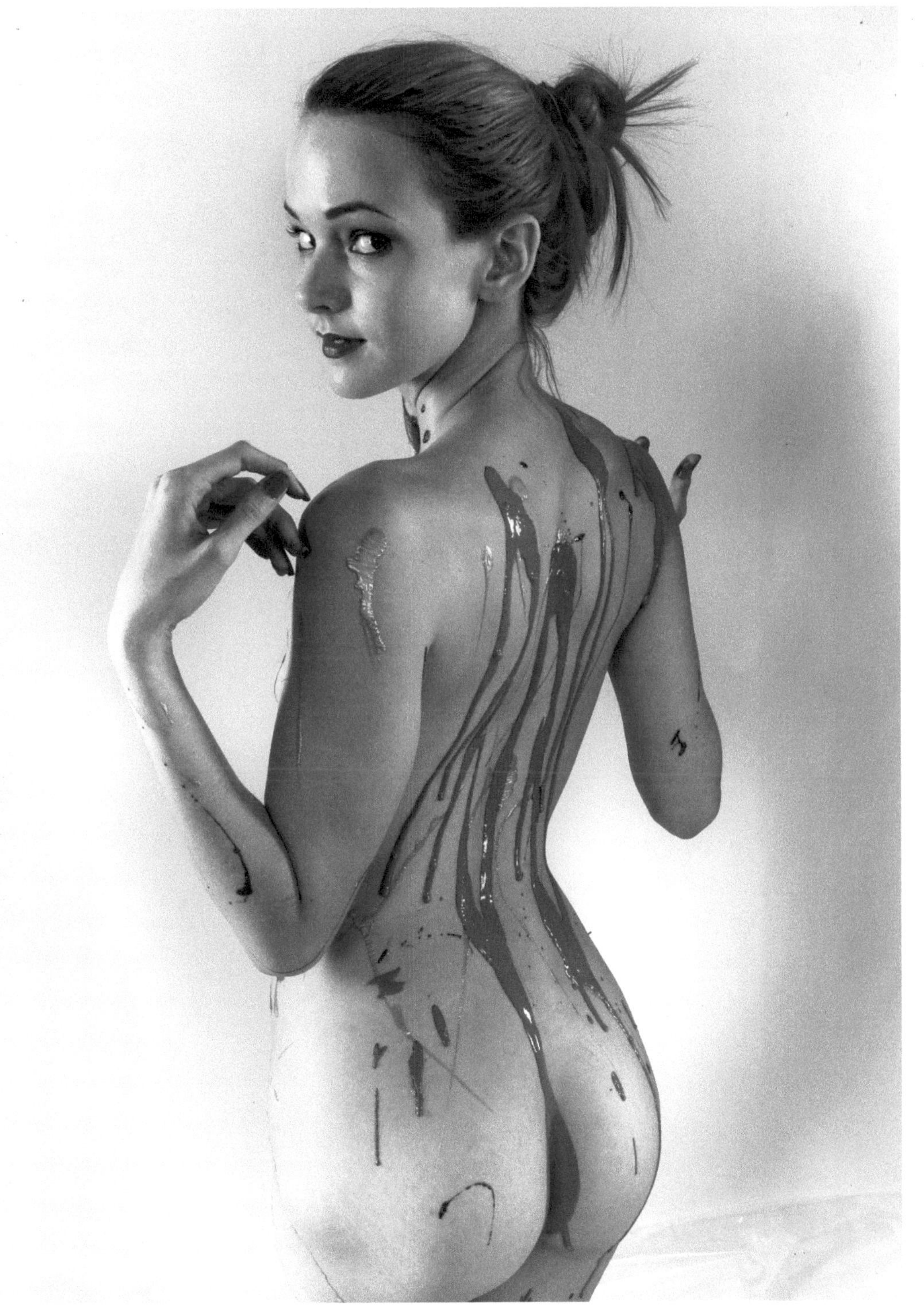

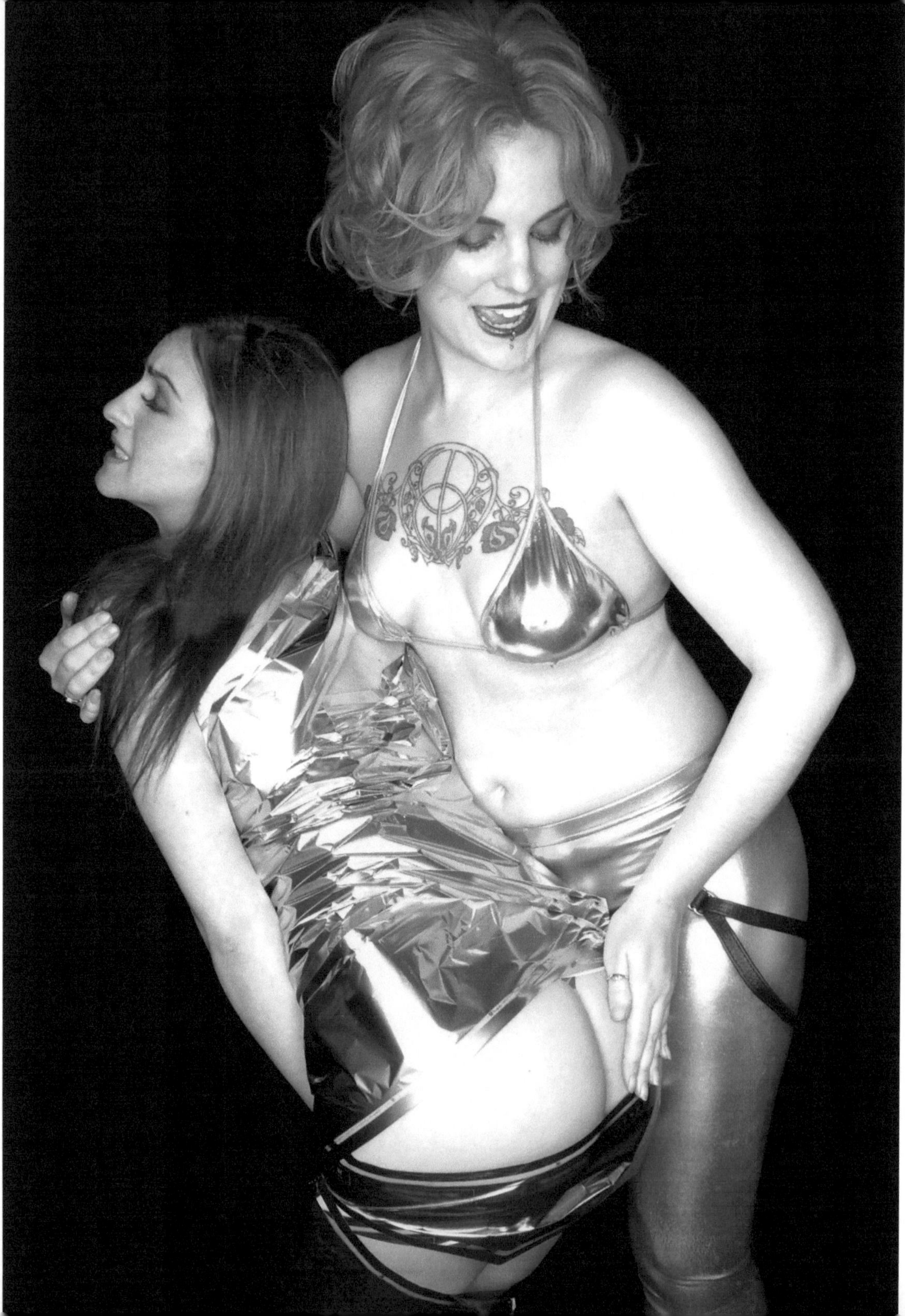

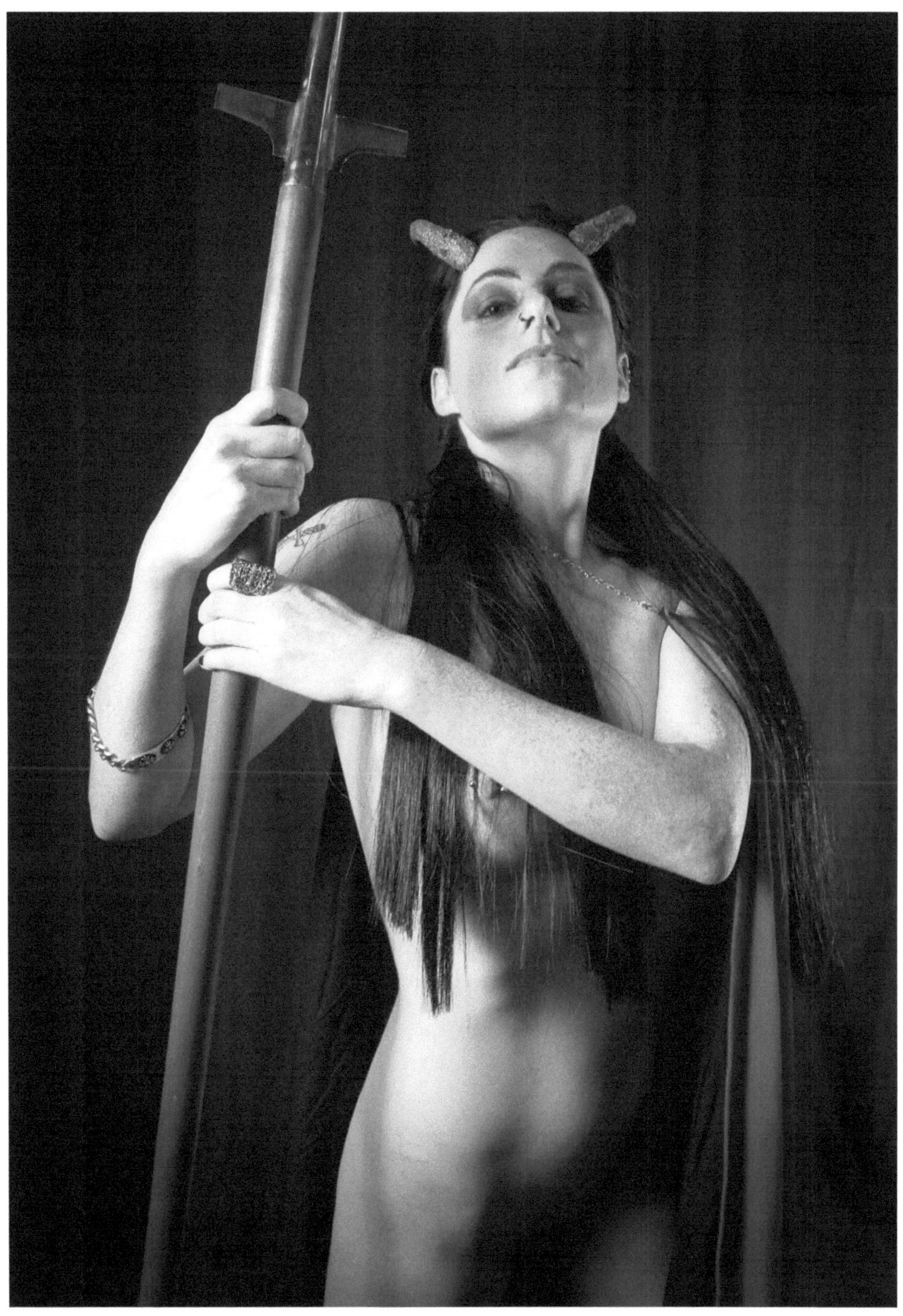

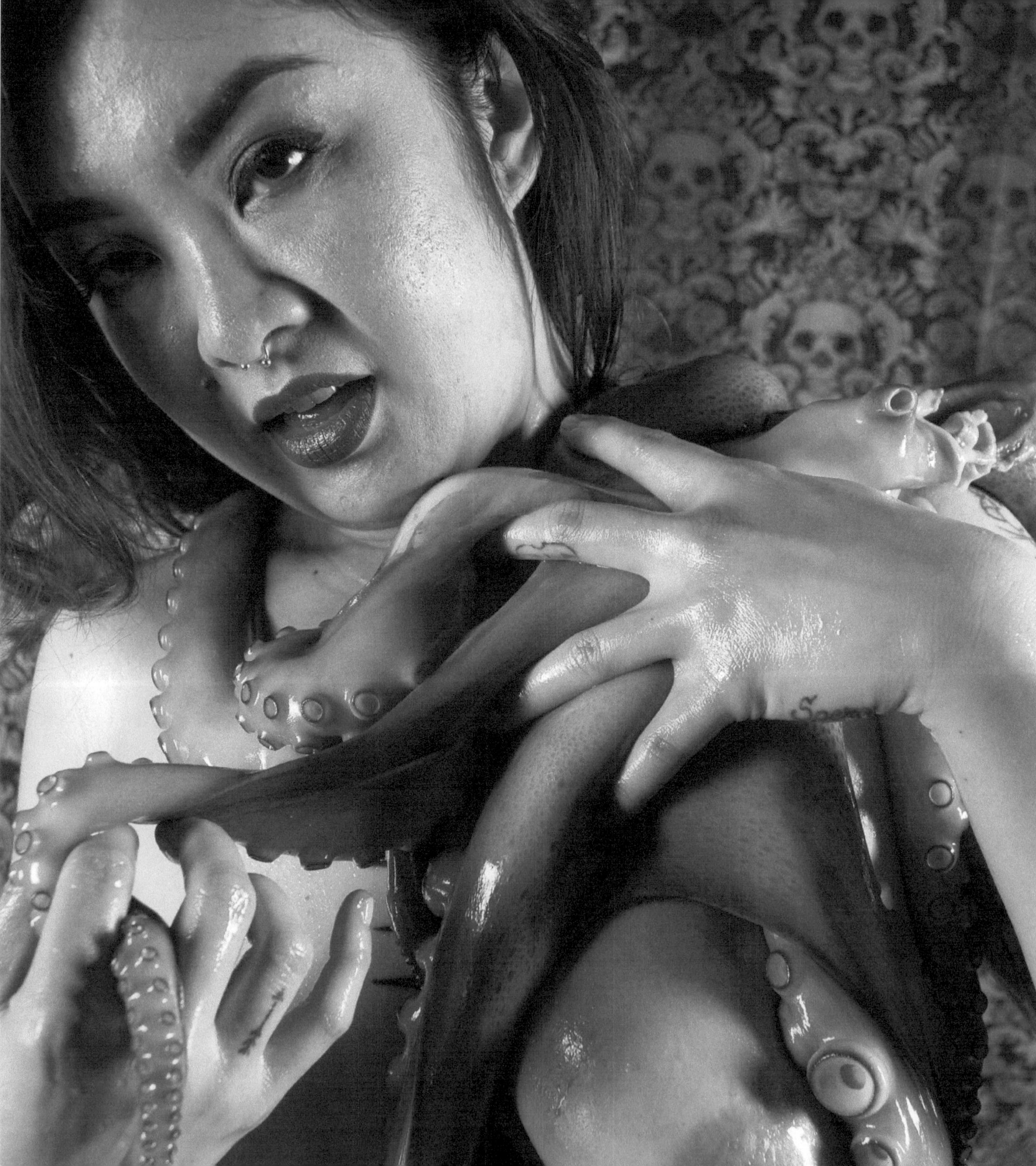

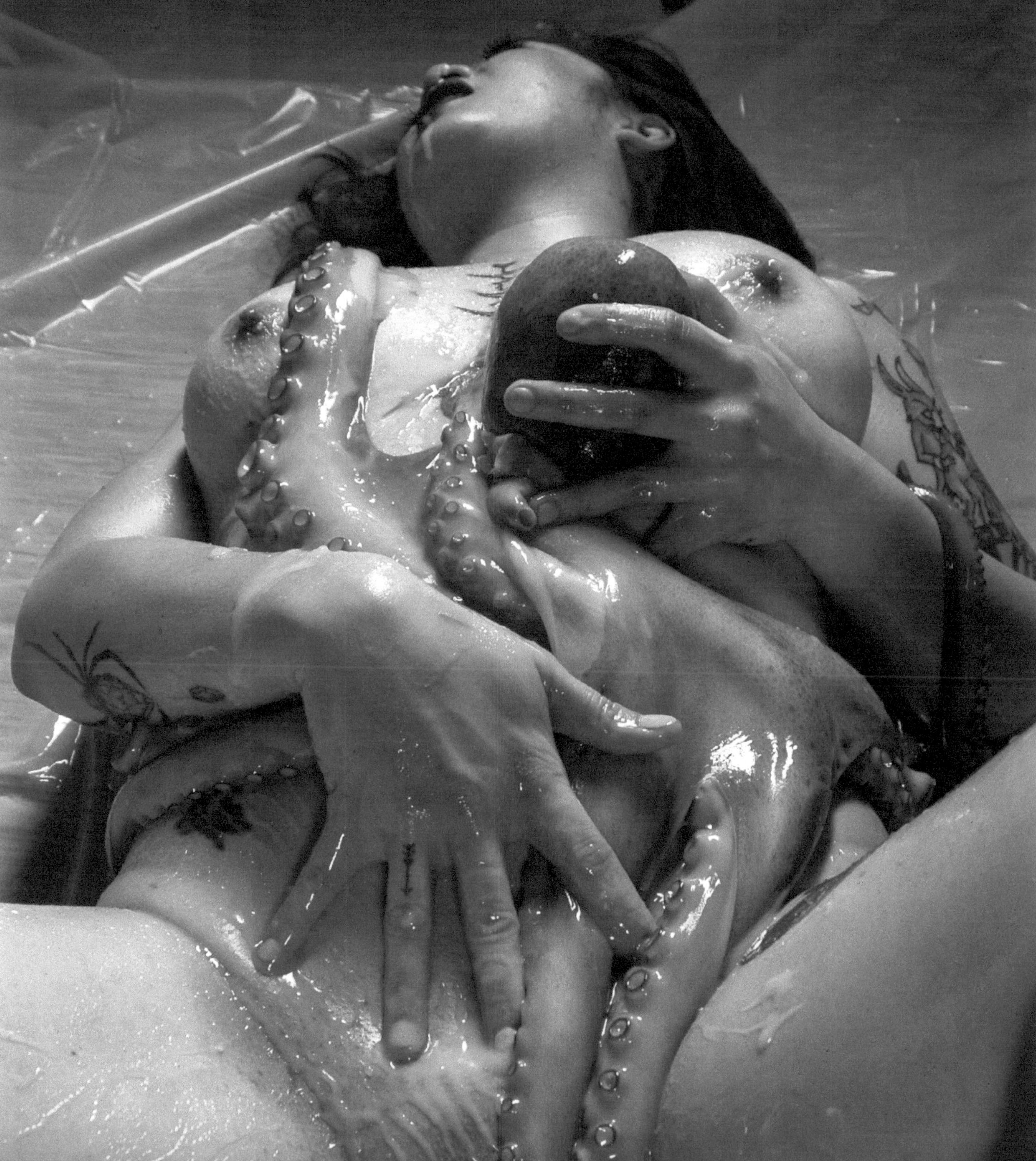

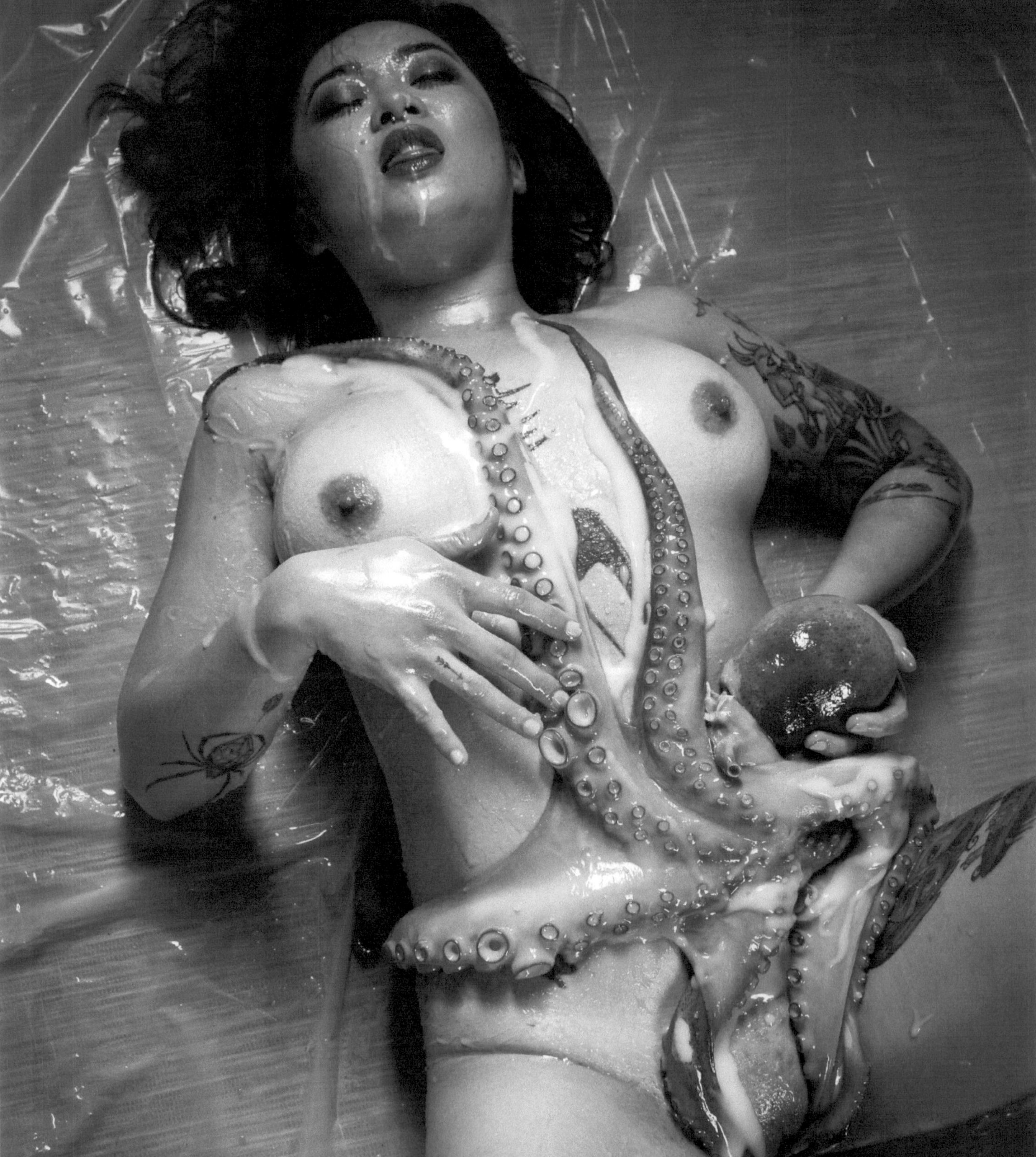

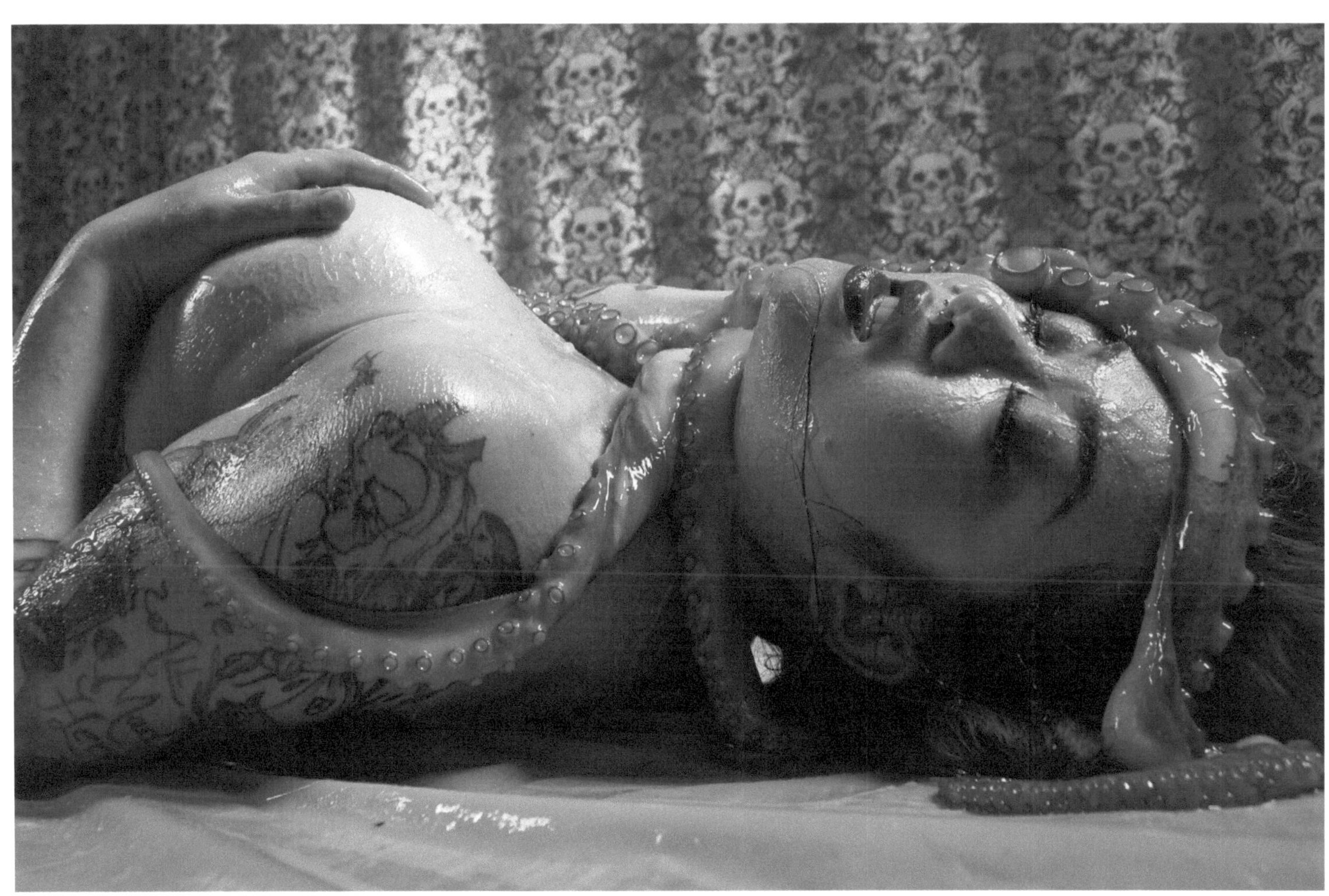

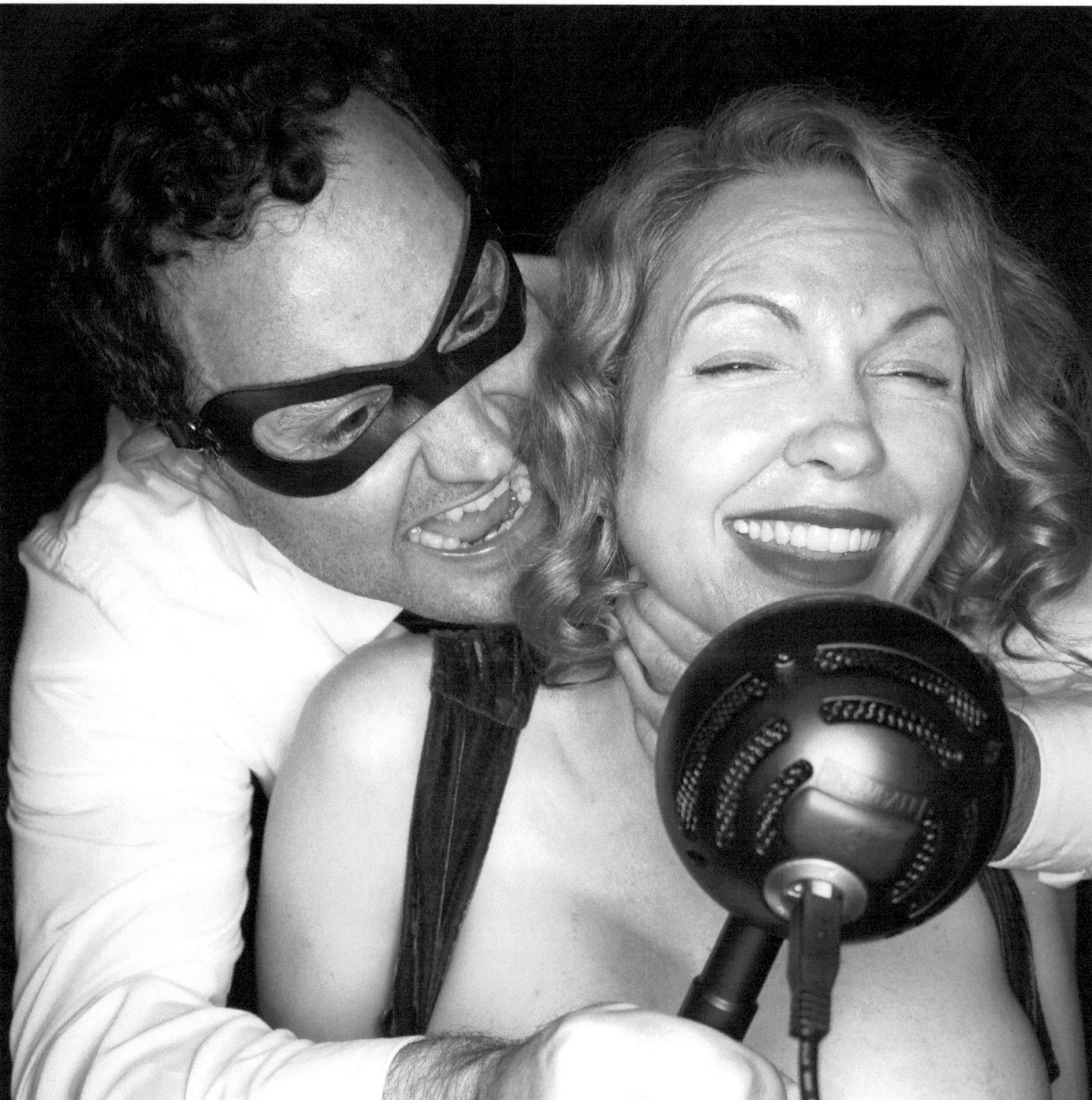

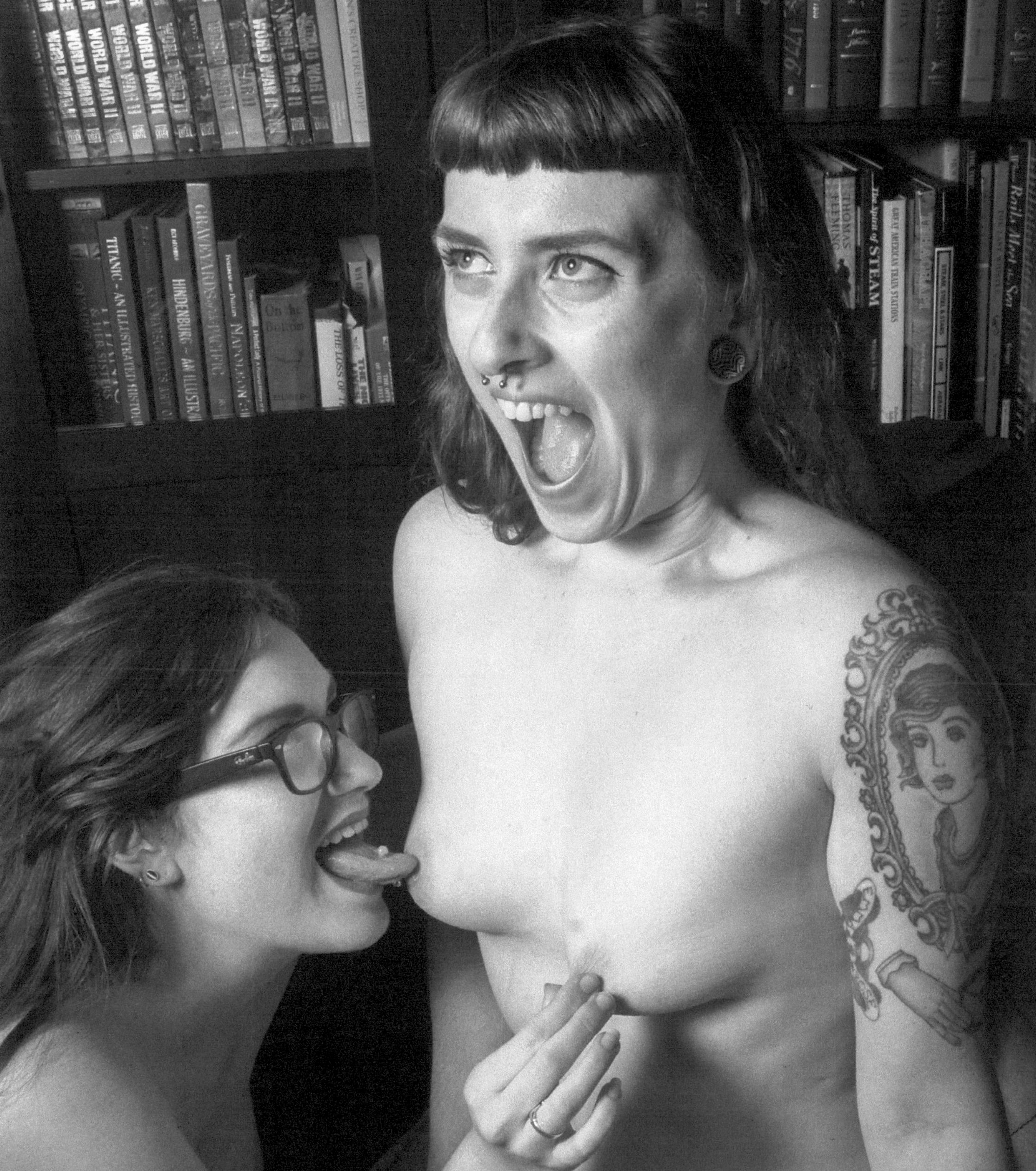
WORLD WAR II
TITANIC – AN ILLUSTRATED HISTORY
HINDENBURG – AN ILLUSTRA
GRAVEYARDS of the PACIFIC
On the Bottom
THE LOSS OF T
1776
THOMAS FLEMING
The Spirit of STEAM
GREAT AMERICAN TRAIN STATIONS

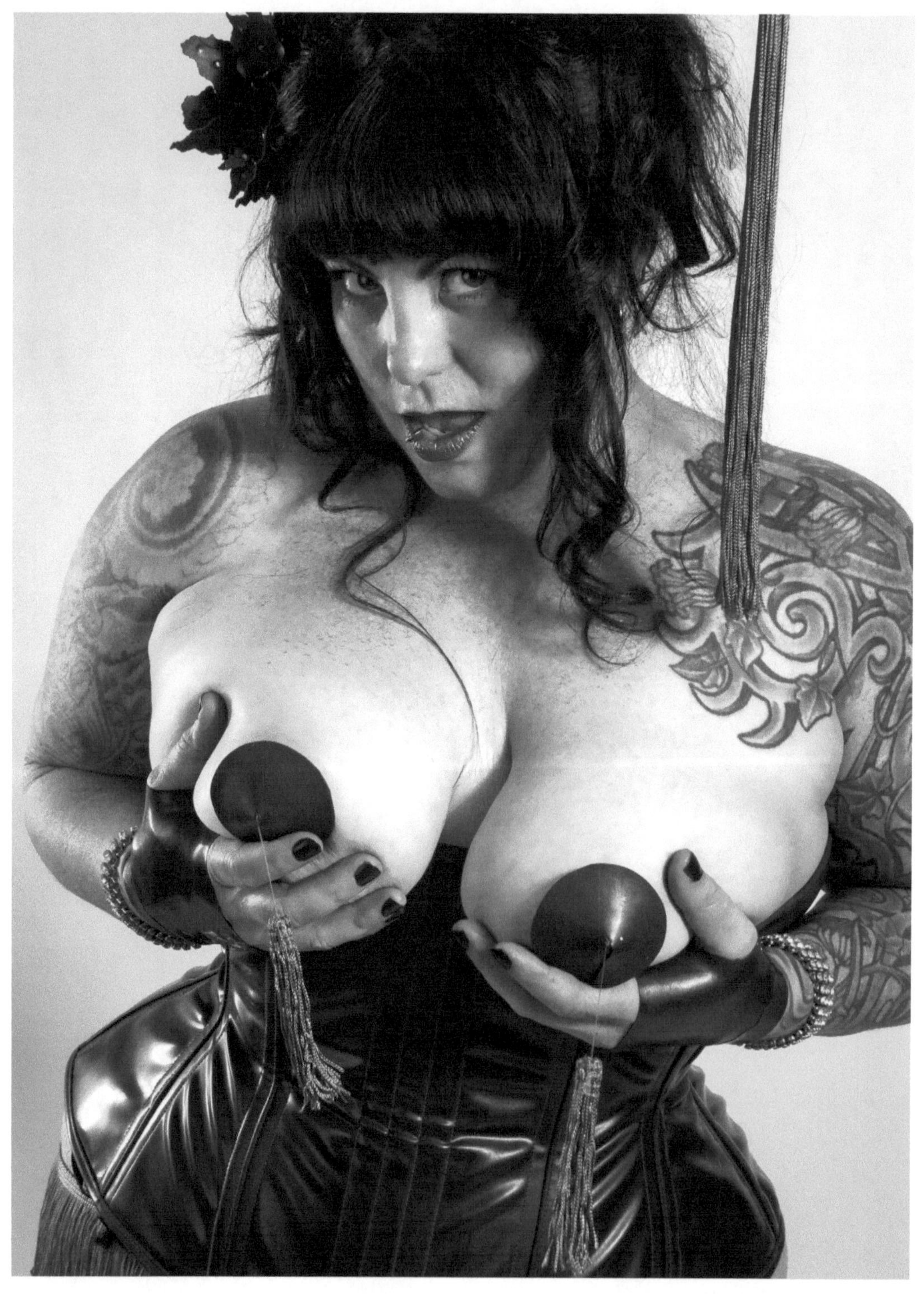

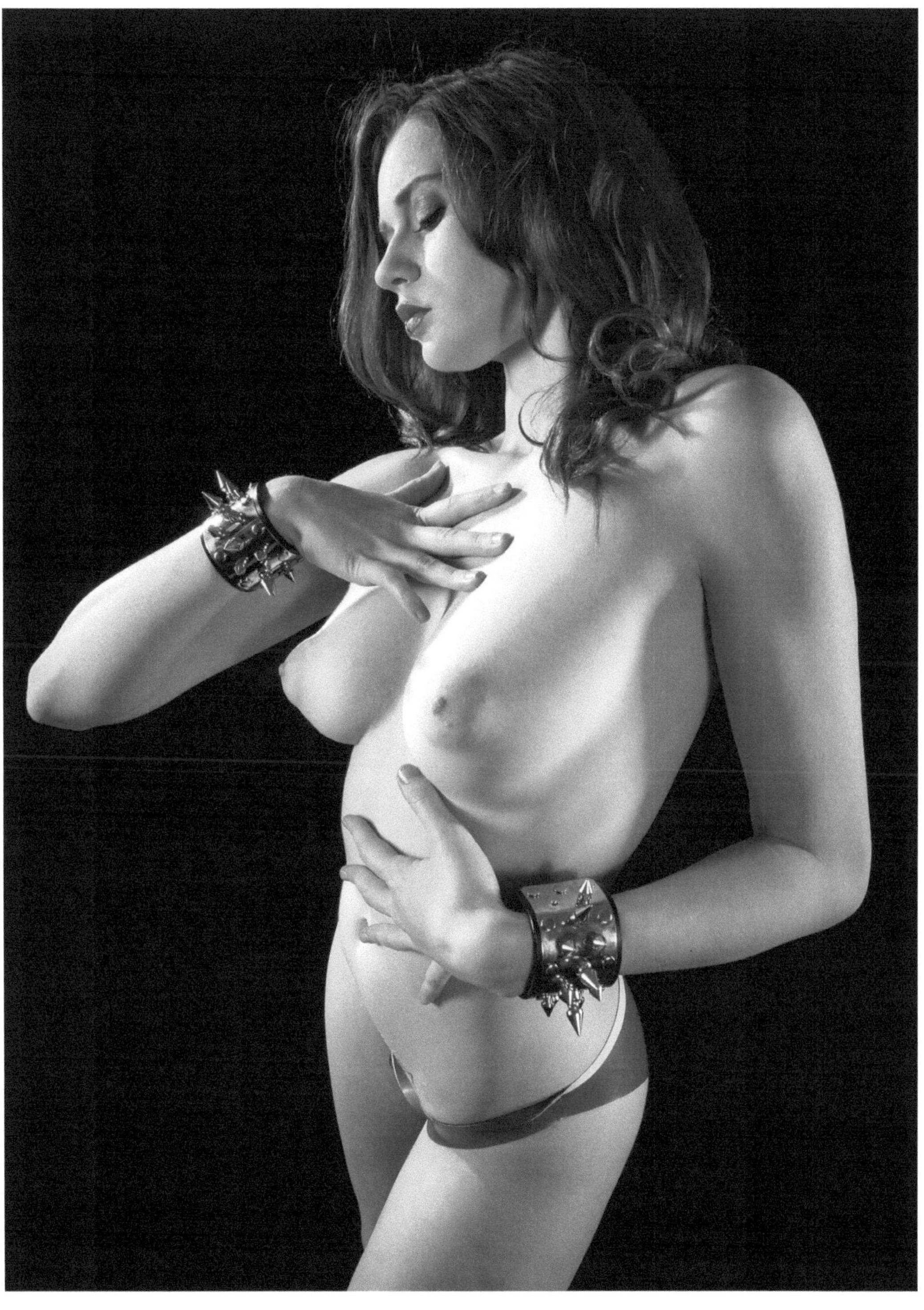

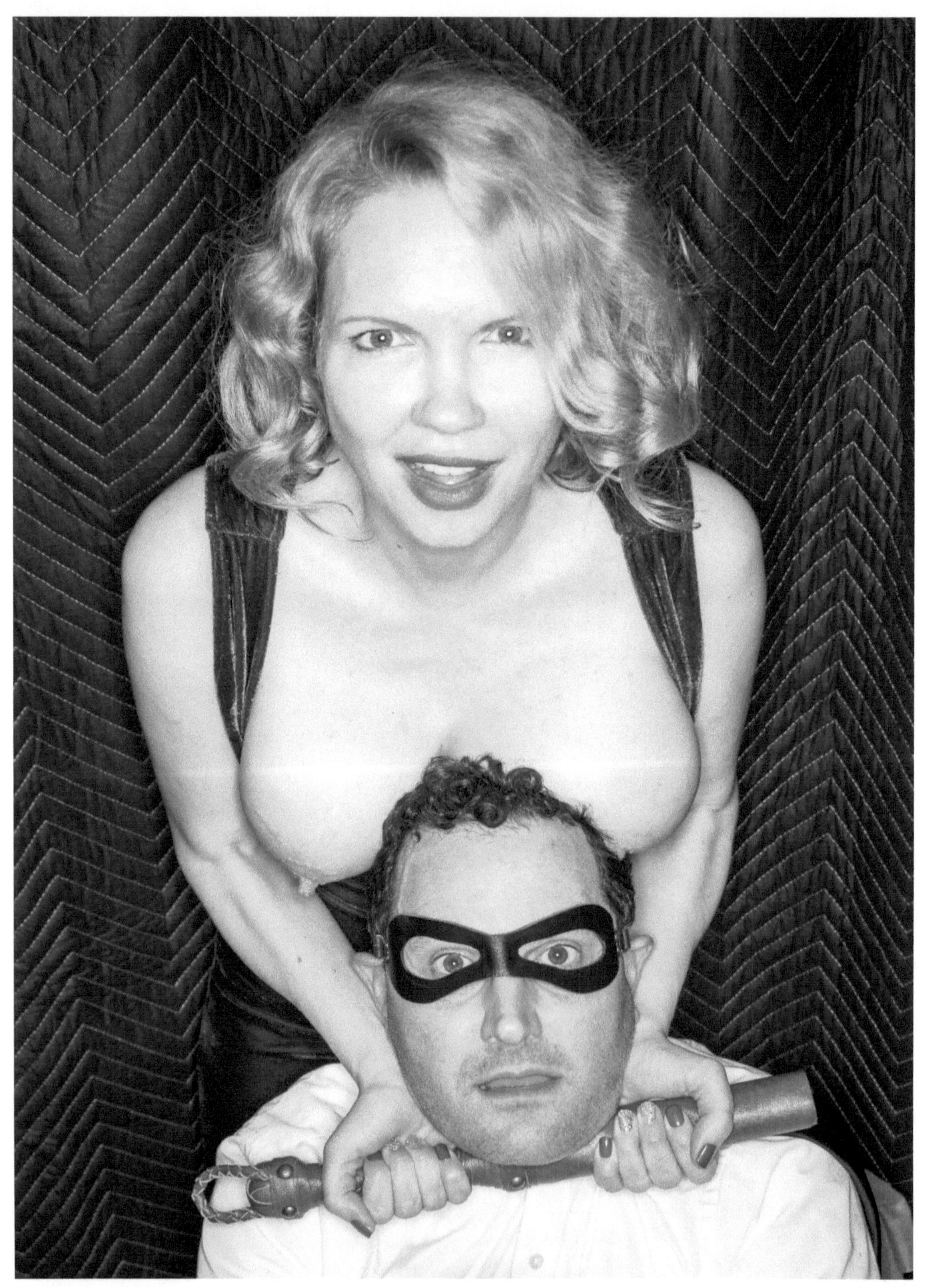

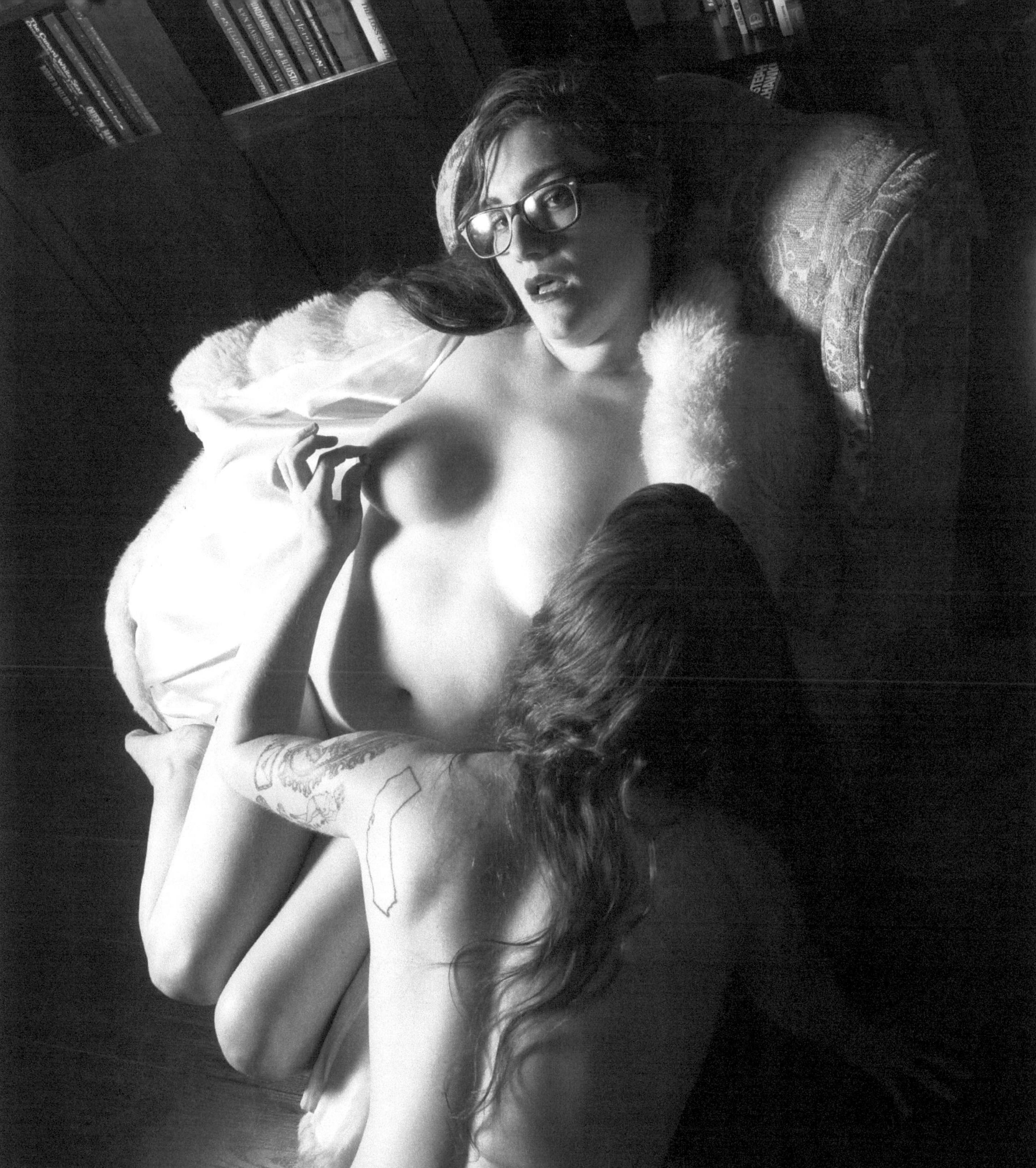

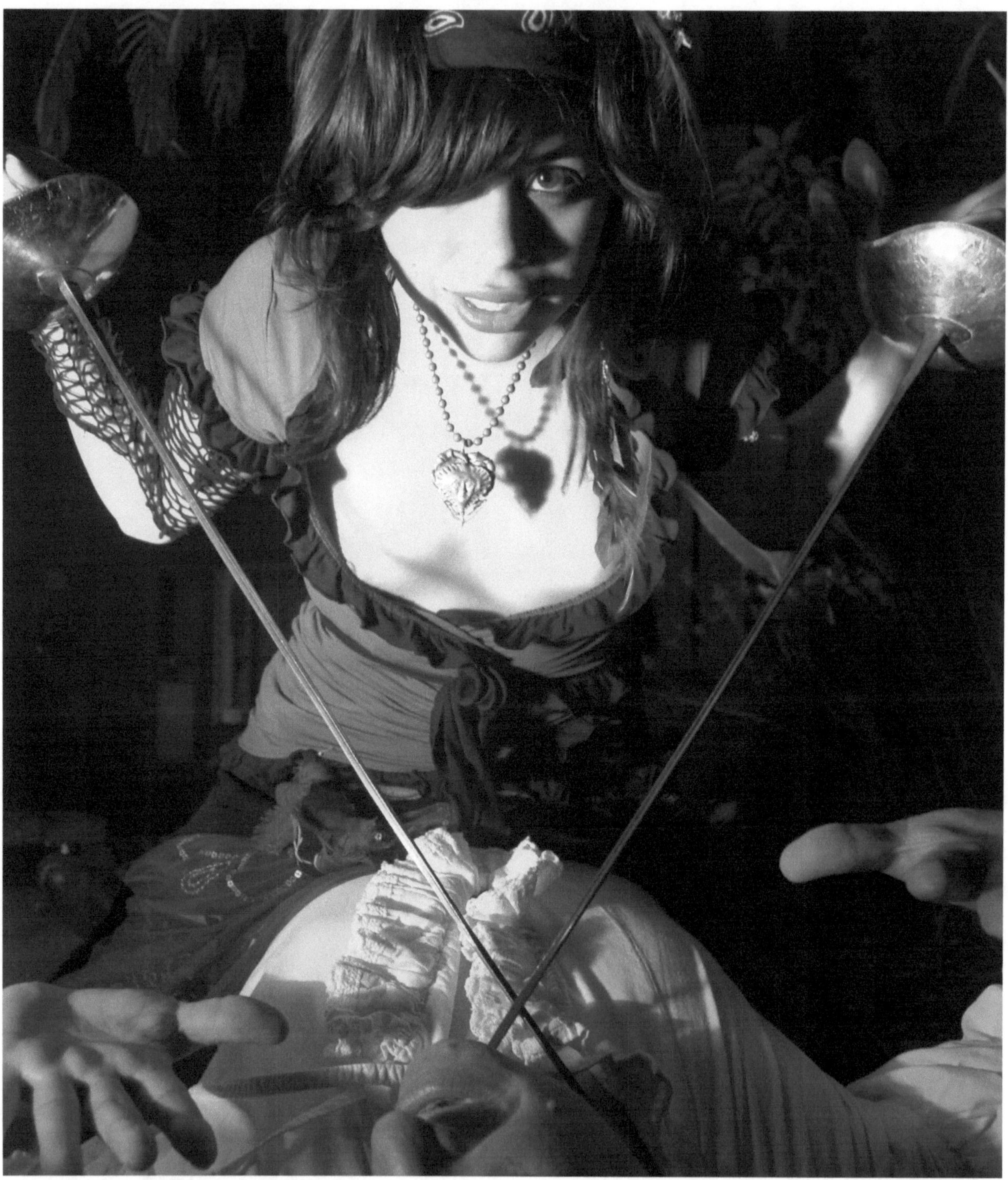

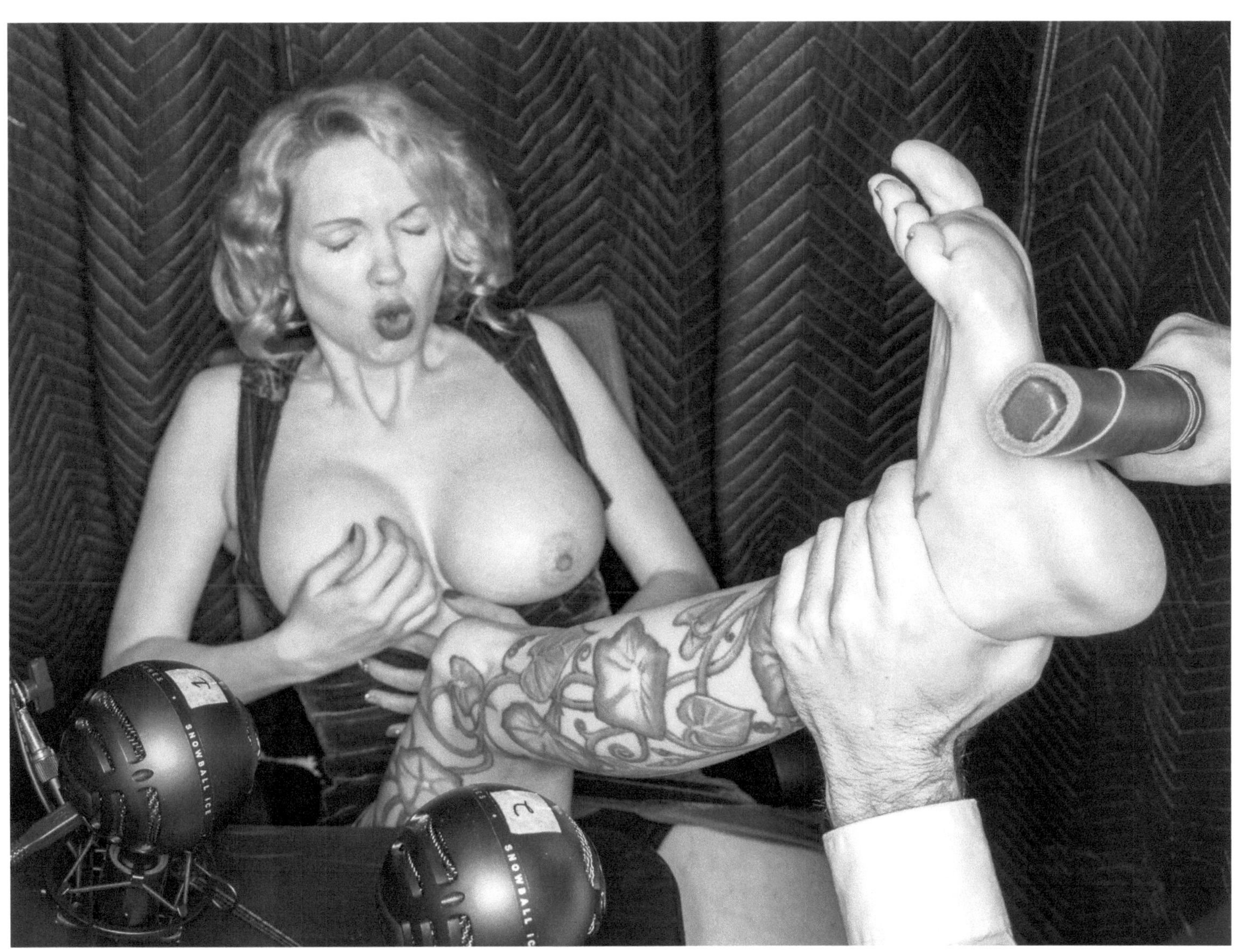

SNOWBALL ICE
SNOWBALL

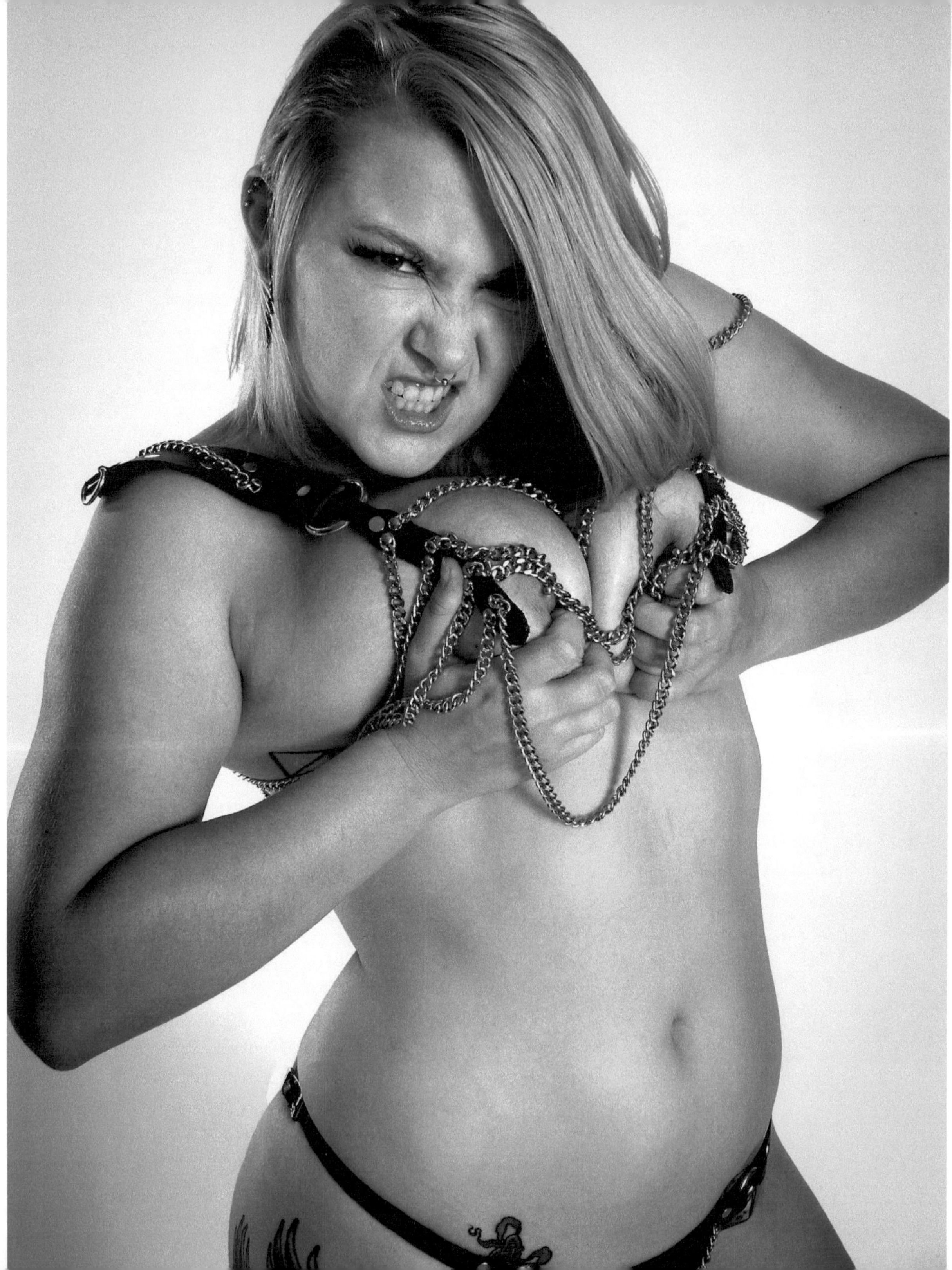

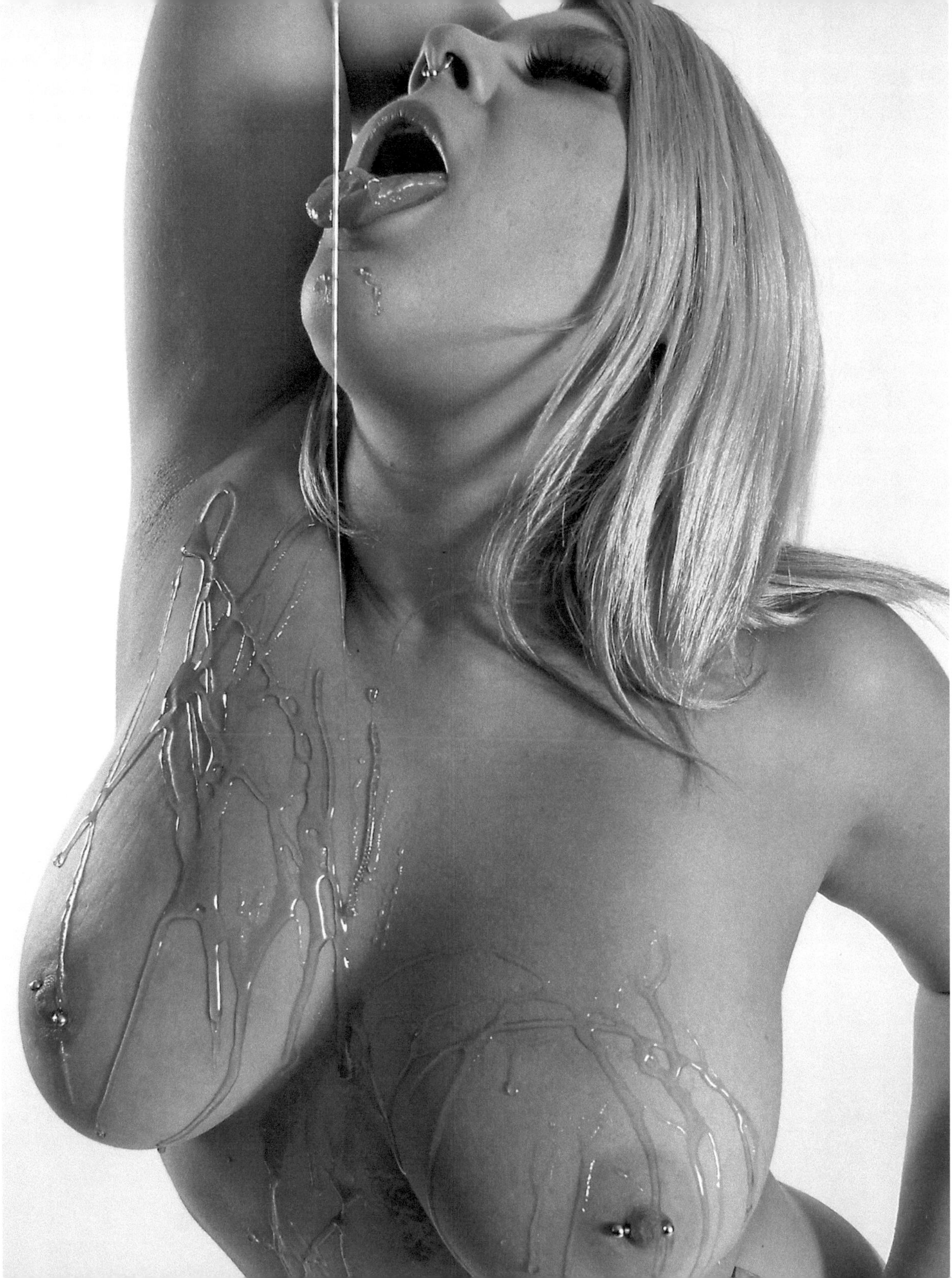

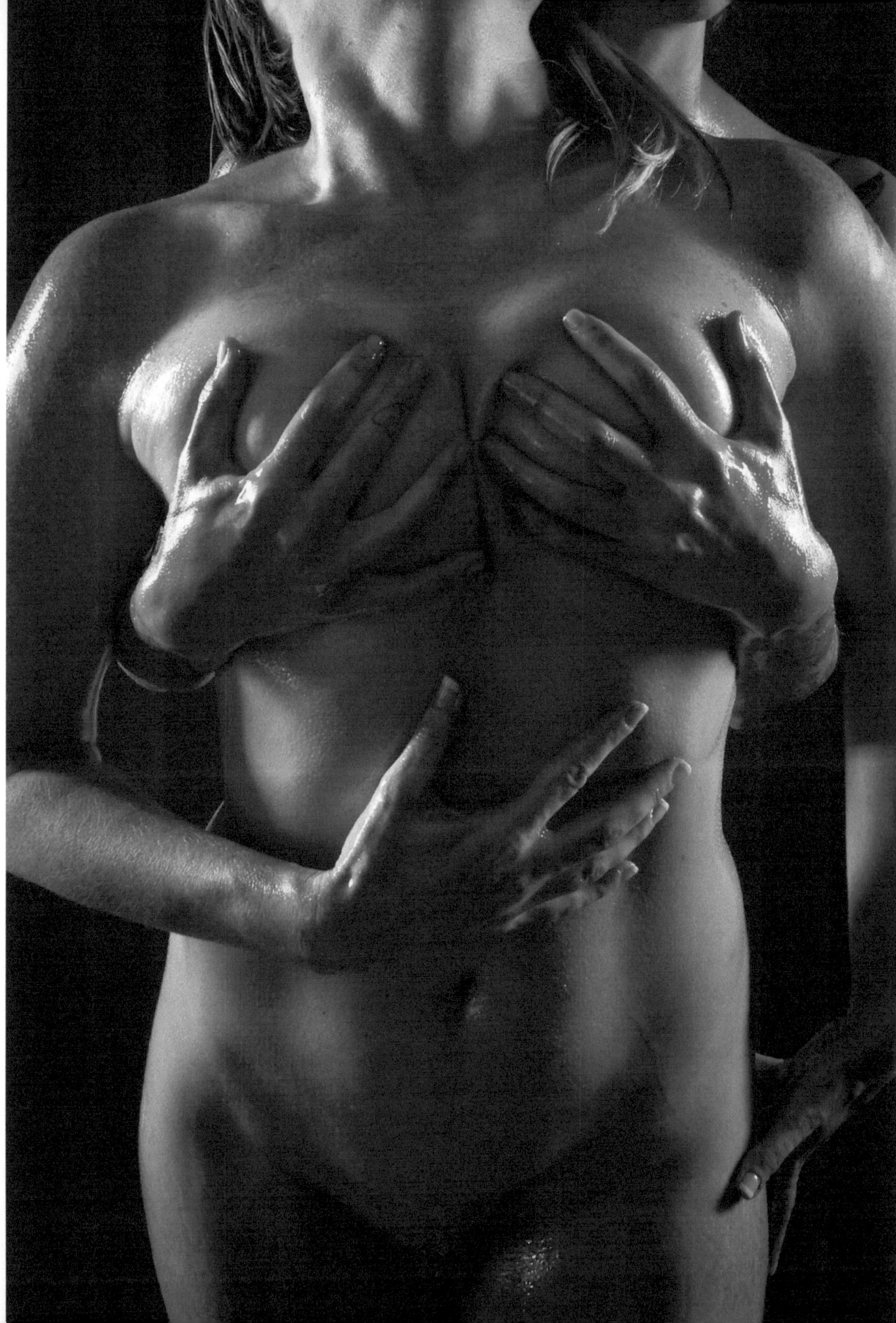

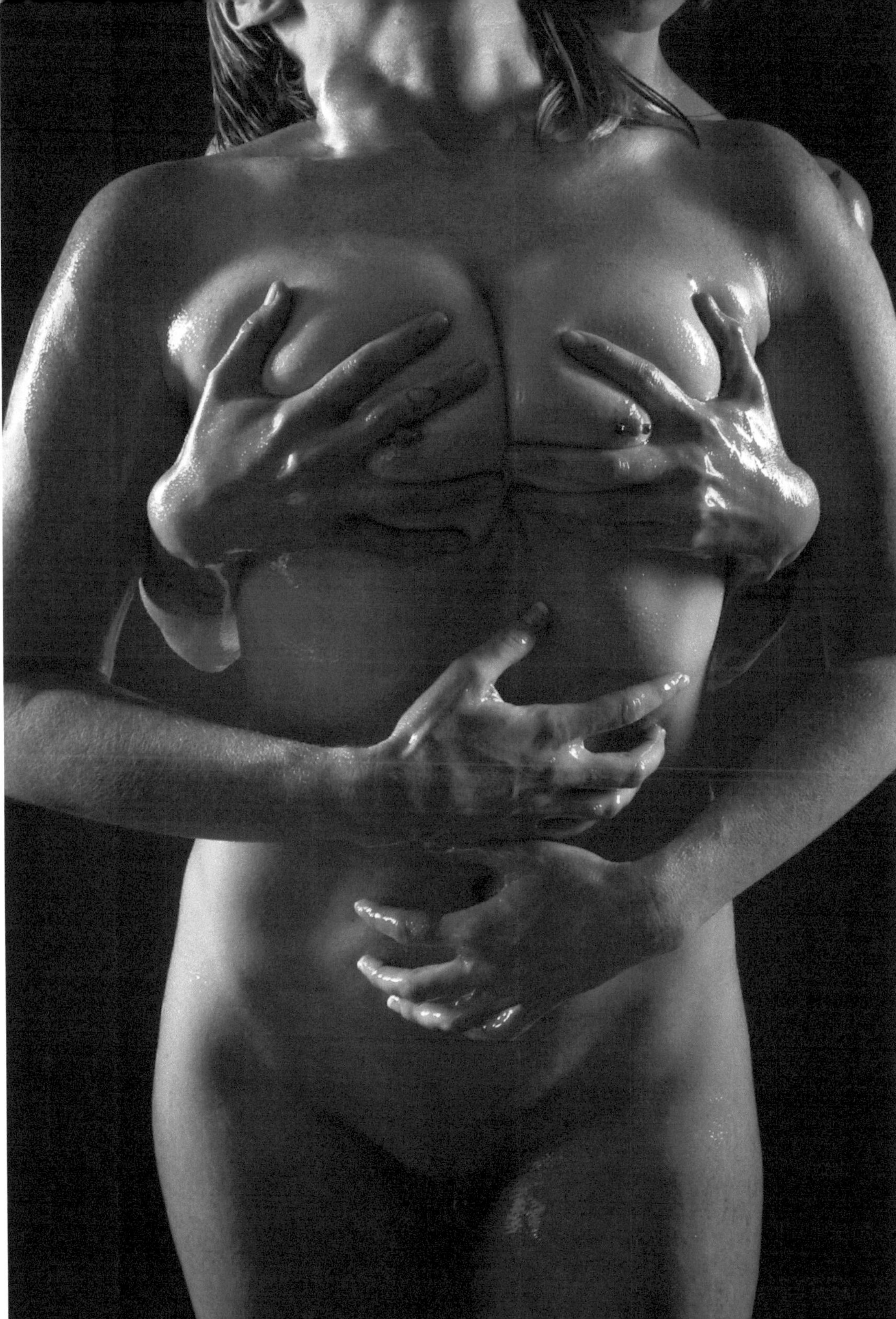

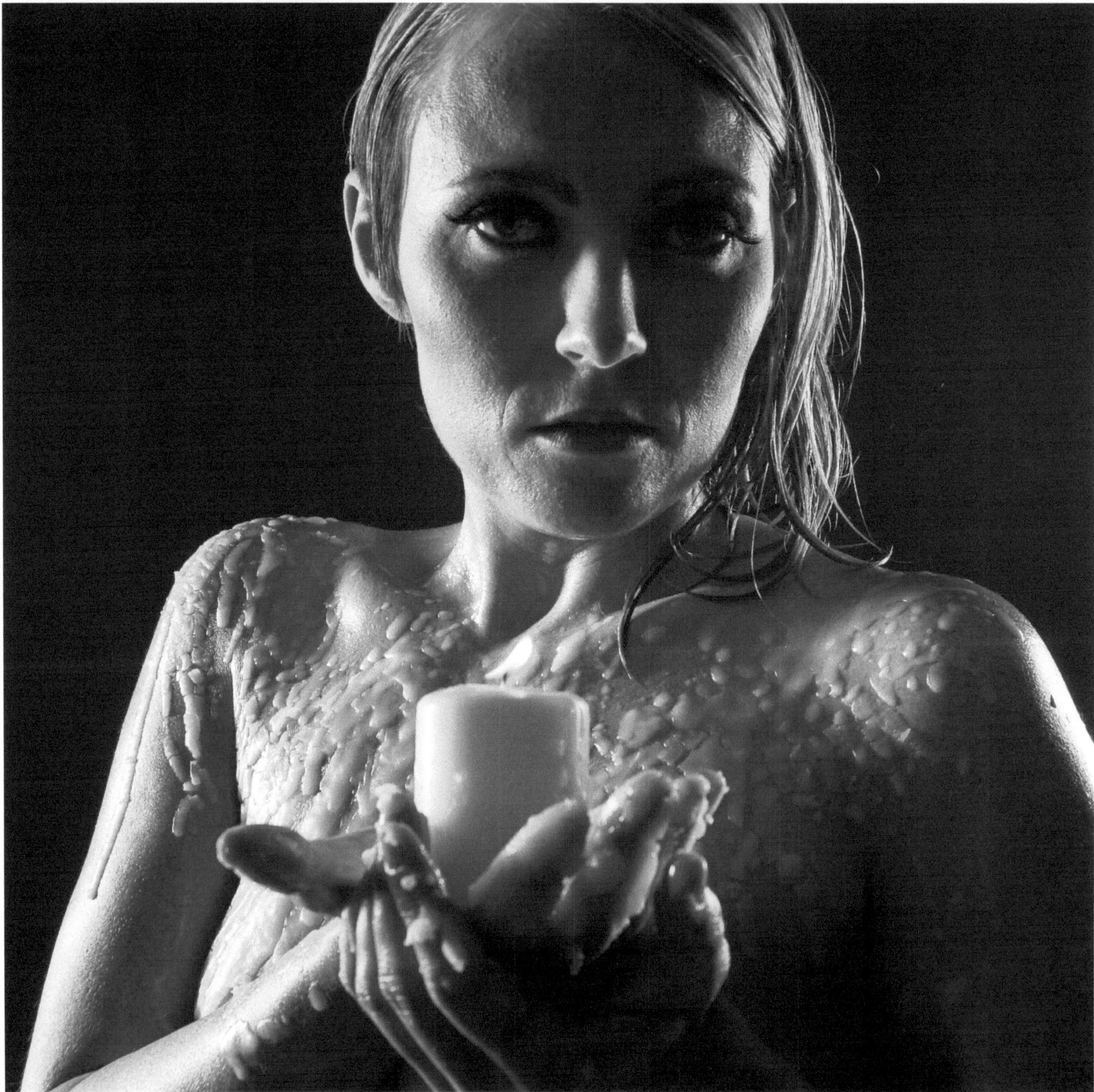

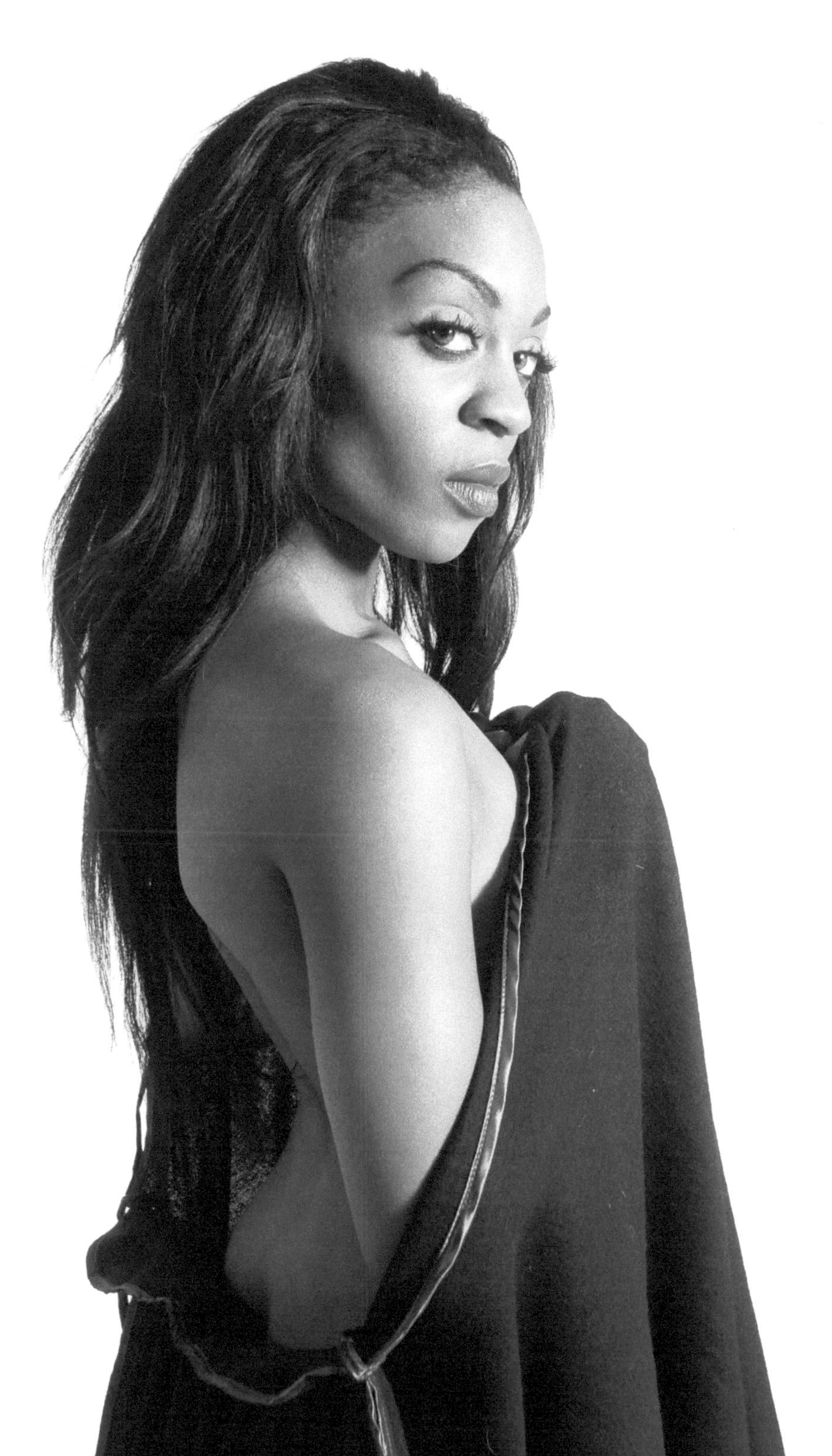

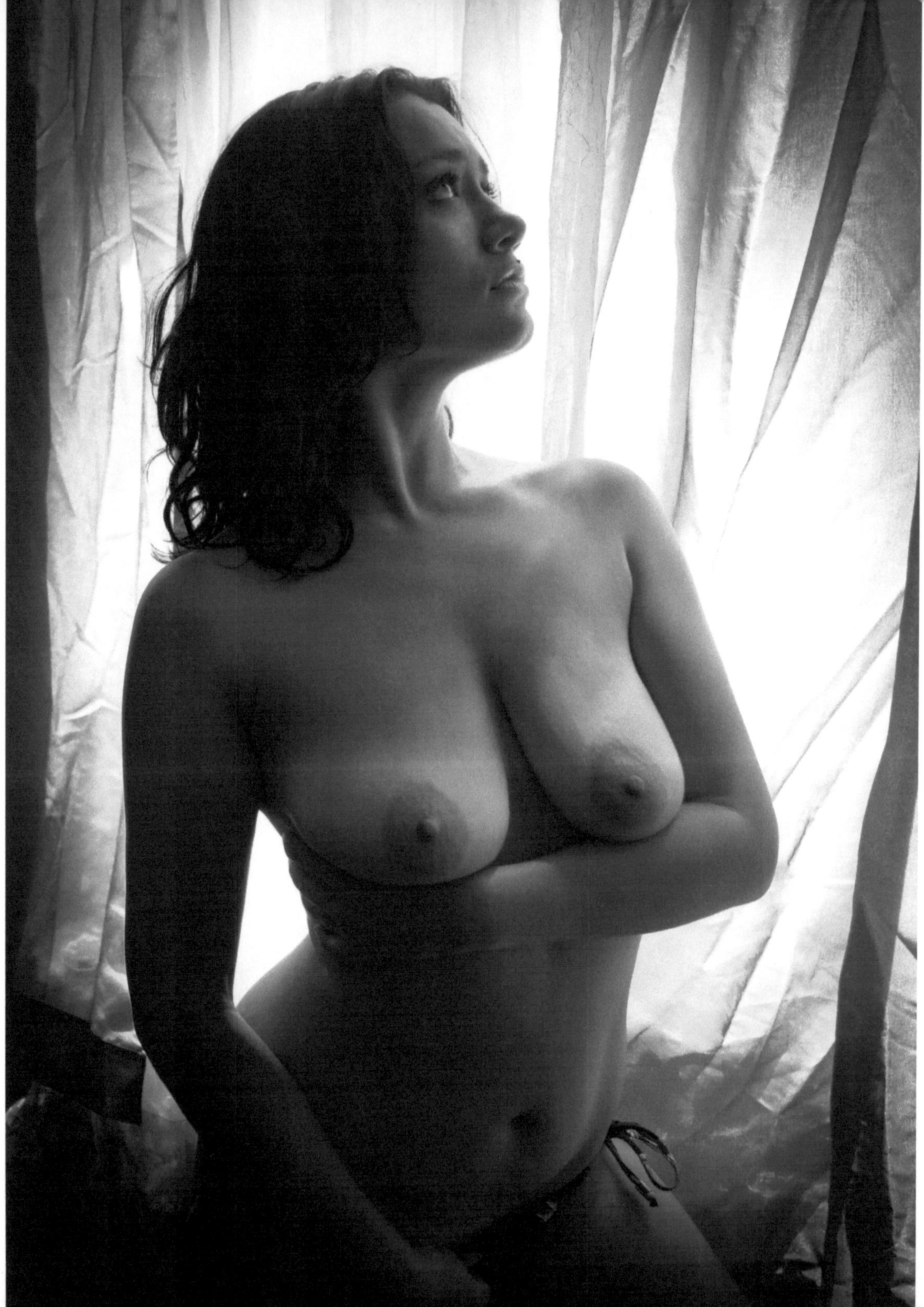

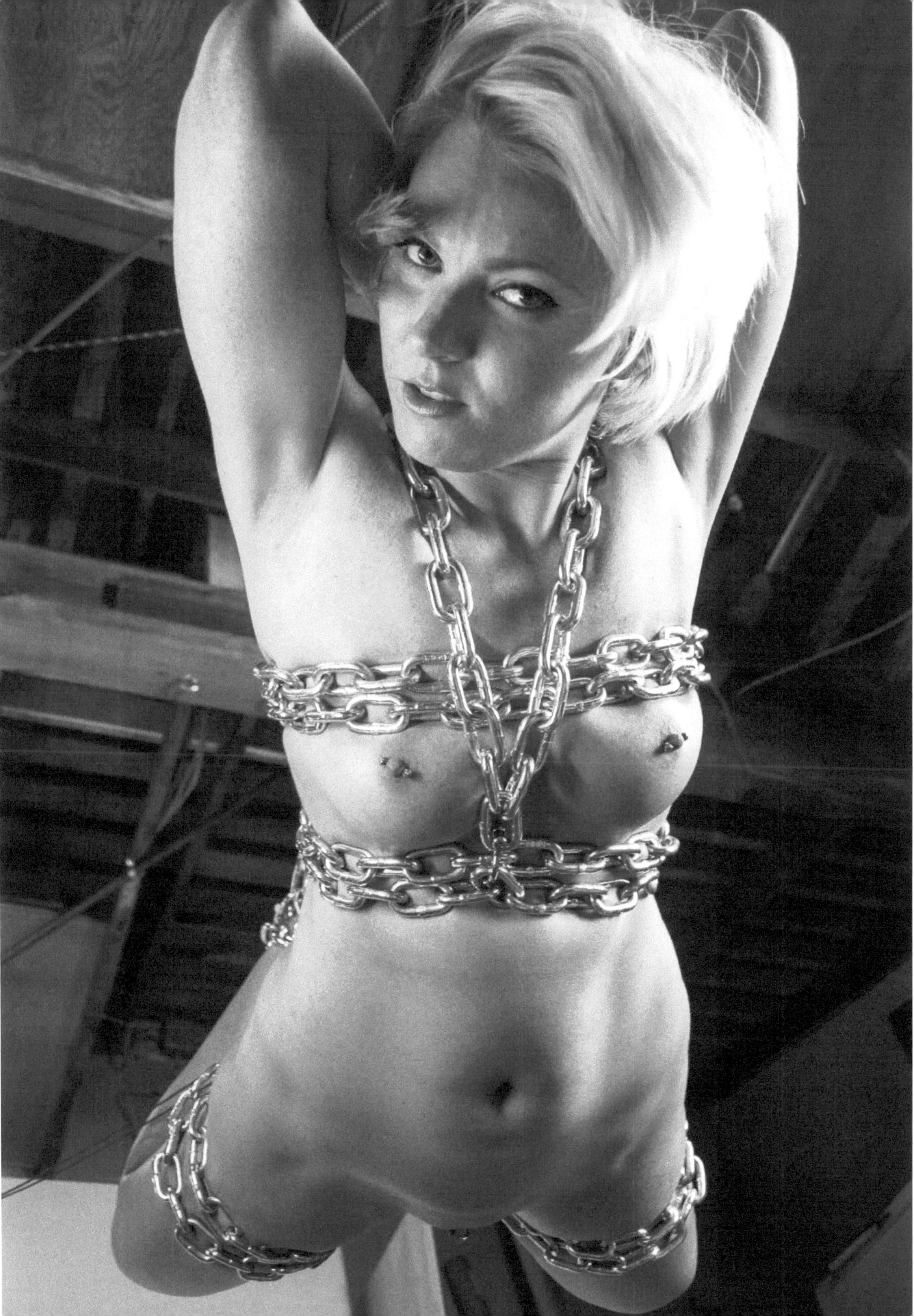

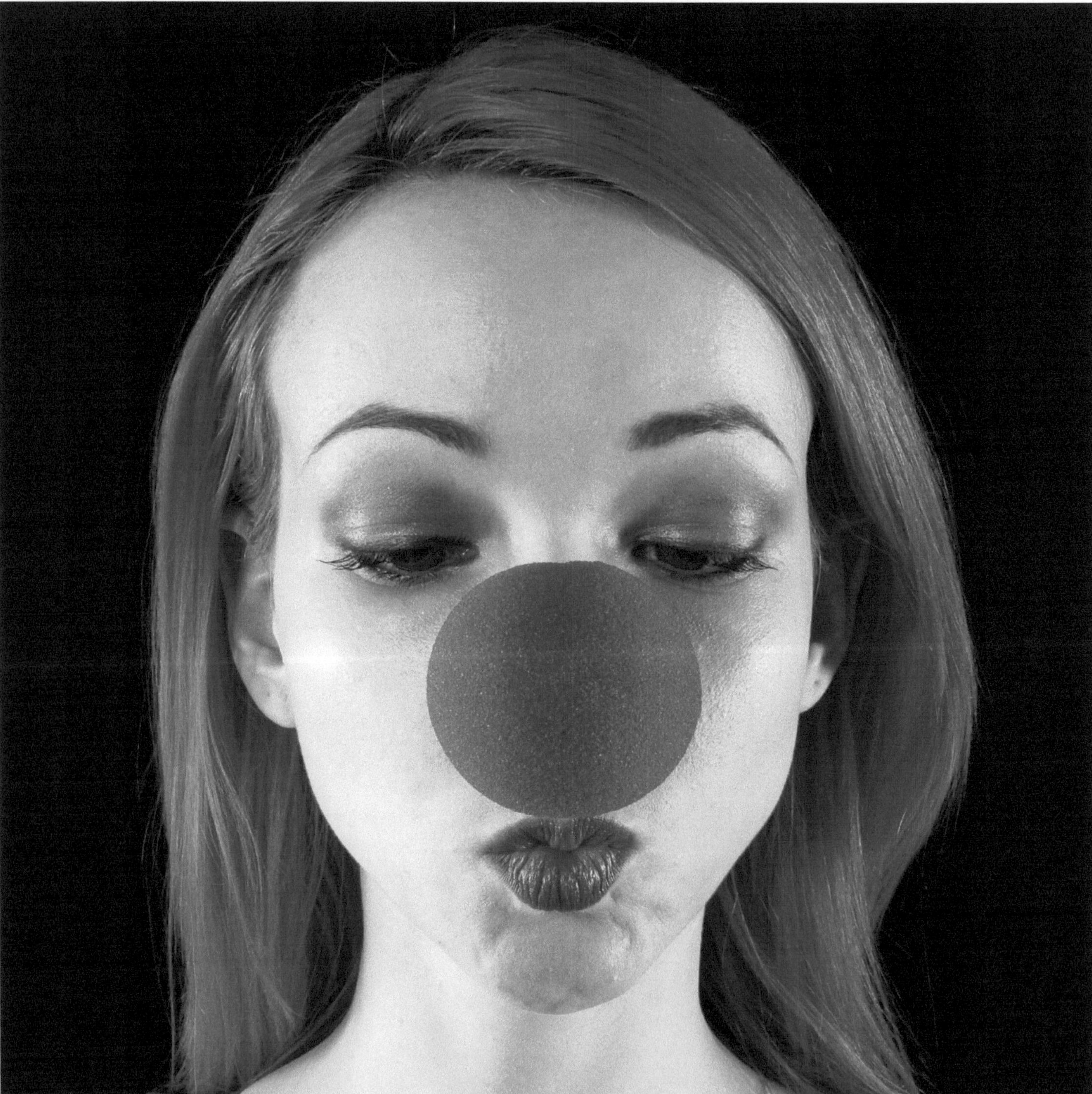

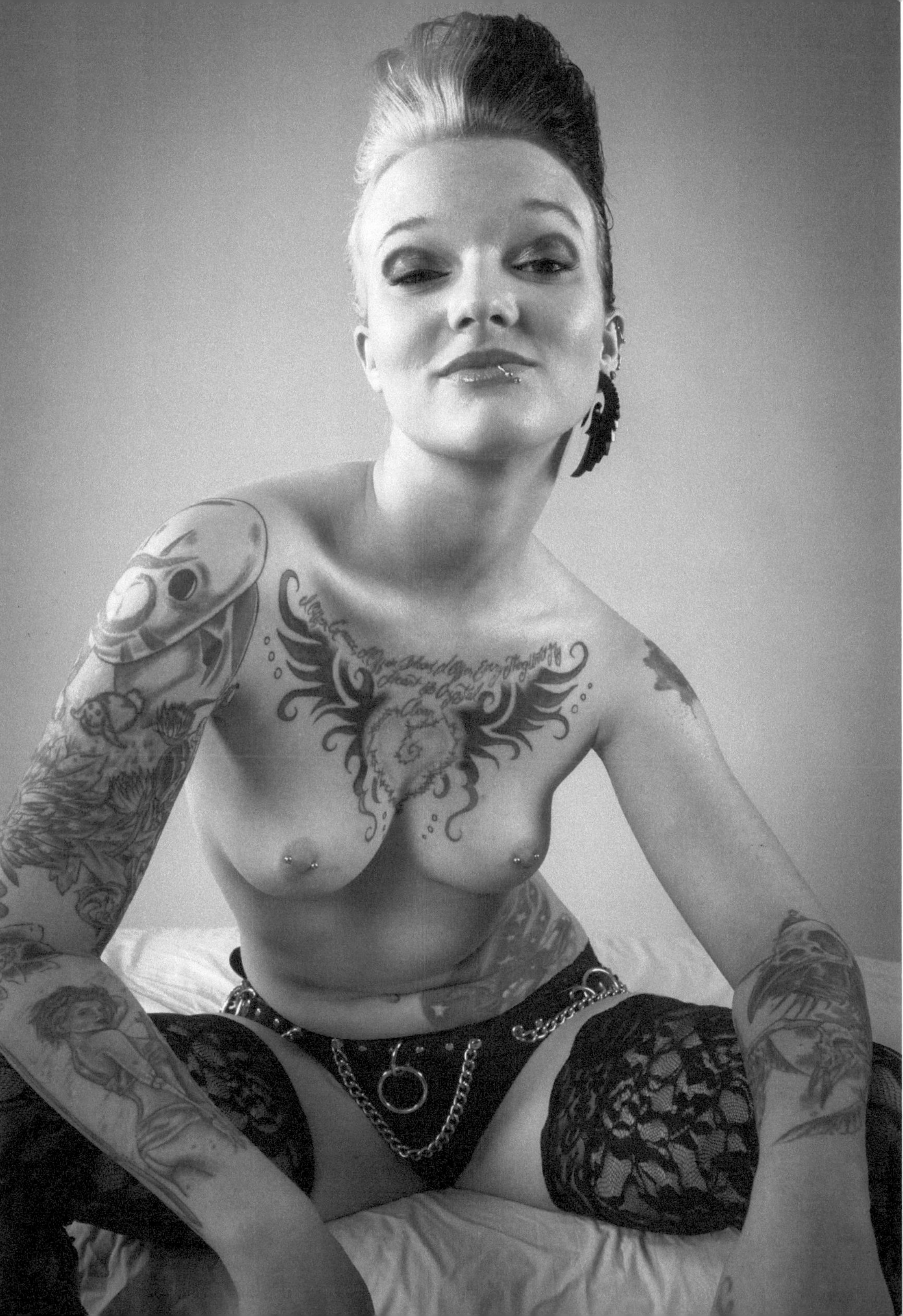

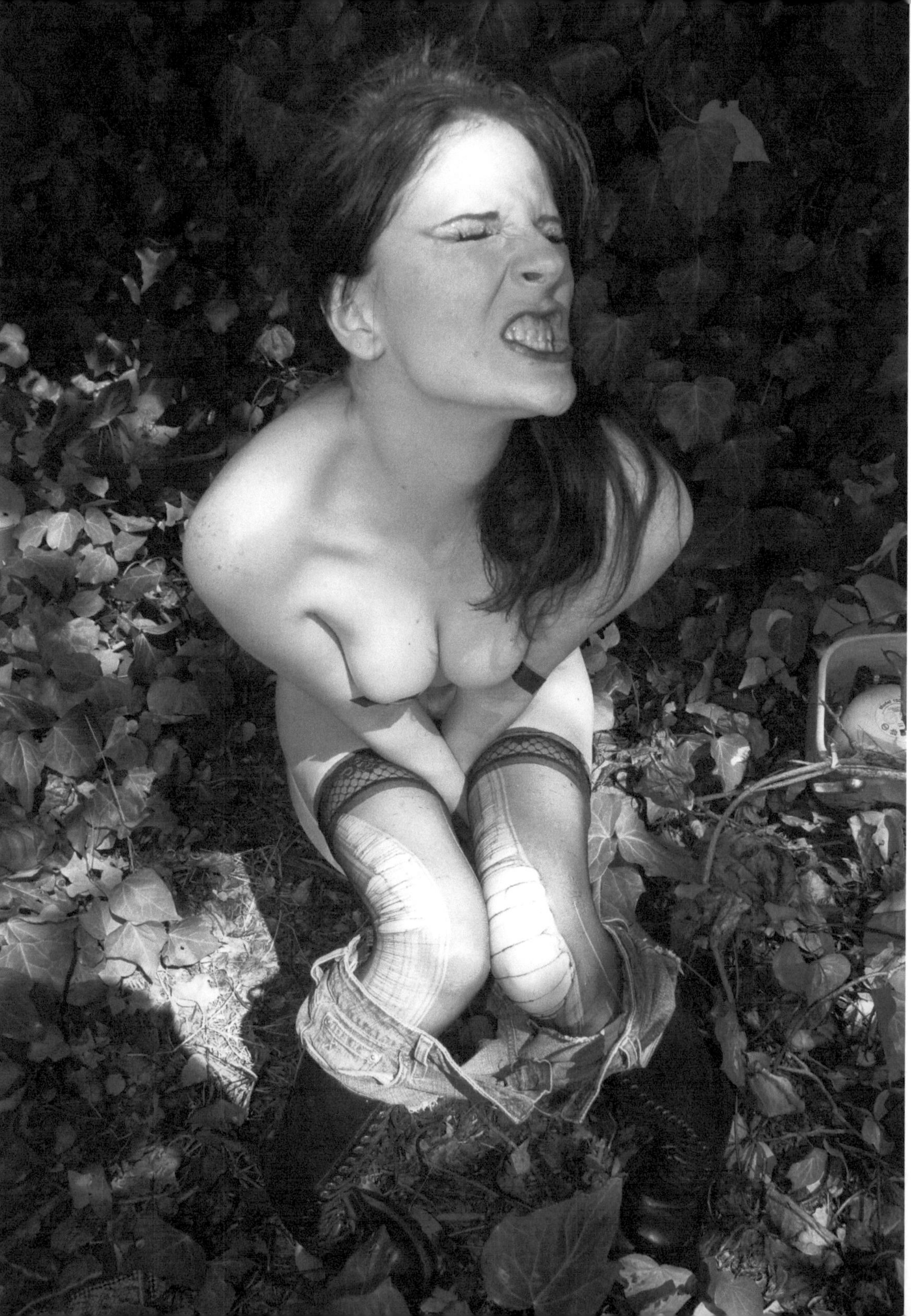

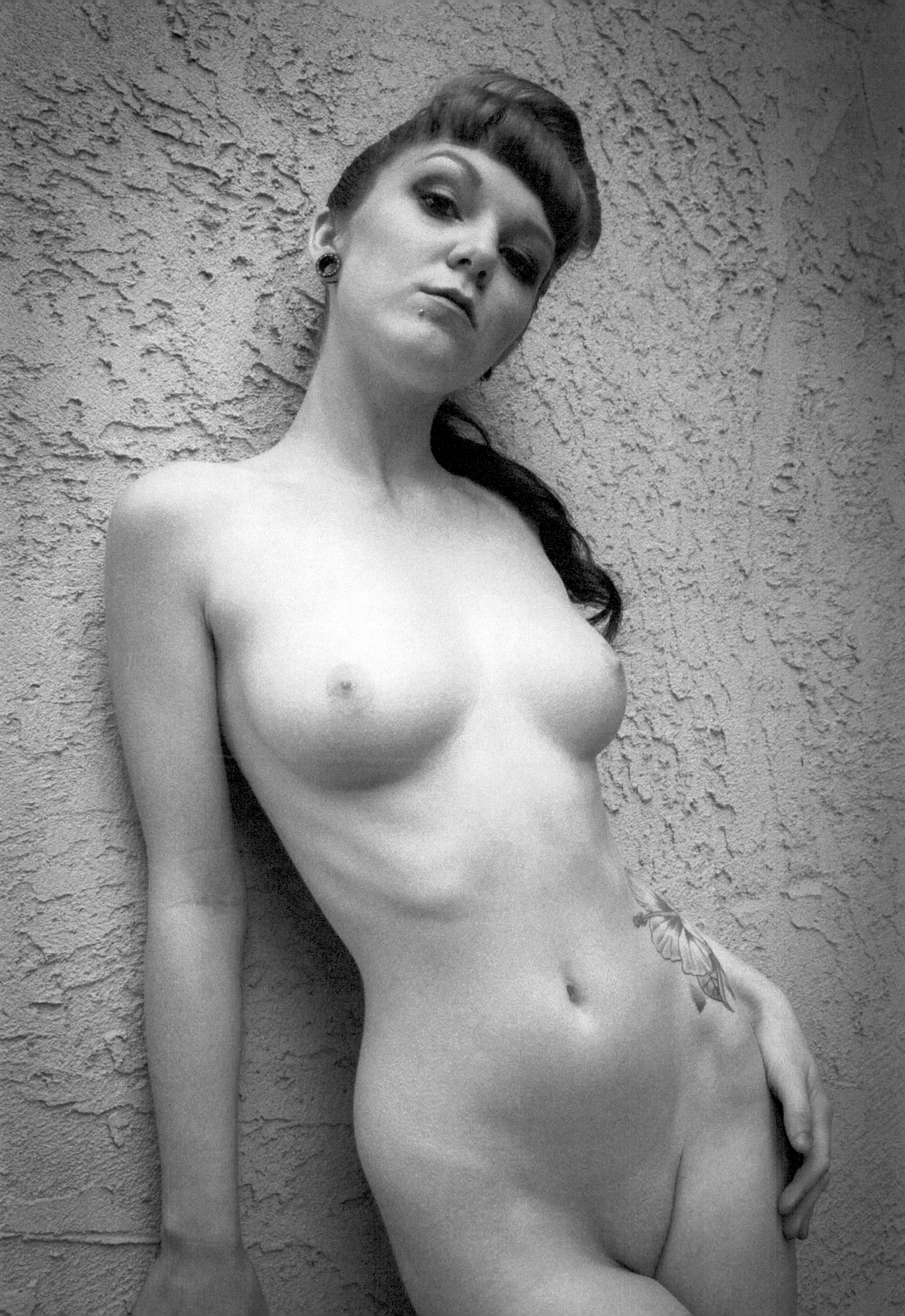

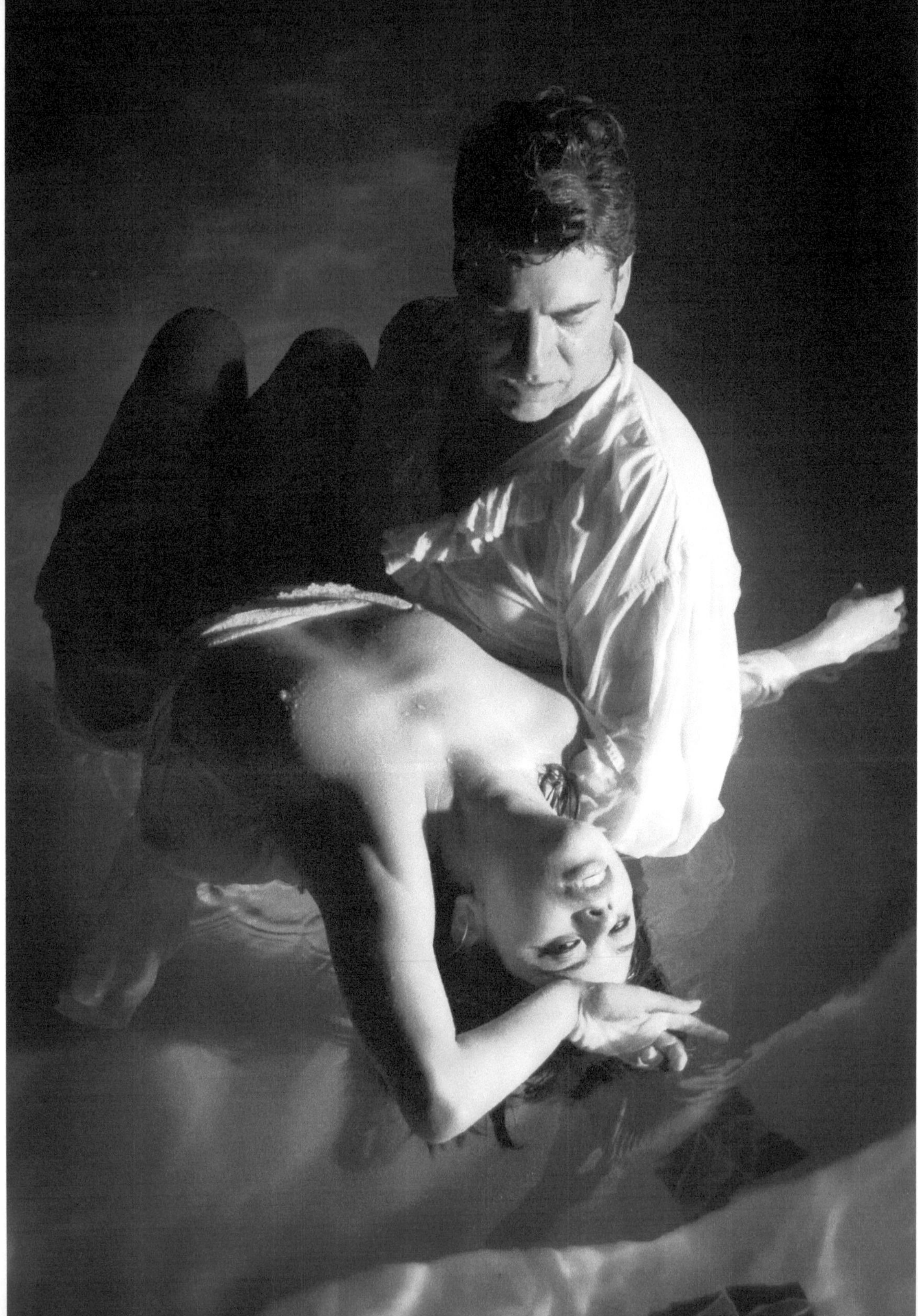

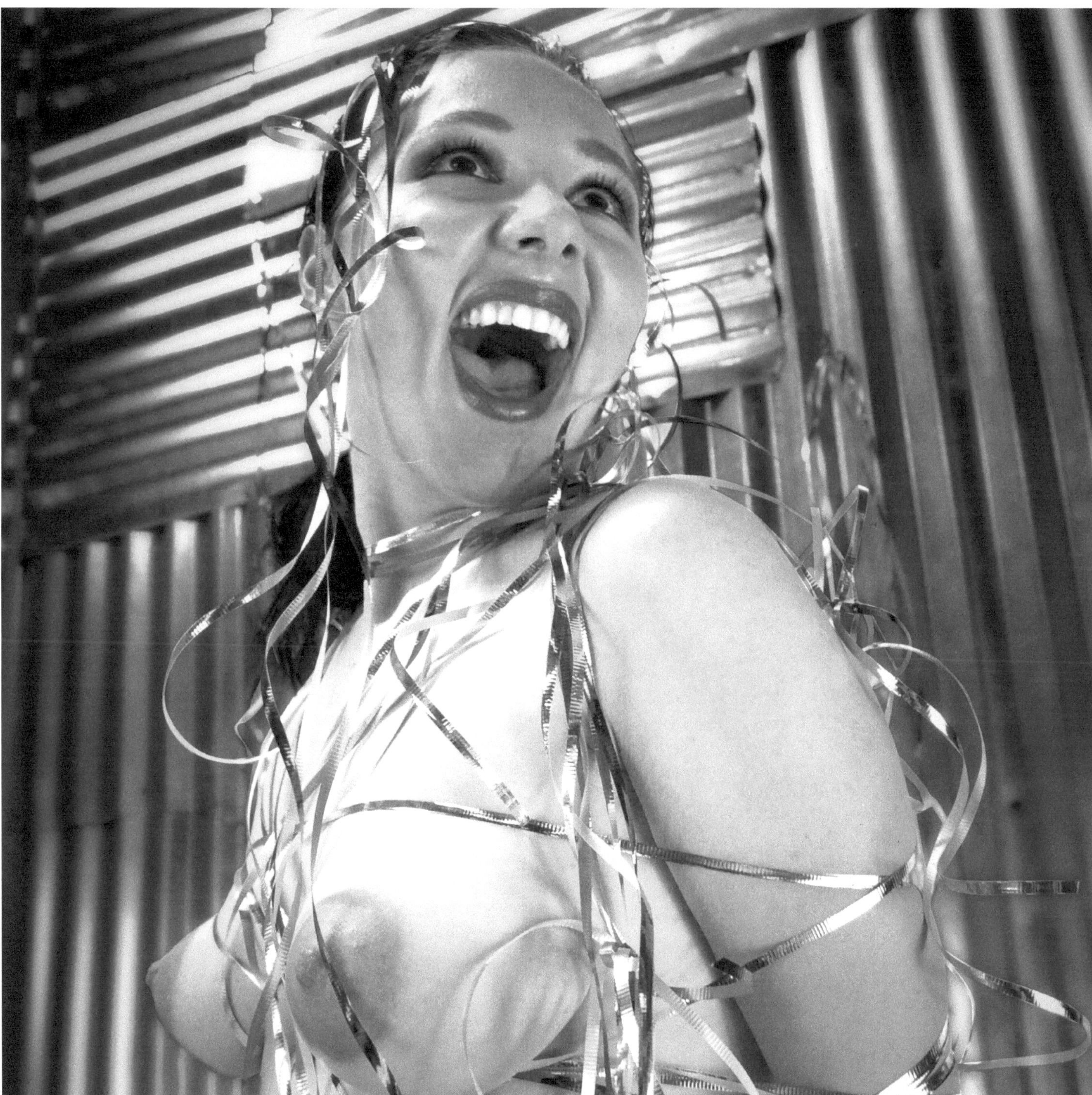

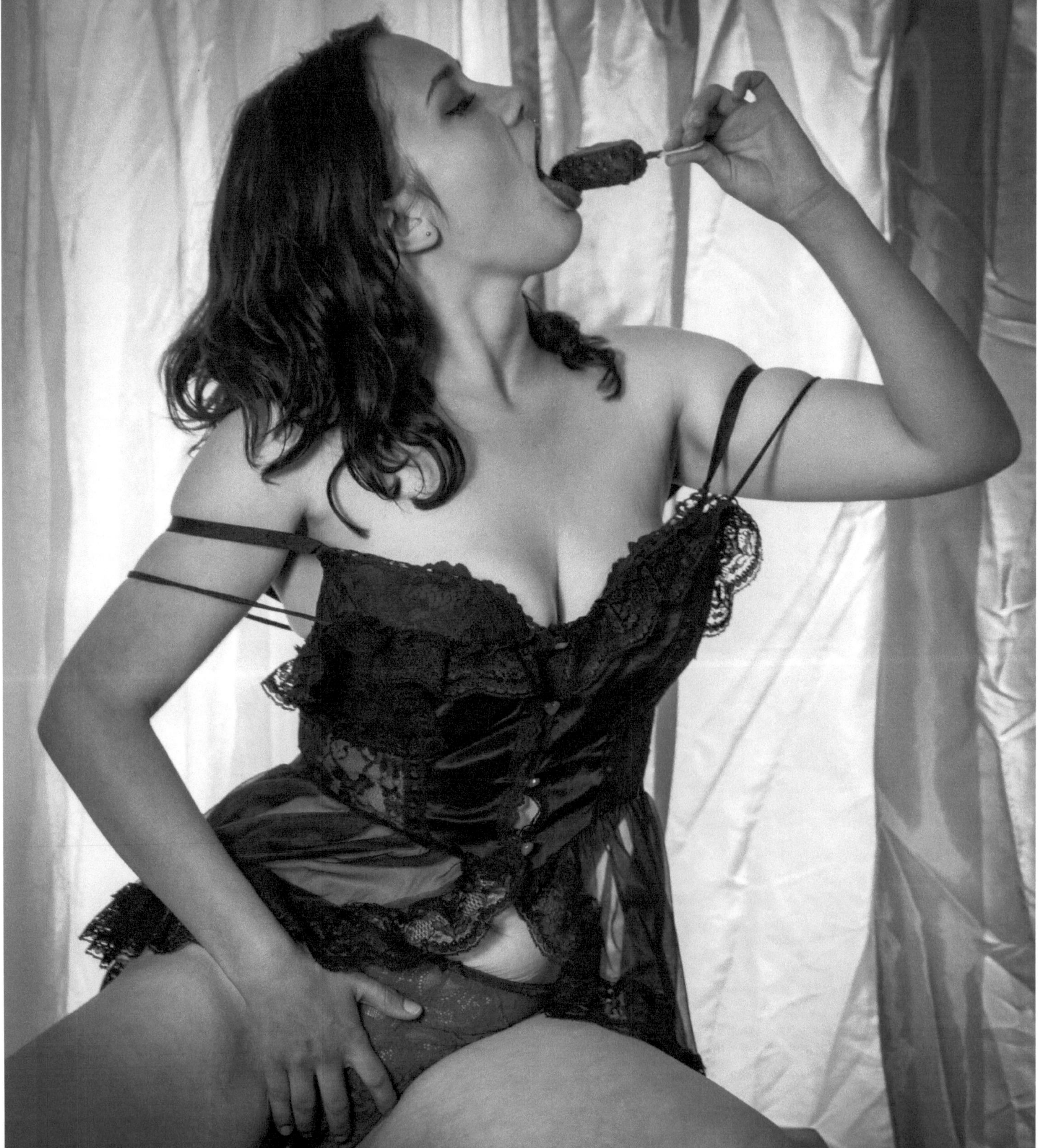

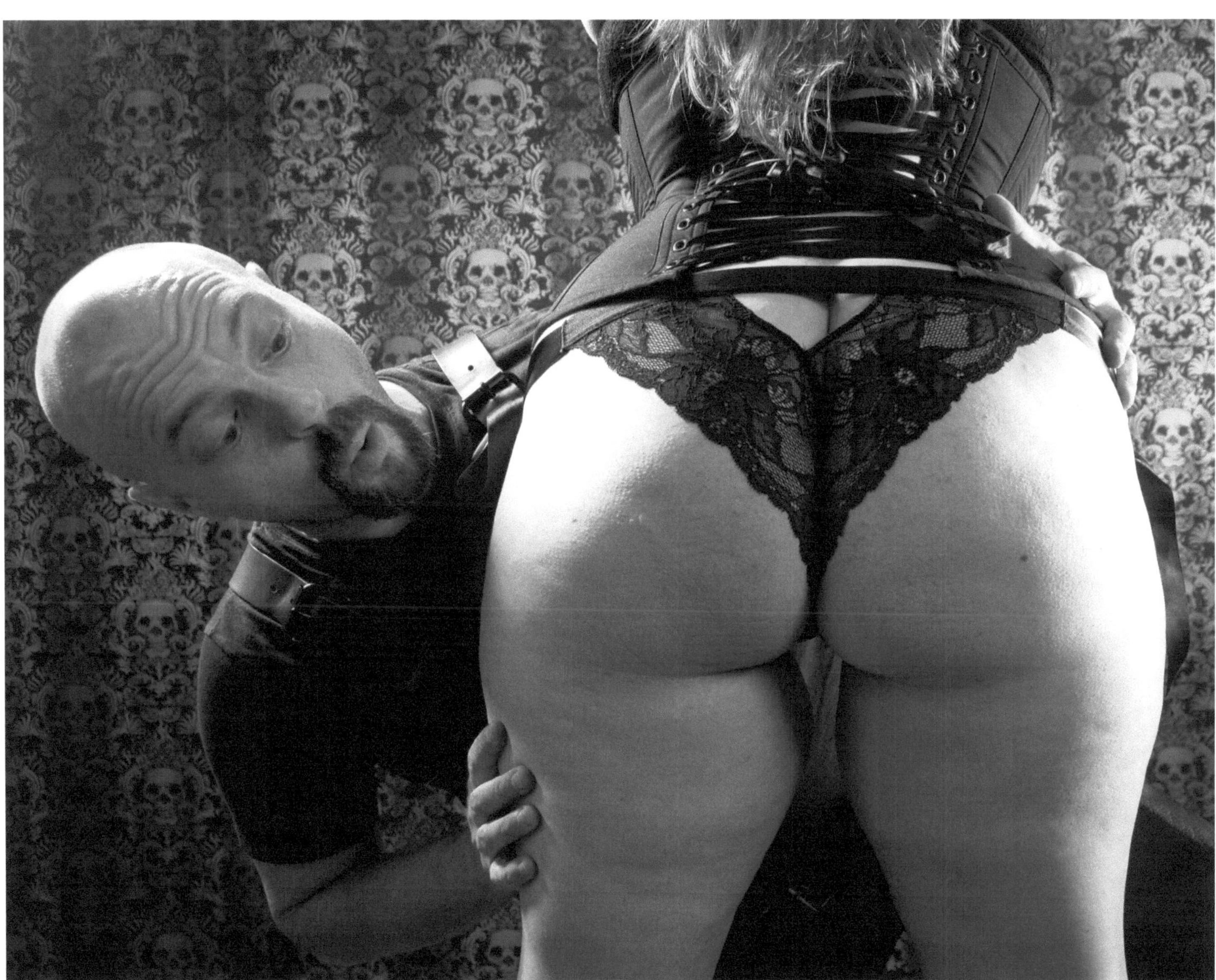

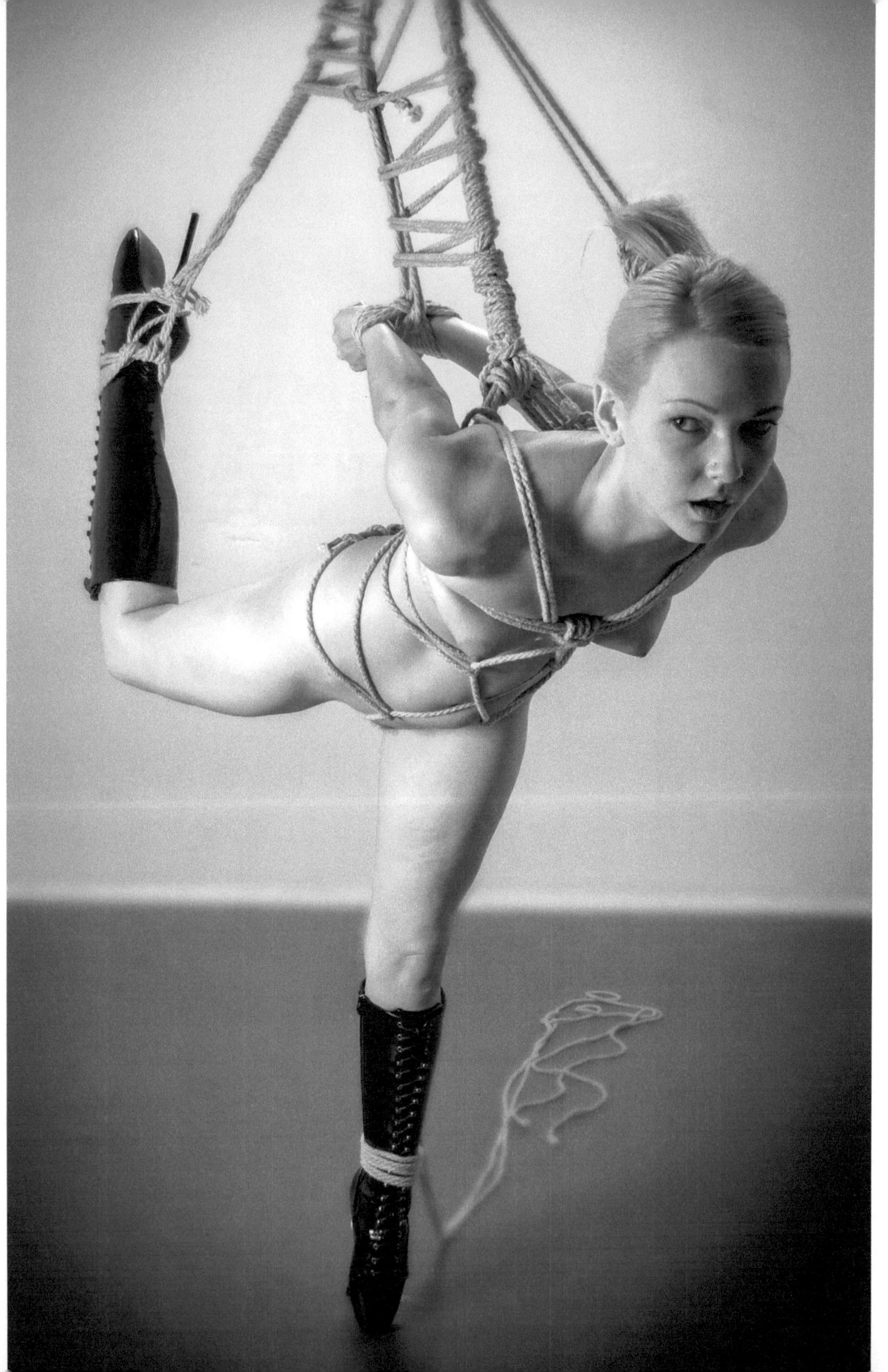

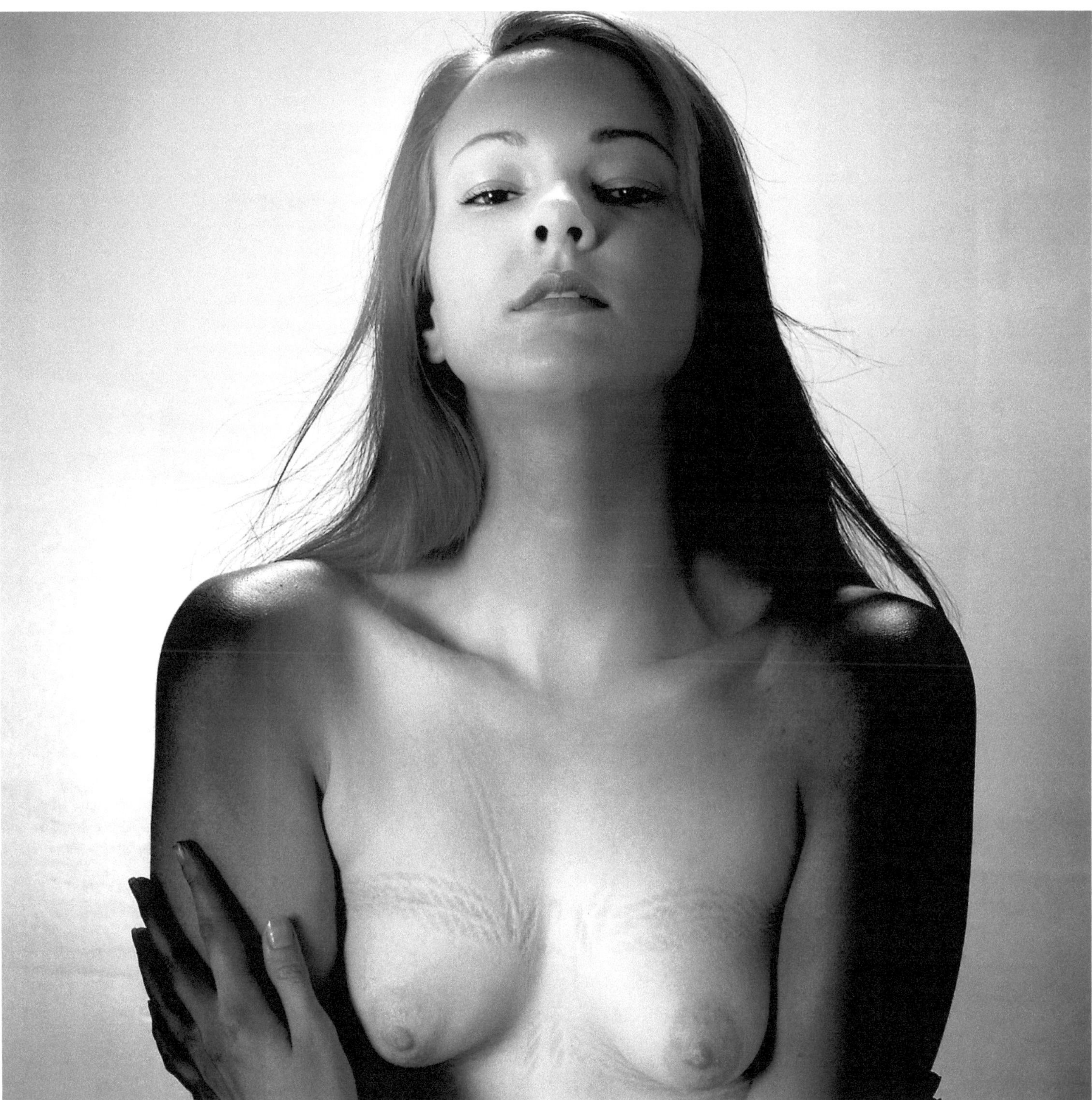

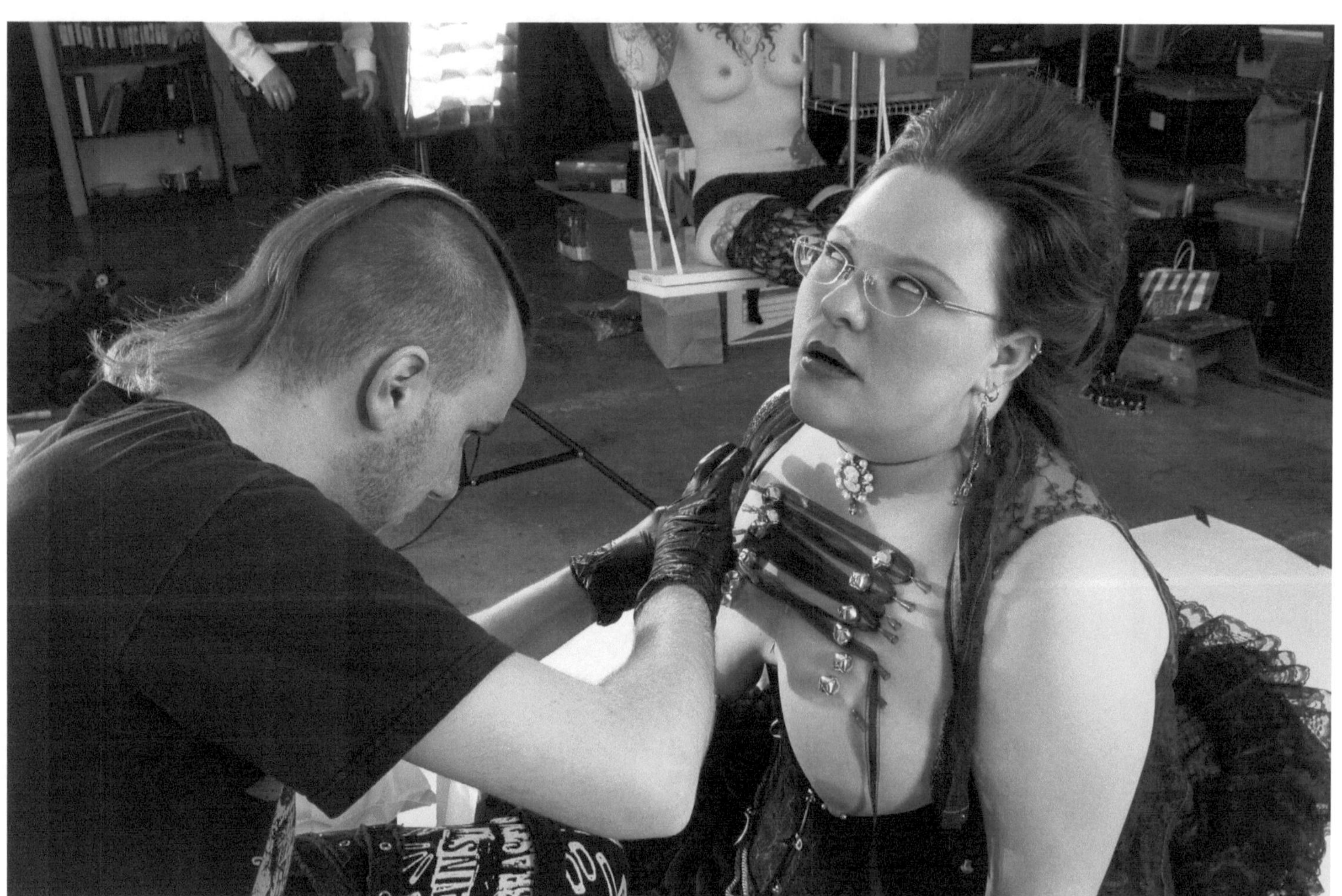

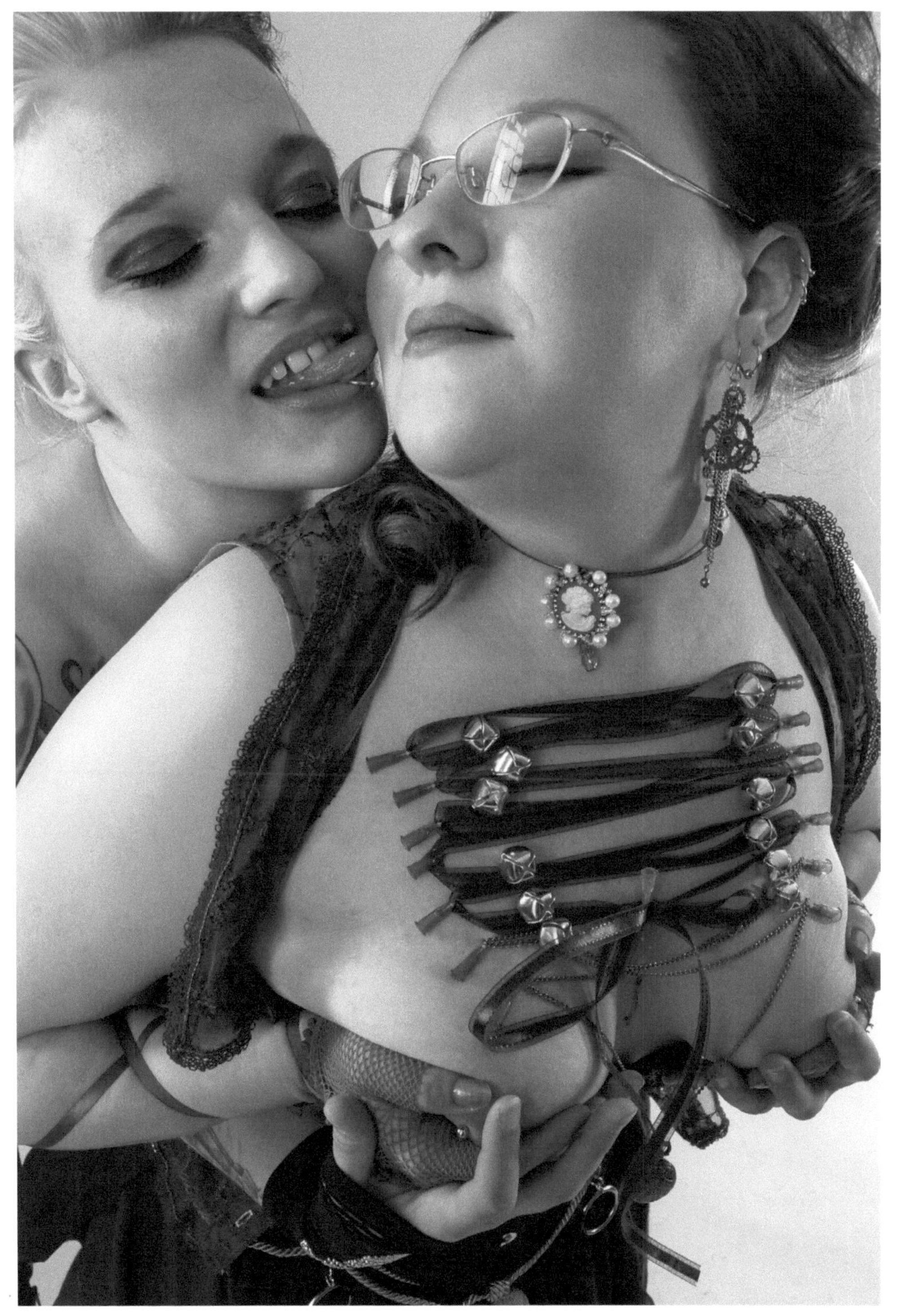

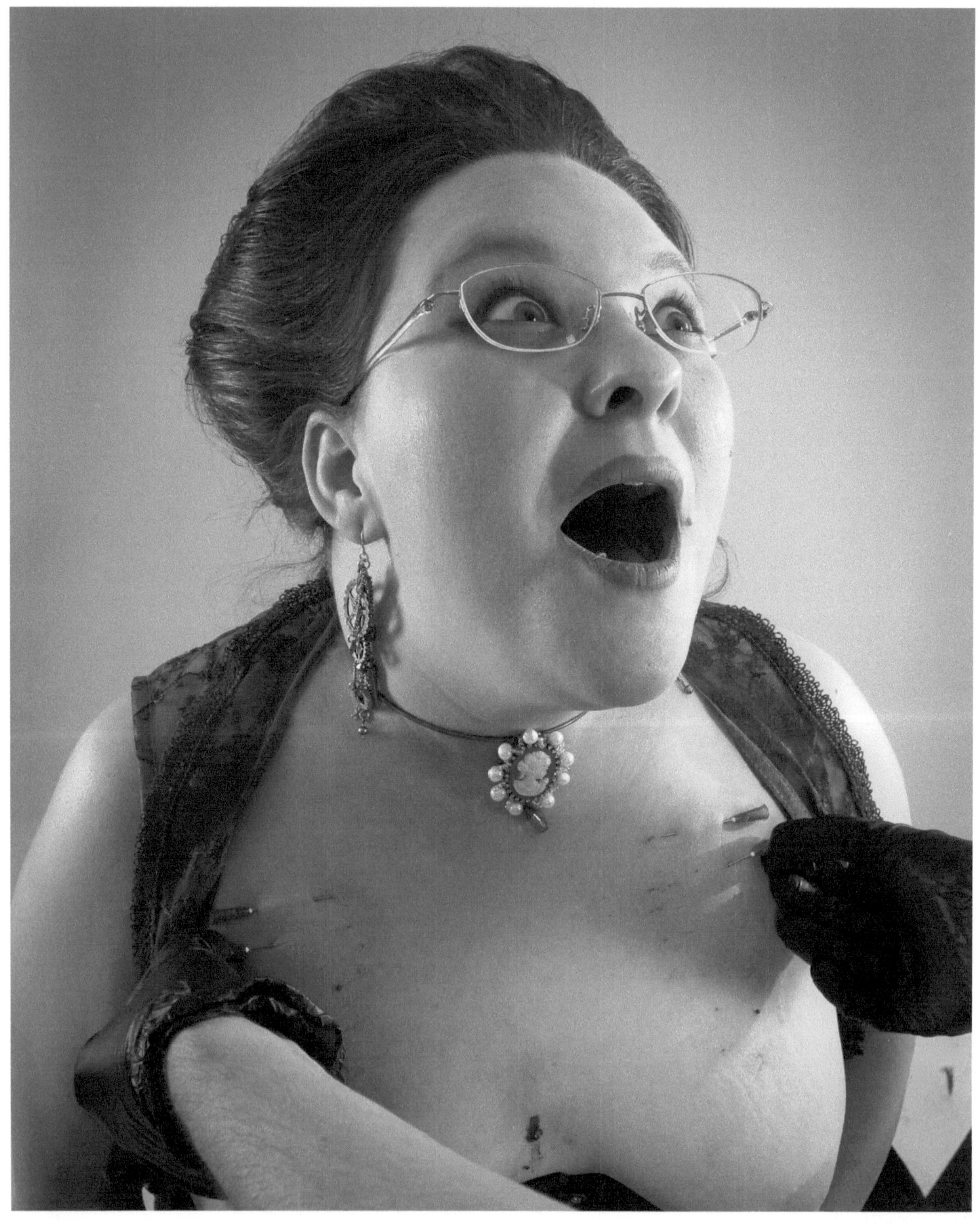

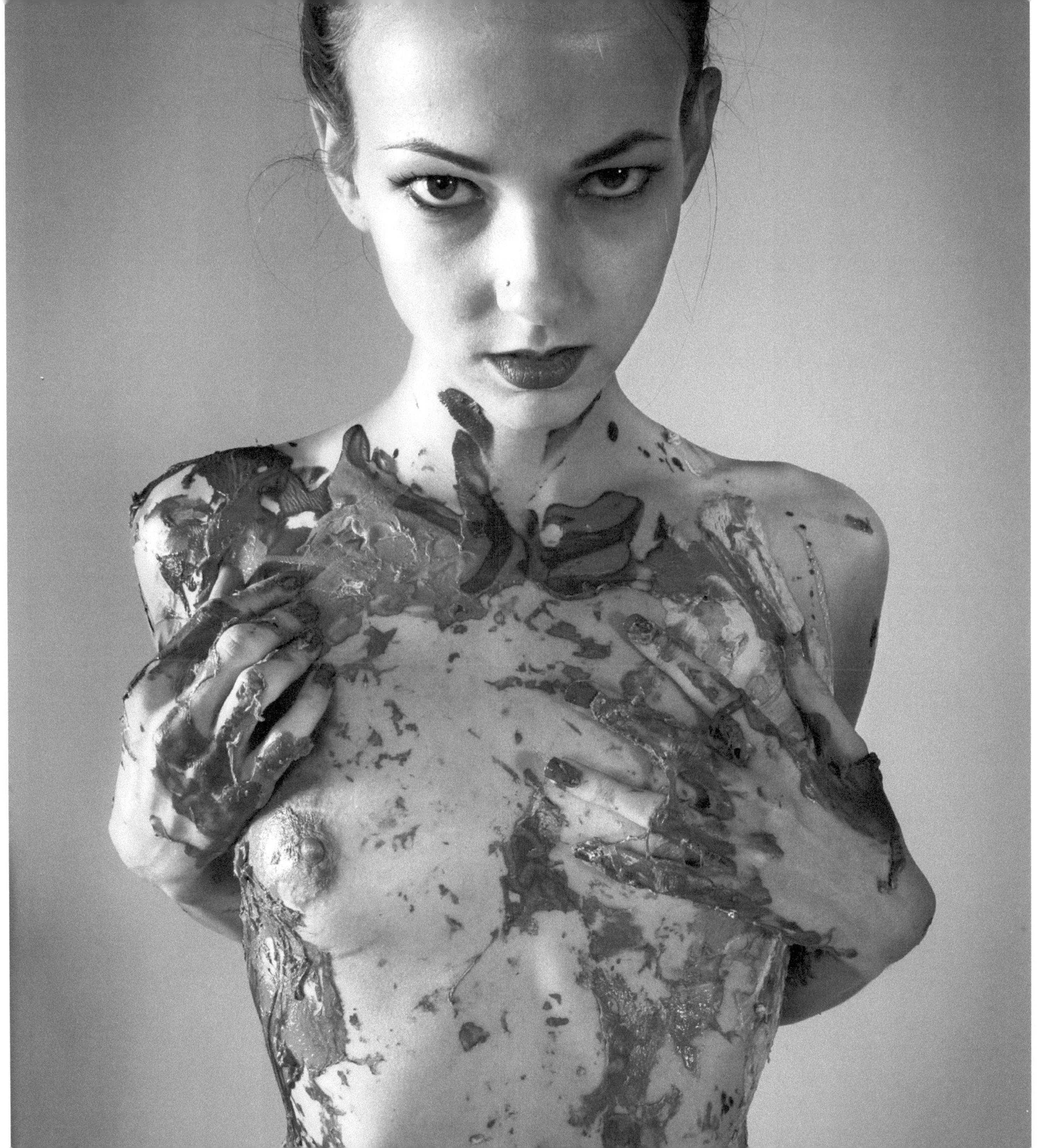

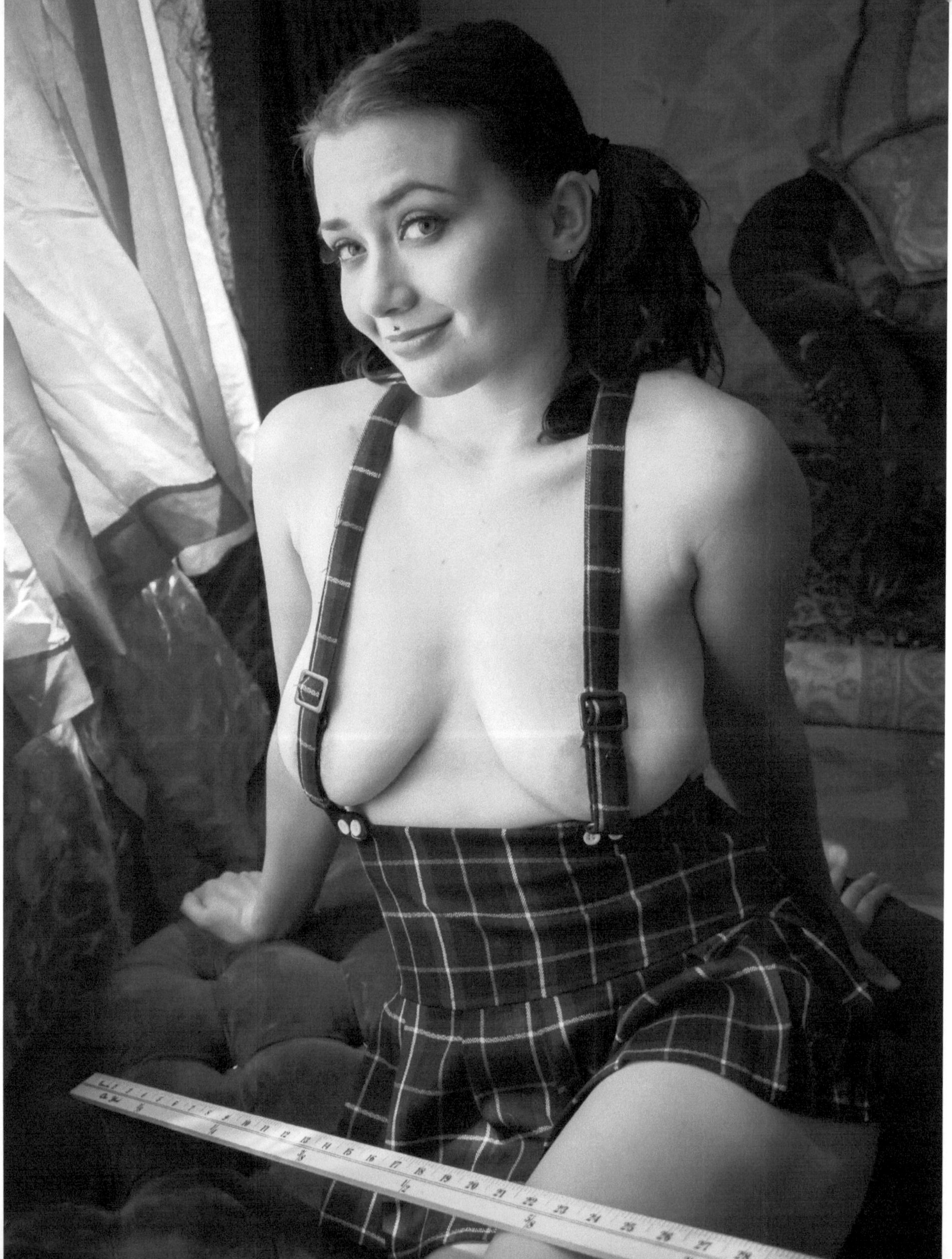

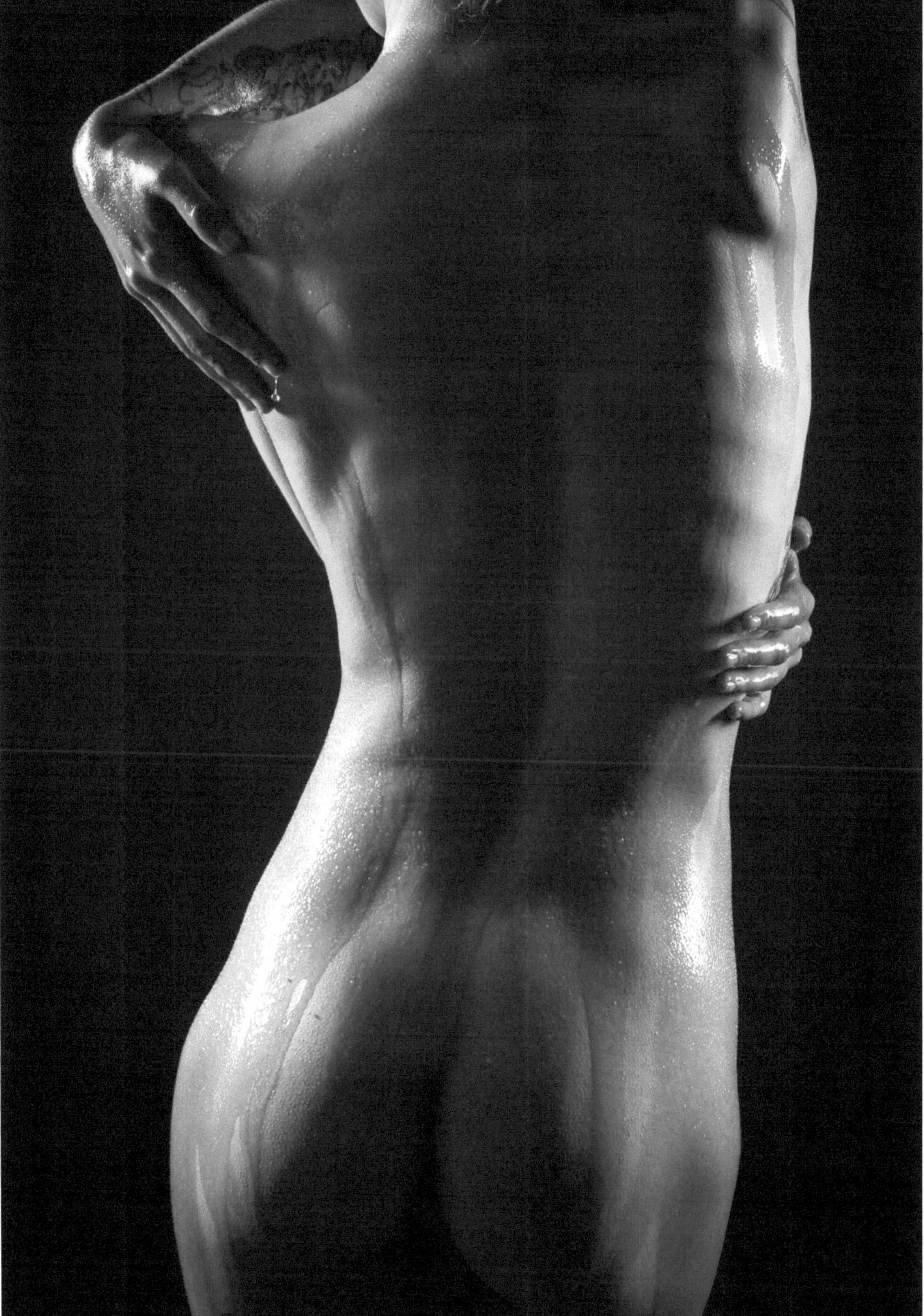

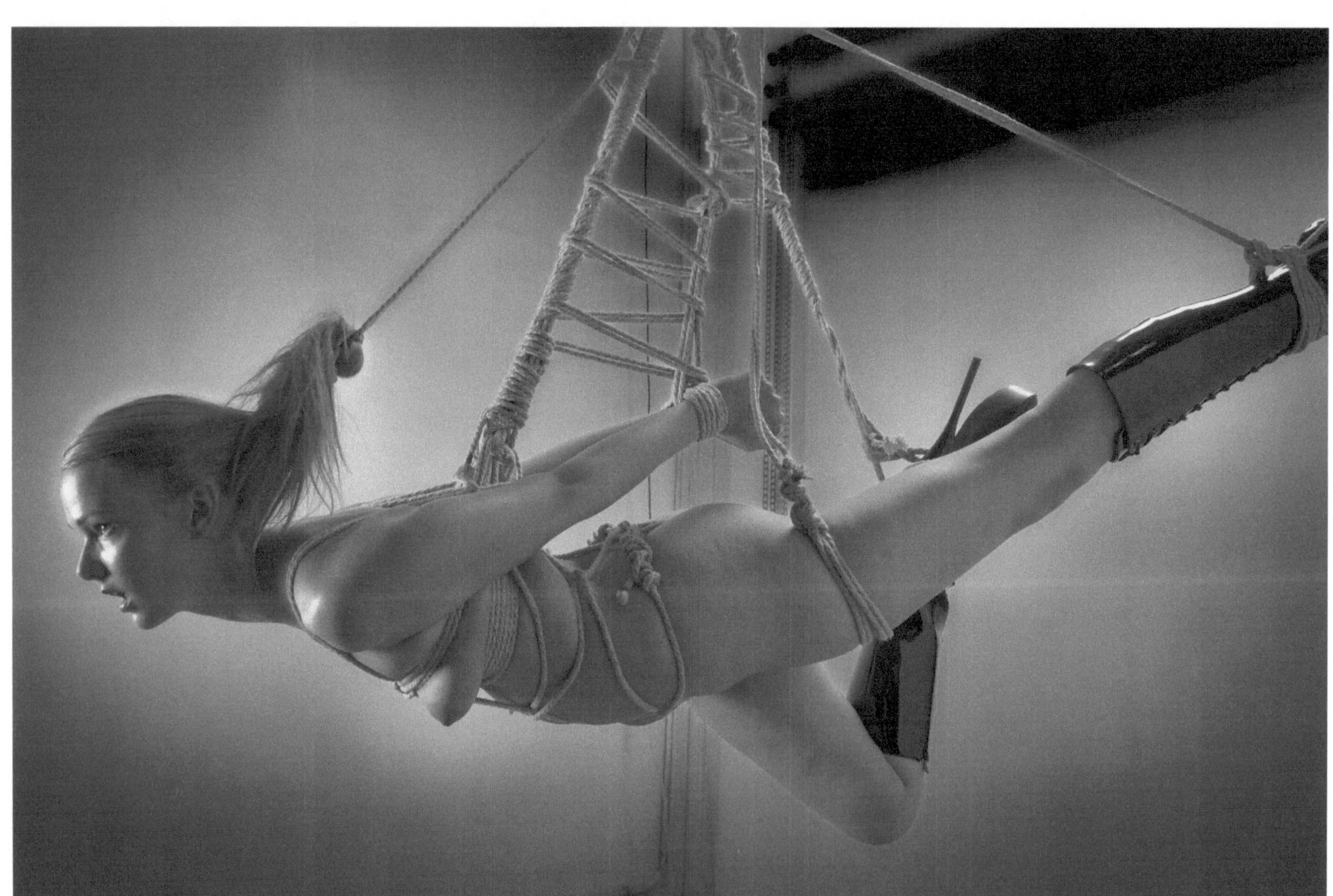

Acknowledgments

Models:

Kitty Litterpaws
Christina
Maggie Mayhem
Raven Le Faye
Wunderpanties
FreakMar5
Basha
Chelsea Christian
The_Facilitator
Dani Red
-Promethea-
-Pervette-
Daisy Knight
Girlcub
Courtney Cass
Ms. Catonic
Alexander_Lucard
Penny Poundcake
Libby Loo
Eleanor
Kitty Meow
Melisande
Cat Rich
Arcadia Kane
Iyah
Jessica
Katy
Scarlet Faux
nano_bites
Rain DeGrey and Chris
Jeff Cathcart
Tia Leigh
Purrplexitty
Eastbaysinner510

Crew:

Make-up artists:
HisDame
Tasha Lopez

Hairstylists:
Justina Downs
HisDame

Rope Rigging:
CorruptMorals

Needles:
Eastbaysinner510

Special Thanks to...

JD Lenzen
Jeff Cathcart
Sharon Cathcart
Lisa Rigdon
Owen Johnson
Zille Defue
Michael Rosen
Little Boxes Theater
Mariah Carle
Amani Wade

Check out these other books by James Courtney.

The Kinky Coloring Book
The Kinky Coloring Book #2
The Kinky Coloring Book #3
The Kinky Coloring Book #4
The Burlesque Coloring Book

www.ingramcontent.com/pod-product-compliance
Lightning Source LLC
LaVergne TN
LVHW070127110826
845147LV00002B/206